# Victorian Hauntings

## Spectrality, Gothic, the Uncanny and Literature

Julian Wolfreys

palgrave

First published 2002 by
PALGRAVE
Houndmills, Basingstoke, Hampshire RG21 6XS and
175 Fifth Avenue, New York, N.Y. 10010
Companies and representatives throughout the world

PALGRAVE is the new global academic imprint of
St. Martin's Press LLC Scholarly and Reference Division and
Palgrave Publishers Ltd (formerly Macmillan Press Ltd).

ISBN 0–333–92251–4  hardback
ISBN 0–333–92252–2  paperback

This book is printed on paper suitable for recycling and
made from fully managed and sustained forest sources.

A catalogue record for this book is available
from the British Library.

Library of Congress Cataloging-in-Publication Data
Wolfreys, Julian, 1958–
   Victorian hauntings : spectrality, Gothic, the uncanny / Julian Wolfreys.
     p. cm.
   Includes bibliographical references and index.
     ISBN 0–333–92251–4 — ISBN 0–333–92252–2 (pbk.)
     1. English literature—19th century—History and criticism. 2. Supernatural in
literature. 3. Ghost stories, English—History and criticism. 4. Gothic revival
(Literature)—Great Britain. 5. Ghosts in literature. I. Title.

PR468.S86 W65 2001
820.9'37'09034—dc21                                                   2001036

10   9   8   7   6   5   4   3   2   1
11   10   09   08   07   06   05   04   03   02

Printed in China

*. . . yet when she spoke that name that named nothing, some impalpable but real thing within him responded as if to a summons, as if it had heard its name spoken.*

John Banville, *Doctor Copernicus*

*. . . come back, we are disghosted . . .*

James Joyce, *Finnegans Wake*

*But let's not act as if we know what a phantom or a phantasm was . . .*

Jacques Derrida, *The Rhetoric of Drugs*

# Abbreviations and a Note on References

The abbreviations below are used throughout the book with reference to the principal nineteenth-century texts under discussion. Initial reference to all other cited works is provided in the endnotes, with appropriate abbreviations being given in the notes and used subsequently throughout the text when the work in question is cited throughout the chapters. Where a work is referred to more than once within a chapter, the author's name and part of the title are given parenthetically.

**Charles Dickens**

CC    *A Christmas Carol*, in *The Christmas Book*s, ed. Ruth Glancy (Oxford: Oxford University Press, 1988), 1–80.

GE    *Great Expectations*, ed. Margaret Cardwell, int. Kate Flint (Oxford: Oxford University Press, 1994).

LD    *Little Dorrit*, ed. John Holloway (London: Penguin, 1988).

MC    *Martin Chuzzlewit*, ed. Patricia Ingham (London: Penguin, 1998).

NN    *The Life and Adventures of Nicholas Nickleby*, ed. Michael Slater (Harmondsworth: Penguin, 1986).

OMF  *Our Mutual Friend*, ed. Adrian Poole (London, Penguin, 1997).

OT    *Oliver Twist*, ed. Peter Fairclough, int. Angus Wilson (London: Penguin, 1988).

PP    *The Pickwick Papers*, ed. James Kinsley (Oxford: Oxford University Press, 1988).

UT    *The Uncommercial Traveller and Reprinted Pieces*, int. Leslie C. Staples (Oxford: Oxford University Press, 1987).

**George Eliot**

LV    *The Lifted Veil*, in *The Lifted Veil and Brother Jacob*, ed. Helen Small (Oxford: Oxford University Press, 1999), 1–44.

**Thomas Hardy**

MC    *The Mayor of Casterbridge*, ed. Dale Kramer (Oxford University Press, 1987).

**Alfred, Lord Tennyson**

IM    *In Memoriam A. H. H*, in *Tennyson: A Selected Edition*, ed. Christopher Ricks (Berkeley and Los Angeles: University of California Press, 1989), 331–484.

# Contents

# Acknowledgements

There are numerous ghosts haunting the pages of this book, the most obvious being those whose works I have cited, directly or indirectly, and who return here in various guises, put to work in commentaries, as well as in other less immediately apparent ways.

More immediately, there are those who have offered help, remarks, criticisms, suggestions, along with everything else. I would therefore like to thank William Baker, John Brannigan, Marsha Bryant, Martin Coyle, Mark Currie, Pamela Gilbert, Susan Hegeman, Jim Kincaid, John Leavey, Martin McQuillan, John Peck, Nils Plath, Ruth Robbins, Nicholas Royle, Peter Rudnytsky, John Schad, Andrew Smith, Chris Snodgrass, Geoff Wallace, Phil Wegner, Kenneth Womack.

I would especially like to thank Barbara Cohen and J. Hillis Miller for inadvertently having caused these essays to take quite another turn, in what now appears to be the most uncanny of manners. Because of them, and through them, the ghosts of T. J. Clark, Tom Cohen, Arkady Plotnitsky, and Andrzej Warminski in particular have left their mark.

I would also like to thank Margaret Bartley, Felicity Noble, and Gabriella Stiles at Palgrave, for their continued help.

Earlier, different versions of several of the chapters were originally published elsewhere; each has been revised and, in some cases, significantly extended. I would like to acknowledge and thank the editors for their comments on particular essays: Chapter 1 appeared as '"I wants to make your flesh creep": Notes towards a Reading of the Comic-Gothic in Dickens', in *Victorian Gothic: Literary and Cultural Manifestations in the Nineteenth Century*, ed. Ruth Robbins and Julian Wolfreys (Basingstoke, 2000); Chapter 2 appeared as 'The Matter of Faith: Incarnation and Incorporation in Tennyson's *In Memoriam*' in *Bodies of Christ*, ed. John Schad (London, 2001); Chapter 5 appeared as 'Haunting Casterbridge or, "the persistence of the unforeseen"', in *Thomas Hardy: The Mayor of Casterbridge: New Casebooks*, ed. Julian Wolfreys (Basingstoke, 2000). I am grateful to the various editors and publishers for permission to reprint.

# Preface: on Textual Haunting

Can we speak of 'ghosts' without transforming the whole world
and ourselves, too, into phantoms?
> Jean-Michel Rabaté, *The Ghosts of Modernity*

... ni vivant ni mort. C'est spectral.
> Jacques Derrida, 'Marx, c'est quelqu'un'

What does it mean to speak of spectrality and of textual haunting?
What does it mean to address the text as haunted? How do the ideas
of haunting and spectrality change our understanding of particular texts
and the notion of the text in general? These questions shape this book.
They return repeatedly even though you won't necessarily see them
clearly, if at all. Perhaps though, before anything, it should be asked
why, and with what legitimacy, one can claim to talk of the textual, of
textuality generally, as haunted, as being articulated – and disrupted –
by the spectral, the phantom, the phantasm, the uncanny, the ghostly?

We can situate some tentative answers in the light of the work of
Jacques Derrida, who, like the instituting questions of this volume,
haunts these pages, occasionally as its subject, sometimes as the ghost
in the machine. Derrida, as he himself admits, has interested himself
for a long time in the matter of spectrality and its effects in various
media, forms or discourses, whether one considers his publications on
aesthetics, phenomenology, the literary, virtual and tele-technologies,
politics or writing. Indeed, it is arguably because of Derrida's interest,
particularly in the manifestation of what is felt to be his untimely intervention in the question of Marxism today and its problematic heritage
in *Specters of Marx*, that critical attention has turned to the spectral.

However, while Derrida turns up frequently, and with a frequency
that is positively spectral throughout these pages, this is not a sustained consideration of Derrida's concerns with matters of haunting.
That remains as another project, to come. Nevertheless, as an opening
to the question of haunting, I would like to draft some possible responses to the question of what constitutes the textual as being haunted
through the example of certain remarks of Derrida's on the subject of
the spectral, taken from a short essay, 'Marx, c'est quelqu'un'.[1]

The problem of defining the spectral, of addressing spectrality, is encountered immediately because, for Derrida, the spectral is a concept without concept (Mcq 23). It is a concept or, more accurately, a quasi-concept, which, as Derrida puts it with regard to the notion of iterability, 'marks both the possibility and the limit of all idealization and hence of all conceptualization'.[2] '[H]eterogeneous to the philosophical concept of the concept' (*LI* 118), spectrality resists conceptualization and one cannot form a coherent theory of the spectral without that which is spectral having always already exceeded any definition. Indeed, the problem is such – or, to put this another way, the condition of haunting and spectrality is such – that one cannot assume coherence of identification or determination. Epistemological modes of enquiry implicitly or explicitly dependent in their trajectories and procedures on the apparent finality and closure of identification cannot account for the idea of the spectral. Having said that though, consider what seems to be a definition and yet which articulates the experience of the undecidable within what Derrida names the classical or binary 'logic of all or nothing of yes or no' (*LI* 117): the second epigraph to this preface, where Derrida suggests that the spectral is that which is *neither* alive *nor* dead (Mcq 12; emphases added).

The identification of spectrality appears in a gap between the limits of two ontological categories. The definition escapes any positivist or constructivist logic by emerging between, and yet not as part of, two negations: *neither, nor.* A third term, the spectral, speaks of the limits of determination, while arriving beyond the terminal both in and of identification in either case (alive/dead) and not as an oppositional or dialectical term itself defined as part of some logical economy. As paradoxical as this might sound, Derrida pursues his exploration in these terms, in response to asking himself what a spectre might be, and what one might call by this strange name, spectre (Mcq 23). Of course, says Derrida, the spectre is something between life and death, though neither alive nor dead: 'La question des spectres est donc la question de la vie, de la limite entre le vivant et le mort, partout où elle se pose' [the question of spectres is therefore the question of life, of the limit between the living and the dead, everywhere where it presents itself] (Mcq 23).

Thus, to reiterate the point, the question of spectres is a question of speaking of that which presents itself or touches upon itself at and in excess of the limits of definition. To speak of the spectral, the ghostly, of haunting in general is to come face to face with that which plays on the very question of interpretation and identification, which appears, as it were, at the very limit to which interpretation can go. Moreover, the question is more radical than this, because it touches on the very question of the appropriateness of naming. Names, conventionally applied, fix the limits of an identity. Yet this 'strange name' – *spectre* – names nothing as such, and nothing which can be named as such, while also naming something which is neither something nor nothing; it names nothing which is neither nothing nor not nothing. The idea of the spectre, spectrality itself, escapes even as its apparitional instance arrives from some other place, as a figure of otherness which traverses and blurs any neat analytical distinction. The spectral as other in this case is not, then, simply a dialectical figure, that which returns from the dead for example to haunt life as simply the opposite of life. For, as Derrida's seemingly paradoxical formula makes clear, the spectral is, strictly speaking, neither alive nor dead, even though this condition that we name spectrality or haunting is intimately enfolded in our understanding of life and death.

What does this have to do with texts, though? We speak and write of texts in strange ways. We often place them in a heritage or tradition, much as we would our ancestors. We archive them, we keep them around, we revere them. As John Updike has recently commented of books, 'without their physical evidence my life would be more phantasmal'.[3] Books appear to have a material presence, without which anchoring that such materiality provides, our lives would assume a ghostly condition of impermanence; or, rather say, as does Updike, *more ghostly, more phantasmal.* Thus the book, as one finite identity for textuality, seems to keep us in the here and now by remaining with us from some past, from our pasts, from the past in general.

At the same time, books comprise texts extending beyond the borders of a particular publication or imprint, however bound, framed or produced. There is thus already at work here a certain troubling, a trembling, in the idea of text itself, something which can appear to be both real and phantasmic, and yet simultaneously neither. Textuality is a figure, to borrow a remark of Nicholas Royle's, 'irreducible to the psychical or the real'.[4] We announce in various ways the power of texts to survive, as though they could, in fact, live on, without our help, without our involvement as readers, researchers, archivists, librarians or bibliographers (and we all engage in these pursuits whether or not these are our professions). Shakespeare, it is said, is not for an age but for all time. So, in some kind of rhetorical legerdemain, we keep up the plot, the archival burial ground, saying all the while that the life or afterlife of texts is all their own, and not an effect of the embalming processes in which we engage. In such pursuits, and in the paradoxical dead-and-alive situation by which texts are maintained, we find ourselves forced to confront the fact that what we call texts, what we constitute as the identity of texts is, in the words of Jean-Michel Rabaté, 'systematically "haunted" by voices from the past . . . this shows in an exemplary way the ineluctability of spectral returns'.[5] Such voices are the others of the very texts we read in any given moment. Texts are neither dead nor alive, yet they hover at the very limits between living and dying. The text thus partakes in its own haunting, it is traced by its own phantoms, and it is this condition which reading must confront.

That acts of reading anthropomorphize the text suggests how uncomfortable we are with ghosts. We want to bury the text, to entomb or encrypt it, in the name of tradition or heritage for example, and yet we cannot quite live with such *necrobibliography*. As with John Updike's wholly typical if not symptomatic example, we maintain the text so as to keep the ghosts at bay, as though keeping the haunted form with us were in some strange way a means of disregarding the frequency of the spectral. So we frequently reanimate the text. We speak of the text as 'saying something', we write that the text does things or makes things occur, as though it had a life or will of its own; or, what is even more uncanny when you come to consider it, we substitute the author's proper name in rhetorical formulae such as 'Dickens comments', 'Tennyson says that', 'George Eliot remarks', as though the text were merely a conduit, a spirit medium if you like, by which the author communicates. Thus, even while this return of the author appears a little ghostly, it is a gesture within an acceptable range of oscillations. In speaking of a voice we implicitly assume some presence, form or identity which was once present and which was once the origin of any given text. We thereby locate the potentially haunting effect in a once-live presence. This keeps the haunting at arm's length through the promise that the text can be subordinated or returned to the idea at least of a living form. We all do this; I have probably had recourse to such phrases as those above, along with others like them, countless times throughout *Victorian Hauntings: Spectrality, Gothic, the Uncanny and Literature*.

Such procedure is simultaneously the most commonplace thing in the world of criticism and yet the most irrational. We accord writing – that which, strictly speaking is neither alive nor dead, neither simply material nor immaterial – life and volition through a critical response which does not or cannot acknowledge fully its own complicity in acts of uncanny revivification – how gothic – and at the same time make believe that the writer continues to speak to us, as though we had no role. However, what reading does in effect is to bear witness to the existence of something other, which is neither 'read into' the text nor of the text itself in any simple fashion. The question of the text therefore, like the question of spectres, reconfigures the question of the limit between the living and the dead, which everywhere, in every textual encounter, presents itself. It is not that the text is haunted by its author, or simply by the historical moment of its production. Rather, it is the text itself which haunts and which is haunted by the traces which come together in this structure we call textual, which is phantomatic or phantasmatic in nature while, paradoxically, having an undeniably real or material effect, if not presence.

Whether one speaks of discourse in general, or of text in the particular sense of the web of words which make up and yet are irreducible to a book, one is forced to concede, from the perspective of considering the notions of haunting and the spectral, that the idea of text is radically unstable. What constitutes text, textuality, as an identity is, in the final analysis, undecidable and irreducible to any formal description. Our experience of reading relies on a blurring, which is also a suspension, of categories such as the real or the imaginary. Textuality brings back to us a supplement that has no origin, in the form of haunting figures – textual figures – which we misrecognize as images of 'real' people, their actions, and the contexts in which the events and lives to which we are witness take place. We 'believe' in the characters, assume their reality, without taking into account the extent to which those figures or characters are, themselves, textual projections, apparitions if you will, images or phantasms belonging to the phantasmatic dimension of fabulation. And it is because they are phantasmic because they appear to signal a reality that has never existed, that they can be read as all the more spectral, all the more haunting. Such uncanny figures or characters can be comprehended as phantasmatic in fact because, as with the nature of the spectral, they are readable in their acts of textual oscillation as undecidable, suspended, to draw from the essay by Derrida already cited, 'between the real and the fictional, between that which is neither real nor fictional' (Mcq 24). We cannot resolve this problem, which is the problem of haunting itself, for even as the figures of the text remain and return as held in suspension, so they also suspend our ability to read them, finally. Here, once again, is the *experience of the undecidable*. And so we continue to bear witness to the signs of spectrality, seeking to read that which resists reading, that haunts not only textuality, but also ourselves.

# Introduction

## ON HAUNTING

It is, perhaps, something of a truism to state that there have been ghosts, spirits, phantoms. It is nonetheless accurate to suggest that there has been an interest in haunting generally, for as long as there have been narratives. It is not inaccurate to say that tales of terror and uncanny manifestations which resist rational explanation and empirical verification abound in many cultures, whether one speaks of the persistence of the spectral as a seemingly intrinsic component of religious or cultural belief, or whether one is speaking of sensationalist journalism and the tele-media's perpetuation of narratives of the unexplained and other-worldly. While there is a risk in resorting to the truism above, what is striking is that it is undeniably true in large part: ghosts are always with us, and perhaps now more than they have ever been before.

Whether one refers to the text in the narrow sense of a printed book or whether one uses the term to identify film or video; or whether, in speaking of text, one speaks more broadly of a virtual network of spectro-technical relations as does Jacques Derrida, it is the case that haunting remains in place as a powerful force of displacement, as that disfiguring of the present, as the trace of non-identity within identity, and through signs of alterity, otherness, abjection or revenance. Indeed, according to Derrida, haunting is not simply a thing of the past or, indeed, something from the past. Instead, the experience of haunting has never been greater: 'Contrary to what we might believe, the experience of ghosts is not tied to a bygone historical period, like the landscape of Scottish manors, etc., but on the contrary, is accentuated, accelerated by modern technologies like film, television, the telephone. These technologies inhabit, as it were, a phantom structure.'[1]

Clearly, ghosts cannot be either contained or explained by one particular genre or medium, such as gothic narratives. They exceed any single narrative modality, genre or textual manifestation. It is this which makes them ghostly and which announces the power of haunting. Derrida makes this plain, connecting modern technology to the matter of re-production (and so, implicitly, to matters of repetition and representation): 'When the very *first* perception of an image is linked to a structure of reproduction, then we are dealing with the realm of phantoms' (GD 61).[2]

The spectral nature of modern technologies of reproduction is high-
lighted by others.

Speaking of the 'tendency of television to *decorporealize* the vision
that it is transmitting', Samuel Weber remarks of television transmission that its realist mode hides its ghostly and phantomatic aspects.[3]
Avital Ronell addresses the spectral condition of television and of its
haunting power, which it uncannily perpetuates through the limitless
dissemination of incorporeal images without origin.[4] There is, to speak
simply, no simple first time without a simultaneous displacement of
the first time through reproduction. In this remark, which seems to
invoke or otherwise be haunted by the ghost of a text by Walter Benjamin[5]
(to which Derrida's remark is merely, in part, the response to and
recognition of the spectral effect as a counter-signature to Benjamin's
own ghostly trace), we see mapped out that haunting is not some anterior effect. The ghost does not arrive after the fact, after the so-called
reality of a situation. It is, we must understand before we proceed any
further, the condition or possibility of any mode of representation. The
spectral is that which makes possible reproduction even as it also fragments and ruins the very possibility of reproduction's apparent guarantee
to represent that which is no longer there fully.

Another way to approach this question of haunting might therefore
be to suggest that all forms of narrative are spectral to some extent.
Moreover, any medium through which we seek to communicate today
that involves a narrativization of our identities in relation to others not
immediately present is inescapably spectral. We might take Derrida's
speculation cited above further. Not only is it not the case that ghosts
do not simply belong to the past and narratives told in the past, as in
the phenomenon of the rise of gothic fiction at the end of the eighteenth century. Instead, the proliferation of phantoms and the effects of
haunting are undeniable aspects of the identity of modernity. To borrow and develop a pun of David Punter's on the nature of the gothic,[6]
the spectral is the parasite within that site, or, that *para*-site, which we
call modernity. Haunting exists in a certain relation to the identity of
modernity which both informs the narratives we construct of modernity and as those which are produced within the space and time of the
modern; and it is a sign of the hauntological disturbance that, because
of the various spectral traces, we can never quite end the narrative of
modernity. We cannot with any confidence narrate to ourselves a tele-
ology of the modern, whether we are seeking a narrative beginning or
a moment of narrative closure. Haunting disrupts origin and eschatology

(from the start we might say). A spectre haunts modernity, and the spectral is at the heart of any narrative of the modern.

Furthermore, to tell a story is always to invoke ghosts, to open a space through which something other returns, although never as a presence or to the present. Ghosts return via narratives, and come back, again and again, across centuries, every time a tale is unfolded. This return, a figural or rhetorical effect marked by what Peggy Kamuf has described as 'repetition and difference',[7] is arguably the trace of haunting itself, and of narrative's always being haunted in its very condition. There can be no narrative, in short, which is not always already disturbed and yet made possible from within its form or structure by a ghostly movement.

Furthermore, the movement of the return is not simply that, for that which is spectral is only ever perceived indirectly by the traces it has left. It has, in returning, already begun to retreat. There is no ghost but only, to employ a somewhat awkward formula, the ghost of a ghost or, rather its trace. The idea that all narrative, that all structure perhaps, is haunted, and that haunting or spectrality constitute in part, even as they haunt, the condition of narrative or structure will of course need qualifying and it is in part the purpose of the present volume to offer such qualification, if not to assert such a statement. But for now, what I want to propose is the idea already intimated, hardly original but worth exploring nonetheless, that all stories are, more or less, ghost stories. And, to reiterate another principle: all forms of narrative are, in one way or another, haunted.

## ARCHITECTURE AND HAUNTING

A woman is sitting at home alone, one Saturday morning just before midday, when, unexpectedly, a knock comes at the door. On opening the door she finds, much to her surprise, an old friend whom she has not seen for some time. Inviting her friend in, they talk of a number of things, until, over an hour later, her friend must leave. The woman wonders about this visit, wondering also about the condition of her friend who appears to be either ill at ease or unwell. A day or so after this encounter, the woman finds out that her friend had died on Friday, the day before the visit had apparently taken place.

This is a true story, allegedly. There is textual evidence to support the facts. The short narrative just recounted was first printed anonymously in pamphlet form in 1705, as 'A True Relation of the Apparition of One Mrs. Veal the Next Day after Her Death to One Mrs. Bargrave at Canterbury the 8th of September, 1705'.[8] Shortly afterwards republished as a companion piece and advertisement for a translation of Charles Drelincourt's *The Christian's Defense against the Fears of Death*, it was not until 1790 that the 'author' of this tale was discovered to be Daniel Defoe.[9] Corroborating, independent evidence supporting the claims of the story was first published in 1895, by Defoe scholar George Aitken. This evidence was an anonymous account, written in Latin, and found by Aitken in a copy of the fourth edition of the 'True Relation'. However, the account was not contemporary, but was dated 1714, claiming to be an interview with the woman, Mrs Bargrave, who encountered the ghost. Subsequently, two letters have been discovered, both dating from the year of the apparition, which further support, if not the validity of Mrs Bargrave's claims, then, at least, the persistence of her narrative.

What is of interest here is the very persistence of the narrative in its various forms or manifestations. Beginning with haunting, it is the act of haunting which returns, insistently, as though haunting were un-cannily bound up in the narrative act. Specifically, it is the process of haunting as process and the disturbing sensation created which is of interest. For every time the story is retold – even in paraphrase in this introduction – the effect of spectral manifestation takes place, every time as first time, but, in being narrated, re-presented, never as a first time as such. The veracity of the ghost of Mrs Veal is neither here nor there. It is certainly not the ghost we encounter, and lack of empirical 'proof' does nothing to detract from the story's power to disturb or otherwise to create an uncanny effect. What is important, to make the point again, is that the moment of haunting is not available as some origin for the tale but only exists in a haunting fashion through various textual traces: Defoe's retelling, the 'interview' with Mrs Bargrave, and the subsequent documentary evidence which has allegedly come to light.

Three aspects of this narrative should interest us. First, there is the textual relay and, with that, the network of texts which, in composing the relay, maintain the spectral albeit in a somewhat disjointed fash-ion, rather than explaining it away. This is achieved in part by the observed processes of fragmented and discontinuous communication. The story returns over and over, unexpectedly, out of the blue in different registers, each reflecting another perspective entangled in a skein of cultural interests.

Then, in the story itself is the temporal disruption of which we should take note. The ghost appears – and indeed this, to state the obvious, is a condition of ghostly apparition – after Mrs Veal has died. But what unsettles is the fact not of the ghostly appearance: for, if we are to reorder the story temporally, when Mrs Veal appears Mrs Bargrave has no knowledge that her friend is dead. Defoe is careful to stress this and this feature of the narrative is, in turn, verified by subsequent accounts. Thus, the appearance of the haunting woman is not in itself haunting, it can be argued. What is uncanny is the act of telling, the narrative act of bringing the ghost back in a temporally disjunctive manner, which destabilizes the cognition of temporal order as a perceived sequence of events. The spectral is, therefore, a matter of recognizing what is disorderly within an apparently straightforward temporal framework. The reader or audience are discomposed in their perceptions by a process of revelation, the act of 'unfolding' to borrow the verb employed by Hamlet's father's ghost, old Hamlet. This process never stops taking place, even though the ghost appears only the once. What is truly spectral is the apparitional event, which, like an analogue tape loop or stuck vinyl recording, replays itself.

The final aspect of the story which is of interest is the question of where haunting takes place. The ghost of Mrs Veal appears in her friend's house. The spectral effect thus needs structure, within which its efficacity assumes maximum disruption. The act of haunting is effective because it displaces us in those places where we feel most secure, most notably in our homes, in the domestic scene. Indeed, haunting is nothing other than the destabilization of the domestic scene, as that place where we apparently confirm our identity, our sense of being, where we feel most at home with ourselves.

The haunted house is a stock structural and narrative figure, whether one thinks of Henry James' *The Turn of the Screw*,[10] Charles Dickens' *A Christmas Carol*, or Stephen King's (and Stanley Kubrick's) *The Shining*, to take some obvious examples. As Jacques Derrida puts it, in a commentary on Freud's reading of Jensen's *Gradiva*, 'haunting implies places, a habitation, and always a haunted house'.[11] Indeed, as we shall encounter below in this introduction as well as in other chapters, the Freudian uncanny relies on the literal meaning and the slippage of, and within, the German *unheimlich*, meaning literally 'unhomely'. For Freud, that which is unhomely emerges in the homely. Haunting cannot take place without the possibility of its internal eruption and interruption within and as a condition of a familiar, everyday place and space. By the same token, there is no space or place which is not available for the event of haunting.

We shall see this repeatedly, whether speaking of homes and gardens as in the texts of Charles Dickens or in towns and their spaces, as is the case with Thomas Hardy. We shall also encounter spectral oscillations within the supposedly familiar space of the home we name our identity, in Tennyson and George Eliot, and we shall encounter the effects of haunting within the familiarity of textual forms, within the conventions of thought, and in the protocols by which, to make for the moment a somewhat artificial distinction, 'literary' and 'critical' modalities function. What this always comes down to, though never in exactly the same manner, is the eerie efficacy of the spectral as an inescapable condition of the forms which we inhabit, literally or metaphorically, which we need to get along, at home, at work, and in the ways in which we make sense of ourselves in relation to the world. The 'architecture' of every form, everything we understand as 'reality', whether it be that of the house, the town, the novel, subjectivity or being, is traced by a double, an incorporeal phantom or phantasm,[12] or a 'gap', to use Nicolas Abraham's word,[13] within the structures we mistakenly believe to be unities, complete, whole, and undifferentiated.

Yet – and we must insist on this – haunting is irreducible to the apparition. The spectral or uncanny effect is not simply a matter of seeing a ghost. The haunting process puts into play a disruptive structure or, to consider this another way, recalling the idea of the phantom or phantasm as 'gap', a disruption that is other to the familiarity of particular structures wherein the disruption is itself structural and irreducible to a simple, stabilized representation. As Rodolphe Gasché remarks of the idea of the phantasm, 'the phantasmatic "structure," puts in play not the phantasm itself – there never could be one – but one of its figures . . . the phantasmatic is the space in which representation is fragmented'.[14] The efficacy of haunting is in its resistance to being represented whole or undifferentiated, or being 'seen' as itself rather than being uncannily intimated.

To 'see' something is, however precariously, to initiate a process of familiarization, of anthropomorphizing domestication. The spectral or haunting movement which opens the 'gap' already there is far more troubling because, despite the apparent fact of perception, the estranging materiality of the spectral persists in its disturbance, even though we can only acknowledge its effect at the limit of comprehension. What is all the more perplexing, to make this point once more, is that the phantom or the spectral is not alien to the familiar space, even if it is other, but is as much at home within the architectural space as we are (if not more so), wherein its motion causes what Mark Wigley describes as that 'uncanny internal displacement'[15] which belongs so intimately to the domestic scene. We may inhabit the spaces and places in question (whether we refer to our sense of identity or our homes, which indeed we also comprehend as belonging to a sense of selfhood), but the spectre, though incorporeal, is incorporated into the very economy of dwelling, even as its otherness both exceeds and serves in the determination of the identity of place. And if language is the house of Being as Martin Heidegger has famously suggested, it is a house notorious for slippage, excess and difference, wherein we are always displaced by a ghostly alterity.

## SPECTRALIZED GOTHIC

The figure of the haunted house and its structural dislocation, is, along with variations such as castles and monasteries, the favoured site for gothic narrative. It is the place where the blurring of boundaries is given its most literal depiction, in the motion of ghosts through walls, as though the psychic or phantasmatic required a manifestation in the form of representation if only so as to be able to pass over that which otherwise cannot be spoken. What we are confronted with is a matter of process and transition. The gothic is itself one proper name for a process of spectral transformation. We will see the spectralized, translated gothic at work in various chapters of *Victorian Hauntings*, and it is thus necessary to consider the spectralization of the gothic, to understand how that which haunts the gothic as genre returns after the demise of the gothic as a vital literary form, as a number of apparitional traces and fragments in discourses of the nineteenth and twentieth centuries. Cast out of its familiar places, the gothic is dematerialized into a somewhat unpredictable tropological play; or, more radically yet, this dematerialization takes place through an irreversible displacement from the tropological – a more or less contained series of effects governed by and recognizable within the laws of a particular paradigm – to the performative, a disturbing iterability the singular events of which announce a somewhat lawless relation to the laws of a system which they exceed. Exorcised from its haunted houses, the spectral-gothic takes on its most *unheimlich* aspects.

It is generally agreed amongst critics that the gothic, understood narrowly as a narrative form or genre given principal expression through the novel, had a life-span of approximately 56 years. It was given life in 1764 with the publication of Walpole's *The Castle of Otranto*. It died allegedly somewhere around 1818 or 1820, with the publication of, respectively, Mary Shelley's *Frankenstein* or Charles Maturin's *Melmoth the Wanderer*. Recent reassessments of Thomas De Quincey's *Confessions of an English Opium Eater* (1821) such as Margaret Russett's *De Quincey's Romanticism* may allow us another provisional moment of 'conclusion' for the Gothic.[16] The gothic is informed by what Russett calls a 'degraded sensibility' (17). At the same time, it is, says Fred Botting, 'a mode that exceeds genre and categories'.[17] Degradation speaks at one and the same time of certain psychological and corporeal conditions, to consider the figure for the moment in a gothic vein. Such breakdown or decomposition is what makes the mode (if it is possible to speak in the singular) excessive of itself. As James Kincaid has argued of the gothic, 'these discourses were radically unstable, still are.'

> Partly that's because they are discourses of the unknown and unknowable. Consider the gothic: it's got always to reach towards what cannot be spoken; if all can be spoken, then there is no gothic. It can gesture towards the sublime, towards the blasphemous, or towards the magical, but it must never fall into the prosaic: the gothic has to alert us of agencies we cannot explain. We cannot explain them because they lie outside the realm of the explicable, outside of language. It's not just that we don't know enough; knowledge is not the issue. If the gothic can be explained, it is no longer gothic.[18]

The 'internal' instability signals something in the gothic which, while perceived as of the gothic, is also other and therefore in excess of any normative gothic or the definition of such – hence the degradation, the excessive and unstable aspects of which the critics speak. The gothic is clearly always already excessive, grotesque, overspilling its own boundaries and limits. The impropriety of gothic sensibility is such that, even before the genre's historical or cultural demise, or, to put this another way, dying even from its first moments of animation, it leaves its traces in its audience, to return again and again. Even at the moment when it appears to have given up the ghost the gothic keeps on returning, as it dies or appears to be decaying. It starts to be celebrated or perhaps fed upon, by criticism for example, or else it feeds upon itself adopting a knowingly self-referential manner. What we observe therefore is that a spectralization of the gothic takes place; that this phantomization is always already at work within the very identity of the form.

The death and spectralization of the gothic perhaps takes place in the publication of Thomas de Quincey's *Confessions of an English Opium Eater*, in 1821. If *Confessions* is readable as the genre's conclusion of sorts, its publication and discourse also mark the return of the gothic or, at least, the gothic's others. This work, though not a novel, is clearly disturbed in its narrative identity by traces of the gothic, from the first instances of the seemingly haunted house in Soho and the equally haunted, haunting anonymous girl, to the perpetually haunting figure of Anne who returns to disturb De Quincey's troubled psyche and who is endlessly reiterated not only as a phantasmal figure in the author's memory but also through the endless series of interchangeable, anonymous female images in London. Even the city of London itself, with its dark passages and labyrinthine streets, is constructed by De Quincey in a knowingly gothic fashion; the city is both mapped and troped by fragmentary instances of the gothic's apparitions which inform and distort the urban rhetoric. The convolutions of the city and its anonymous inhabitants, refigured through the haunting imagos of the urban discourse as a phantom community, in turn inform the often equally labyrinthine structure of the *Confessions'* narrative, with its constant deferrals and displacements of information, its promises of narrative revelations which never arrive, and its passages which, all too often, lead frustratingly nowhere. The spectral-gothic is thus readable as the invisible apparition which transforms the form its tropes come to haunt.

The gothic can then no longer be figured from the 1820s onwards, as a single, identifiable *corpus*; if indeed it ever was simply this, as critics such as Russett, Botting, Kincaid and others make clear. One of the chief features of gothic in its first phase is the frequently fragmentary condition of its narrative, as many critics in recent years have acknowledged.[19] Responding in part to this, the present volume addresses through its readings what remains as the haunting spirit of the gothic throughout the nineteenth century, gesturing in conclusion towards the twentieth. Escaping from the tomb and the castle, the monastery and mansion, the gothic arguably becomes more potentially terrifying because of its ability to manifest itself and variations of itself anywhere. Reciprocally, the texts in which we are interested and which are readable as being traced by the gothic may also be read as embracing the gothic, incorporating its traces into themselves in intimate and disconcerting ways. Each text responds to the possibilities of haunting, as the spectre and the spirit of the gothic is unfolded in myriad strange and estranging ways.

In being so dispersed, in coming to light in numerous, unsettling, and unpredictable ways, assuming new identities seemingly from beyond the grave, the gothic appears to mark nineteenth-century textuality and culture with a haunting promise, which is the promise of a haunting to come, a promise that we will never have done with phantoms or spectres. The gothic becomes other than itself, the meaning of the term changing, metamorphosing beyond narrow definition, promising the destabilization of whatever it comes to haunt, while it is itself destabilized in itself and from itself. At the same time, the promise of the gothic was – and still is – a promise of a certain return, a cyclical revenance. It still remains as this, and its remains are readable as numerous counter-signatures guaranteeing the gothic promise within the text.

However, while for some the gothic as a genre was to become unbearable, first in the 1820s and, subsequently, in the twentieth century through early critical assessment of the gothic, for many others it remained – and continues to remain as a series of not quite proper remains – *unburiable*. The promise and the ghost of the gothic is comprehended in all its uncanny potentiality as both *trait* and *retrait*, the one enfolded *and* revealed in the movement of the other. As the ghost has already retreated, so all that is left is its trait, its trace. The spectral-gothic mode leaves its immaterial yet indelible mark in the nineteenth and twentieth centuries, in the most conventional of narratives and the most unlikely discourses. But even as we read those traces, we only read where the gothic has been, we only comprehend the effect in the places from which the spectral gothic has already retreated. We understand the gothic therefore as always already spectral through and through. All that is left in the text is, once again, that promise of the gothic already announced, the disturbing trace, the haunting absence. Of course, such a narrative about the gothic is itself a gothic narrative, concerned with constant returns, uncanny disturbances, dismembered remains and improper forms, deferrals and differences. Thus, in this rhythm of recirculation we begin to comprehend that the promise of the gothic itself returns once again – to haunt our comprehension, to trouble the certainties on which we rely for our identities, and to continue returning in ever stranger articulations of revenant alterity.

The gothic is to be found everywhere then but never as itself, never in the same form twice. The gothic becomes truly haunting in that it can never be pinned down as a single identity, while it returns through various apparitions and manifestations, seemingly everywhere: in comic discourse, in discourses of history and Christian belief, in the very possibility of the novel in the second half of the nineteenth century, and in countless other discourses and historical, material traces as well, as several of these essays suggest. The effect of the gothic as one phantom of an uncontrollable spectral economy is to destabilize discourses of power and knowledge and, with that, supposedly stable subject positions. The gothic operates through the blurring of vision and the anatomization of experience. Recognizing the signs of haunting it must be concluded that, whether one speaks of the experience of reading or the experience of the materiality of history, one witnesses and responds to ghosts. In these and other disturbing ways, the gothic as so many heterogeneous signs of haunting manifests itself as both a subversive force and a spectral mechanism through which social and political critique may become available and articulable, as we come to apprehend material realities, political discourses and epistemological frameworks from other invisible places.

Thinking the spectralization of the gothic moves the idea of the gothic beyond the narrow understanding of the gothic as narrative or novel form. Coming to terms with this, we recognize the truth of an argument concerning the gothic put by Eve Kosofsky Sedgwick. As Sedgwick argues, the function of the gothic was to 'open horizons beyond social patterns, rational decisions, and institutionally approved emotions . . . [it] became a great liberator of feeling through its acknowledgement of the "non-rational"'.[20] As Sedgwick suggests, if we are to accept this definition of the gothic we must at the very least also acknowledge the radical discontinuity between such a sense of the gothic and its narrow definition, or what Sedgwick describes as the 'Gothic novel proper' (3). It is this very discontinuity – which also marks both an equally radical transition and the suspension of identity – which serves to liberate the spirit of the gothic from its ponderous conventional body. At the same time however, the radical transformation of gothic, which is in turn a gothic transformation, a spectralization within and as a break from itself, makes the definition of the gothic much harder, from certain conventional critical positions; and it is with the provisional identification of the gothic in different and differing ways that criticism has concerned itself. The act of defining the gothic beyond

its narrative conventions is fraught with difficulties, not least because
of what Sedgwick terms the 'conflicting claims of the general and the
specific' (4). Sedgwick's analysis of contingent naming focuses, appropriately enough, on the frequency of the term 'unspeakable' in gothic
narrative. As she argues, the frequency of such a term may be raised
critically to the level of the thematic but, equally, the unspeakable
names a certain play within narrative structure.

If, as Robert Miles suggests, the question 'What is "Gothic"?' seems
easily answered, this is no doubt because of a formalist adherence to
the rote identification on the part of the critic of 'the same plots, motifs
and figures endlessly recycled'.[21] Nothing could be easier, less troubled.
Yet such an approach, if we recall Sedgwick's argument, and to follow
Miles also, falters once we begin to pay attention to gothic's own
hauntings, its affirmative resistances, or what Miles terms 'Gothic's
deep structure'. Gothic writing, Miles argues, following David Punter,
is '"disjunctive", fragmentary, inchoate' (1). Such a formula clearly
recognizes and responds to the phantasmatic condition of the gothic,
of the spectral condition by which the gothic identity partially and
momentarily emerges. Furthermore, Gothic 'worries over a problem
stirring within the foundations of the self . . . [and is concerned with]
the representation of fragmented subjectivity' (Miles 2). There is for
Miles, after Foucault, an 'instability of discourse, its tendency, especially
within the "dialogic" space of narrative, to fragment or round on itself'
(6). Thus for Miles, the gothic is concerned with the self, with the
other within the self, and with what Kelly Hurley terms 'the ruination
of the human subject . . . [through] the spectacle of a body metamorphic
and undifferentiated'.[22] This can only be part of the story however.
There is a danger here of slipping into a critical language of abject and
fragmented corporeality and materiality which, in its quasi-Foucauldian
turn, does not adequately register the degree to which psychic and
bodily identity is produced not by an unequivocally discernible gothic
discourse *per se* but is subject to a gothicization by the invisible trace left
by the disruption of the spectral. What we name the gothic is readable
as a spectro-aesthetic project and, it might be added, a projection also.

The critical move beyond the conventions of gothic narrative is articulated then, at least in part, by the act of reading gothic's own
hauntedness, its revelation of the alterity within subjectivity, and the
alterity which undoes any sense of the subject's own comprehension
of coherence, presence or meaning. Whether it is through the spectro-
poetical manifestations of identity's fragmentation and the future death

of the subject imminent within the endless reproducibility of the image made possible by the technology of cinematography,[23] or whether one considers the uncanny assault on the sense of self by the otherness of the foreign; whether it is through either the withered or corpulent, hectic or abused figure of the grotesque child (as is presented in the chapter on Dickens), or through the projection of spectro–sexual ambiguities; whether it is a matter of the return of the past, the return of the repressed, or the reception of the invisible trace of the otherwise unrepresentable; or, whether it is a matter of that which disturbs history and politics internally and yet is neither, simply, a question of history or politics conventionally considered but is, instead, a matter of the haunting poetics of experience: the comprehension of the gothic is expanded through an understanding of the role gothic effects have to play in the constitution of modern, fragmented subjectivity.

At the same time, the heterogeneity of subjects addressed here point to what Jacqueline Howard terms gothic's – and, by extension, the realm or archive of the spectral's – "'multi-voiced-ness'", its 'propensity for multiple discourse'.[24] Arguably, it is this propensity which serves to mark the gothic from one perspective as a haunted medium, always traced by excess, always exceeding definition; spirited from its embodiment in a discernible genre, the gothic is translatable only through the signs of spectrality. If the body and the subject are fragmented and dispersed, then so too are the voices of the gothic subject. For the spectralized gothic subject, properly understood, is never singular. There are always other voices, other disembodied, ghostly articulations within and against the dream of full, simple, self-evident speech to be read in any apparently stable voice, such as that desired in and for realist narrative. Such qualities in turn speak to the 'plural dimensions of reading' (1) which, for Howard, is also a provisional definition of the gothic mode, all of which resist the imposition of an homogeneous definition of the gothic, while proving 'unsettling for the reader' (12).

However unsettling the haunting of stability, of homogeneity and the self-same may be, it directs us in the gothic context currently addressed to a certain fragmentation of textual form along with the recurrent apparition of other textual fragments, disembodied phantom signatures, whether one speaks of the resonance of names in Dickens, or architectural echoes in Hardy. Not only do fragments of texts reappear, fortuitously or ironically, but fragments are created in their own right, as a textual expression of a spectral-gothic sensibility. The phantom-fragment is a textual, *material* embodiment which, though incorporated, through its apparitional interruption disjoints the implicit laws, logic and economies of the very text it haunts. Such a device echoes with the narrative tendency in gothic to come to an impassable and unspeakable hiatus, spoken of above by James Kincaid, and thus to break down at the limit of representation.

What therefore remains is the work of ghostly textual revenance which must disturb through indirection. Such fragments, and the silences which they generate, speak of the unspeakable, bearing witness to an absence or the unrepresentability at the heart, and as the very limit, of meaning. Reading the gothic fragment is to discern a symptom of haunting, rather than to describe texts as gothic. Wherever narratives cannot speak, there we may respond to the gothic fragment as one aspect of the enormity of haunting, or what might be provisionally described as the spectral sublime. The gothic is thus one name for acts of spectral troping which we otherwise name the ghostly, the uncanny, the phantom.


SPECTRAL PROCESS

Questions of haunting, the gothic, the spectral and the uncanny make themselves available for commentary through process rather than product, through on-going activity rather than static presentation or re-presentation, as we have implied. The various forms of spacing, repetition, doubling and return with which we find ourselves interested are not so much concerned with particular phenomena as they have to do with matters of rhythm and transport. The question of doubling is particularly bound up with a sense of the uncanny.

Samuel Weber comments that: 'The figure of the double . . . of course, is closely associated both with the Freudian (and Heideggerian) motif of the *uncanny, des Unheimlichen*, as well as with a certain relation to death.'

> The double is the ghostlike manifestation of *iterability*, which 'splits' each element while at the same time 'constituting' it through the split . . . the double, the *Doppelgänger*, is the most direct manifestation of this splitting: the *splitting image*, one could say . . . The paradoxical twist however, is that according to the deconstructive graphics of simultaneity, any identity, including the self or the subject, is constituted only in and through this split, this doubling. (*MM* 144)

Weber's remark brings into focus the idea that doubling is not simply a rhetorical device but is the figure of haunting *par excellence*. It is itself not only itself but already other than itself, every instance of doubling being the singular instance of the 'ghostlike manifestation', irreducible to the general law of doubling on which the singular plays. The singular event of duplication (if that is not to put things paradoxically) remarks the text materially while remaining partially other to any conception of an economy of duplication which would take place in the same fashion every time. Thus the singularity of the doubling event redoubles and thereby exceeds the notion of the double. Moreover, in the double there is both that which is familiar enough to be disturbing and strange enough to remind us of the otherness that inhabits the self-same.

Doubling is, however, but one aspect of the uncanny, one process by which the uncanny sensation is felt, and it is to the concept of the uncanny in the texts of Freud and Heidegger that we now turn briefly, in order to see how the uncanny is not merely a category in its own right but is itself another name, an image without image perhaps, for spectrality and haunting.

In his revised essay of 1919,[25] Freud defines the uncanny as a sensation of unease, dread and terror which makes itself manifest within us in particular situations: 'the uncanny is that class of the frightening which leads back to what is known of old and long familiar' (*U* 195). Freud's definition of the uncanny relies in part for its illustration on structural undecidability (*heimlich/unheimlich*; *U* 195–201), as already mentioned, and discussed in Chapter 5 on Thomas Hardy, below. Particularly for Freud, as he reads across a wide range of literary texts,[26] the significant aspects of the uncanny are its powers (as already noted) of doubling, of repetition, and, equally, the ability to disturb not with something alien or strange but, instead, through the return of the all too familiar, that which we have repressed, forgotten; something, which we might describe as a secret: 'this uncanny is in reality nothing new or alien, but something which is familiar and old-established in the mind and which has become alienated from it only through the process of repression' (*U* 217). Yet it must be stressed that the efficacity of revenance is not fixable in some particular image but, rather, in the power of the motion of the sensation itself. The uncanny is thus uncanny in itself in that, in never being itself, it can be pinned down to no one thing. It is this uncanny power which leads Terry Castle to define the uncanny as 'itself a sort of phantom, looming up out of

darkness', the source of which is unrecognizable.[27] Like other manifestations of the spectral, the uncanny returns but is an experience of
revenance cut off from any origin. It is, to quote Nicholas Royle on
the relationship between the sensation of *déjà vu* and that of the uncanny, 'nothing other than supplementarity-as-experience, the experience
of a supplement without origin, a disturbance of any sense of "familiar
ground"' ('*DV*' 11).[28]

As Castle makes clear, therefore, and as Royle implies, Freud's reading
of that strange sensation we encounter is itself apparitional, and Freud's
discourse can in no way control its haunting or spectral condition. So,
it is hardly surprising that Neil Hertz comments of the essay, described
elsewhere by Hélène Cixous as 'less a discourse than a *strange* theoretical
novel' (emphasis added),[29] that its '*invisible energies* are thought of
[by Freud] as those of the repetition compulsion, and the *glimpses* one
gets of them are felt as disturbing and *strange* . . . The feeling of the
uncanny would seem to be generated by being reminded of the repetition compulsion, not by being reminded of whatever it is that is repeated.
The becoming aware of the process is felt as eerie, not the becoming
aware of some particular item in the unconscious'[30] (emphases added).

Both Cixous and Hertz write of that which is strange, though with a
difference. For Cixous it is the essay itself which is strange and, therefore, estranging, within itself. Somehow, Freud's essay is not quite an
analytical discourse but, instead, a disturbing, compelling narrative.
Its scientific identity is haunted by a fictive, narrative other. For Hertz
what is strange is the feeling the uncanny instance provokes when one
encounters it. It is this which Freud's essay brings to light, what its
analytical mode describes, rather than being an incidental effect of the
essay. In the split between the two critical perceptions and the space
which is opened up in that split, something emerges. What we might
read therefore in Cixous' comment is the very feeling as the writer's
eerie response, which is defined by Hertz as 'disturbing and strange',
intending this to be a definition rather than a response. An uncanny
force persists in Freud's writing which does not diminish with rereading. This powerful movement keeps returning to haunt Freud's readers
in the essay's own doubleness, described by Cixous as 'a text and its
hesitating shadow' (FP 525).

Cixous' response in the face of the Freudian text's uncanniness –
and the repetition compulsion it commands in some of its readers – is
to speak of it in haunting terms, in words we might more conventionally apply to a gothic narrative. Indeed, in addressing the ways in which

fiction figures itself as the '[r]eserve or suspension' (FP 546) of the *unheimlich* in Freud's essay, she transforms the text into a haunted fiction as well as a text haunted by the uncanny effects which fiction can produce between 'author and reader' (FP 547). While Hertz appears to maintain a greater critical distance, the same response is also readable in his discourse, which paraphrases and thereby doubles Freud's observations on that which returns and which is *invisible*, and yet of which one is afforded occasional *glimpses*. The 'becoming aware' of an 'eerie' sensation – 'to what arouses dread and horror' (*U* 193) – is all the more marked by the fact that what is uncanny is precisely not some object or, as Hertz calls it, an 'item' but the power of return and reiteration itself. Hertz' remark makes of Freud's essay the ghost story it always already is, addressing the suspension and duplication which traces that *invisible figure* which despite its invisibility is nonetheless momentarily glimpsed. And it is this, arguably, which is reduplicated in the energy spent by criticism in its efforts to explain the effect, as the uncanny is 'finally that which resists analysis and, thus . . . attracts it the most' (FP 547). There is thus a rhythm of haunting, an oscillating frequency constantly crossing and recrossing between the visible and invisible, between life and death.

The notion of the uncanny is also considered by Martin Heidegger in 'The Structure of Uncanniness'.[31] For the philosopher the nature of Being (*Dasein*) is inescapably uncanny. The spectral process, its motion or efficacity rather than the perception of some phenomenal object, a performativity or technicity if you will observed in the text of Freud is also privileged by Heidegger in his consideration, which is described as *Dasein*'s flight from itself (*HCT* 283). The fear we feel in given situations causes us to flee, and yet the fear is a response to nothing as such but rather to that haunting sensation which appears fleetingly, hauntingly, from within our identities, which fear, Heidegger argues, is 'constitutive of the being of Dasein' (*HCT* 283). That such a sensation is the manifestation of the spectral is implicitly acknowledged by Heidegger when he alerts us to the groundless ground of the apparition's manifestation: 'What threatens is nothing definite and worldly, and yet it is not without the impending approach which characterizes the threatening' (*HCT* 289). Of this motion within and yet other than one's being, Heidegger remarks 'We then say: one feels *uncanny* . . . One no longer feels at home in his most familiar environment . . . in dread, being-in-the-world is totally transformed into a "not at home" purely and simply' (*HCT* 289).

Furthermore, in its haunting aspect, the uncanny sensation comes ever closer and is made greater in that it *is* spectral: the apperception of the nothing as nothing 'amplifies its proximity' (*HCT* 290). Yet because apparitions retreat, because what is repressed or hidden *is* forgotten, invisible, such spectres can – *and do* – always return to haunt us. What Freud calls repression, Heidegger names forgetting, which, he argues, is constitutive of the fear that haunts *Dasein* (*BT*, 316). To be haunted is the on-going process of coming to terms with one's being. Concomitantly, the sense of being haunted, of repeatedly encountering intimately the uncanny sensation is, in turn, a recognition of the abyssal nature, the groundless ground of being (*HCT* 291). As Hent de Vries puts it, with reference to Derrida's *Specters of Marx*, '[t]his spectrality is not . . . somehow there, before, behind, aside, or beyond the Dasein it comes to haunt from its very first breath. The Specter is the impossible un-conditionality of Dasein's possibilities.'[32] Where we live, where we are supposedly at home, is in ourselves, and yet being is inescapably a haunted house, constituted structurally only through the phantom nothing and its constant, unending returns. This is the *unheimlich* as phantom, as the serial iterability of phantasms. And what makes this haunting so intolerable is the constant movement. What is unbearable, remarks Cixous, 'is that the Ghost erases the limit which exists between two states, neither alive nor dead' (FP 543). This is the persistence of the spectral process, whether its disruptions are more markedly spatial, as in Freud's essay, or temporal, as in the text of Heidegger.

## DISCONTINUOUS PARABOLA

The imagined figure of the *discontinuous parabola* is meant to suggest the movement and structure of *Victorian Hauntings*. This phantasmic figure describes an arc which bears, however loosely, an apparent resemblance to a seemingly linear historical trajectory. However, this parabola, with its implicit linear historicity is not a continuous, smoothly undifferentiated line. There is not a calm transition or motion throughout the nineteenth century which is not, always already, disrupted, and broken up from within itself. Such disjointing is, furthermore, a manifestation of haunting. How might we describe this?

One of the recurring interests in this Introduction and throughout the various readings is that of return, of revenance, and the disturbing efficacity of such a process. The question of return, of repetition and doubling in specific relation to Freud on the uncanny is first noted by Jacques Derrida in *Dissemination*, where he finds himself returning to Freud's insistent interest in 'the paradoxes of the double and of repetition, the blurring of the boundary lines between "imagination" and "reality"'.[33] As we argue, after Derrida, what returns is never simply a repetition that recalls an anterior origin or presence, but is always an iterable supplement: repetition with a difference. There is, then, an apparently circular or, more precisely, a folding and unfolding motion which in the act of appearing to complete itself moves us somewhere else, so that what we come to read on so many occasions is a figure, to borrow Tennyson's words, of *the same, but not the same.*

Such a movement of apparent circularity that propels elsewhere, which resonates as an other figuration within or disfiguration of the possibility of hermeneutic unity, is arguably that which haunting makes materially possible. Haunting as the immaterial projection of the other is discernible as a material trace and the way in which the spectral is perceived, the ways in which we receive the phantom (indeed if we receive it at all) is a sign of historial intervention. That which haunts therefore is neither absolutely singular nor completely obedient to the laws of the form from which it departs. This is what makes that which haunts so haunting, so uncanny: the apparent familiarity from which there is departure. Haunting and spectral effects are neither simply idiomatic and lawless, and nor do they merely obey the law from which they depart, but operate disruptively from within the most habitual, accustomed structures of identity.

*Victorian Hauntings: Spectrality, Gothic, the Uncanny and Literature* proceeds along its apparent arc, then, by exploring moments of return which are also instances of displacement, differentiation, and deferral. Beginning with the figures of the haunted house and the disfiguration of genre, I look at how various cultural and literary discourses – on the child, faith and Christianity, questions of psychology and subjectivity, the matter of poetic form and the limits of narrative or topographical representation, the question of biography and the burden of the past and what Abraham and Torok term 'transgenerational phantoms' (*SK* 162–205) – manifest the signs of 'phantomatic haunting', otherwise readable as a 'psychic half-life' (*SK* 166–7).

Clearly such considerations have ramifications for fundamental issues of how we think we see, how we believe we read, how we construct commentaries, narratives, histories. Admitting the efficacy of haunting, and opening ourselves to the chance of the phantom, and yet

admitting equally that we cannot control either the manifestations of
the spectral nor how we respond to such instances, we can no longer
discern such figures as controllable aesthetic devices. If the imaginary
figure – a phantom projection? – of the discontinuous parabola maps
anything at all it is an irreversible transition (a transition always already in place, immanent by virtue of the condition of hauntology) in
the nature of haunting: from tropes subordinate to and controlled within
a system of representation to a performative modality which articulates the system of representation and the limits of any such mimetic
architectonics, while being irreducible to that, or, indeed, to any system.

This irreversible shift already at work for example in Defoe and
Dickens – perhaps best described as the hauntological troping of trope
– challenges the efficacy of conventional aesthetic modalities. We come
to understand how we cannot control the spectral through an act of
reading. Attempting to read the historial transition of spectrality as the
rhythm or proliferating *punctum* of discontinuous serial manifestation,
what becomes recognizable is, in the words of Paul de Man, a certain
'complicity of epistemology and rhetoric'[34] when read, according to
de Man, as the kind of shift described here. Moreover, in this reading
and its recognition there are revealed what de Man calls '*historical
modes of language power*' (*RR* 262). Far from being quasi- or pseudo-
mystical, the reading of spectrality, of haunting, of phantasmic and
phantomatic effects addresses the way in which discourse in all its
materiality achieves material effects. And such materiality is all the
more powerful in that its procedures operate between the visible and
invisible, between the living and the dead, without residing or otherwise being assignable to any one location.

For example, take de Man's consideration of the spectral condition
of light (which should be borne in mind when turning to Tennyson in
Chapter 2). In his essay 'Anthropomorphism and Trope in the Lyric',
de Man offers the following commentary on the figure of light in a
reading of Charles Baudelaire: '[t]he philosophical phantasm that has
concerned us throughout this reading, the reconciliation of knowledge
with phenomenal, aesthetic experience, is summarized in the figure
of . . . light . . .':

> Light implies space which, in turn, implies the possibility of spatial
> differentiation, the place of distance and proximity that organizes
> perception . . . Whether the light emanates from outside us before it
> is interiorized by the eye, . . . or whether the light emanates from

inside and projects the entity, as in hallucination or in certain dreams, makes little difference . . . (*RR* 258)

Irreducible to a concept, stable identity or location within the discourse of philosophy, light operates as shifting approximation. The illumination we receive is diffuse, and this is wholly appropriate in describing a figure which in itself has already eluded definition, while enlightenment of the indirect variety comes to be projected in its place. This is, of course, the work of light: to shed light on something else, to allow visualization of the invisible. Light, which figures the phantasm in a certain manner, is also that which makes the phantasm available to sight to an imperfect degree. This at least is the insight we glean from de Man's illuminating formula. There is something in this which is exact in its intimations paradoxically because it is rhetorically imprecise, the very work of the statement exposing the limits of what can be said and brought to light with regard to the question of the phantasm. In discerning the work of the trope, the critic puts the trope to work, irrevocably transforming it in a performative, material fashion. De Man's prose does the work which it has been the project of the essay to unveil. More than this, the phantasm is thereby revealed as occupying a liminal space, as well as moving between two supposedly distinct realms, inside/outside, while being impossible to assign to either. Thus the phantasm haunts any ground on which distinctions are based between what can be felt and what can be known. A limit is marked, a distance acknowledged, however close or intimate sense and knowledge might be presumed to be.

Spectrality has then a life of its own. Or, perhaps more accurately, an afterlife both its own and not its own, an afterlife which is other than the sense of propriety inscribed in the conventionality of 'ownness'. As Derrida suggests in *Specters of Marx*, the question is one of a hauntology irreducible to any ontology. Coming to terms with the wayward power of haunting and pursuing a counter-intuitive analysis of its effects unveils the extent to which the question of the spectre, the ghost, the phantom, the uncanny, is intimately enfolded with issues which not only have to do with the ways in which we see (as suggested earlier), as though this question of perception could itself be reduced to merely formal or aesthetic, ahistorical concerns. What also comes to light is that perception (including, importantly, self-perception), aesthetic and phenomenal judgement and interpretation are caught up in, traced by phantom effects, even as they haunt the material, the ideological, the political, the biographical, the formal, the historical, if not the very idea of history itself. The hauntological transition which the discontinuous arc describes, a transition always already underway, draws our attention to the political, philosophical or ideological through the internal transformation in the 'work of art', the novel, poem, or film. This effect, paradoxically doubled *and* divided within itself, enacts within the scene of reading and writing an act of disfiguration, to borrow from Paul de Man (*RR* 123). Such a disfiguration, according to de Man, 'to the extent that it resists historicism, turns out to be historically more reliable than the products of historical archeology' (*RR* 123).

This leads us to the conclusion, once again, that the tracing of the spectral and the effects of haunting refuse to be generalized into a system. Indeed they exceed all notions of system, even as the hauntological trace informs and makes possible the system and the idea of system as such. This is so – to insist on this matter – because the very condition of spectrality is neither determinable as a single modality nor available as being governed by unchangeable laws. The spectral is thus an intervention and an interruption. Rather than registering this merely aesthetically as a disturbance in the field (see Fredric Jameson's comment at the beginning of the chapter on George Eliot), we should also see such intervention as potentially political. The spectre is, we might suggest, that which haunts politics when politics falls into the unthought and into system, when politics is nothing other than the law and the system, and is therefore available for analysis as that which abandons the political – which is to say the interruption and intervention of the law – in favour of the formal and habitual. Such an act of haunting, that disfiguration spoken of by Paul de Man, is what Ernesto Laclau terms the 'constitutive dislocation', without which 'there would be no politics'. It is precisely that which returns to disrupt identity and yet which is at the 'root of any identity',[35] albeit as an other, a figure of difference from the effort to constitute the identity from those elements considered as homogeneous, that the fracture that we name the political comes to be recognized.

Seeking to read the spectre then returns to discourse the ghostly act of disfiguration, making the invisible visible to reiterate that formula. At the same time, situating the act of reading in relation to the question of the political is to be attentive to the 'anachronism [that] is essential to spectrality' (Laclau 68). Indeed, the figure of the discontinuous parabola by which I describe the trajectory of this book operates both its trace and the fragmentation of that line, through the anachronistic installation and revenance to which reading opens itself and which it, in turn, seeks to open for the reader. Such an act of opening the systems of narrative, discourse, or identity to their own anachronistic constitution is thus to be responsive to the haunting trace. Our reading refigures and configures the disfiguration always already haunting the text.

Reading in this manner is described with approval by Slavoj Žižek, with reference to Paul de Man, as the 'paradox of "truth-in-exaggeration"' which, in the 'violence' of its 'appropriation', unveils what was hidden but there all along.[36] What is hidden is precisely that which haunts all notion of structure, category, or identity as distinct or discrete, self-sufficient or undifferentiated. That which is hidden and which the tracing of disfiguration makes plain is that there is not, simply, a 'sharp distinction between the real and the unreal, the actual and the inactual, the living and the non-living, being and non-being . . . in the opposition between what is present and what is not'.[37]

While signalling disagreements with Derrida in a number of places, Slavoj Žižek nonetheless speaks of the spectral in politics in a manner which acknowledges also that there is no sharp distinction as such. It is particularly over the matter of the 'spectre of ideology' that Žižek reads the ghostly dismantling of distinction (and with it, absolute ontological categorization):

On the one hand, there is the *spiritual element of corporeality*: the presence, in matter itself, of a non-material but physical element . . . On the other hand, there is the *corporeal element of spirituality*: the materialization of the spirit in a kind of pseudo-stuff, in substanceless apparitions . . . And perhaps it is here that we should look for the last resort of ideology . . . in the fact that there is no reality without the spectre, that the circle of reality can be closed over by means of an uncanny spectral supplement. Why, then, is there no reality without the spectre? . . . reality is not the 'thing itself', it is always-already symbolized, constituted, structured by symbolic mechanisms . . . reality is never directly 'itself', it presents itself only via its incomplete-failed symbolization, and spectral apparitions emerge in this very gap that forever separates reality from the real.[38]

In conclusion then, it is the very notion of ghosting, haunting, and of the spectral which disrupts any simple division between the spiritual and materiality. Indeed, what is called the spiritual is not simply a matter of spirit, for the very idea of spirit is only manifest in Žižek's prose through its becoming 'complicated' if you will by the spectre. Neither material nor non-material, the haunting figure uncannily traverses between matter and the abstract, between the corporeal and the incorporeal, incorporating itself within both, while never being available corporeally. Hence the struggle in Žižek's language to come to terms with the question of the spectral, as he shifts between the figure of hermeneutic closure and the aporetic opening, between a kind of Derridean disinterrance and a Lacanian mapping of co-ordinates,[39] which themselves become, in relation to the spectre, an 'incomplete-failed symbolization', a haunted topography of what we call 'reality'. For if Žižek reads the dismantling effected through the reading of the spectre, his own discourse reproduces and thereby suspends distinction through the barely discernible ghostly transference between theoretical discourses. Here we are witness to the blurring, the disturbance in the field of vision, caused by haunting, the merest trace incorporated into language, disruptive of distinctions. And it is this with which we have to deal, for which we are responsible, again and again.

# 1

# 'I wants to make your flesh creep': Dickens and the Comic-Gothic

It is the fear one *needs*: *the* price one pays for coming contentedly to terms with a social body based on irrationality and menace.

Franco Moretti

Gothic novels are technologies that produce the monster as a remarkably mobile, permeable, and infinitely interpretable body.

Judith Halberstam

A baby savage, a young monster, a child who had never been a child, a creature who might live to take the outward form of a man, but who, within, would live and perish a mere beast.

Charles Dickens, *The Haunted Man*

The gothic is always with us. Certainly, it was always with the Victorians: all that black, all that crepe, all that jet and swirling fog. Not, of course, that these are gothic as such, although we do think of such figures as manifestations of nineteenth-century Englishness. These and other phenomena, such as the statuary found in Victorian cemeteries like Highgate are discernible as being the fragments and manifestations of a haunting and, equally, *haunted*, 'gothicized' sensibility. If there is, as I argue in the Introduction, a transition in the nature of gothic from the end of the eighteenth century onwards, an irreversible movement from genre to trope, from structural identity to that which haunts the structures of narrative, it is marked by an inward turn perhaps, an incorporation which is also a spectralization. There is a constant return of the gothic as that which marks national identity without being fixable as a paradigmatic definition of that identity.

The motion of internalization should not necessarily be considered as a denial of the gothic so much as it might be read as a form of

intimacy and haunting. In part, the interest in the traces of otherness
within is often signalled during the Victorian period by an intense
fascination – obsession even on the part of some – with English manners
and all that, while apparently alien to the definition of Englishness, is
nonetheless projected from within that very identity. The phantoms of
English identity, those traces of comic and gothic disturbance, arrive
not from some foreign field. Instead, they return as necessary to the
construction of national identity, while being resistant to unequivocal
identification. For example, it is through what James Twitchell describes
as the sober English concern with darkness, mesmerism and Satanism,[1]
that the gothic aspects of Englishness are revealed. The gothic does
not simply disappear therefore. The gothic, ingested and consumed,
becomes appropriate in its fragmentary materialization, 'a legitimate
subject of literature' to employ Twitchell's phrase (33). Such a 'disappearance' is also an incorporation, as already intimated, so that, though
nowhere to be seen coherently or as such, the gothic in its ingested
and spectralized form leaves its traces on Englishness. In writing of
nineteenth-century literature where writing manifests a gothic return,
there is then to be acknowledged an embrace of the uncanny, a more
or less direct response on the part of certain Victorian writers to the
other within ourselves.

One of the sites of uncanny contestation is the adolescent body or
the figure of the child, a figure, arguably for the Victorians, viewed
communally as uncanny or unnatural because double, being both self
and other: *the same, yet not the same*. In the novels of Charles Dickens
youthful bodies frequently have projected onto and through them the
apparitional traces of gothic and abject otherness. As a consequence,
the young body comes to be presented as in need of discipline or punishment, if its often gothic otherness is not to get out of hand, and if the
child, the adolescent and the teenager (a category not known, of course,
to the Victorians) are to grow into proper Englishmen and women.
However, the haunting and uncanny aspects of adolescent corporeality
which frequently discomfit or perplex Dickens' adults are rendered all
the more ambivalent through the effects of comedy.

Humour already has a ghostly aspect, of course. As soon as one
attempts to analyse it, to explain its slippage and excess, its effects
vanish, as Antony Easthope has argued.[2] Nevertheless, certain charac-
teristics can be sketched, and Easthope risks a definition of the features
of the Englishness of English humour, these being irony, 'the exposure
of self-deception [and] a tendency towards fantasy and excess' (163).

Moreover, caricature is also a culturally prevalent and historically persistent aspect of English comedy, through which the body becomes doubled, an index of both individual and national moral concerns (171). Such a doubling means that the comedic is never simply itself, never containable according to an unequivocal act of definition or analysis. There is that which once again escapes, to return momentarily and to unsettle the certainties of propriety and rational discourse. Like those gothic traces and tropes, the comic works through a process of the material effects it produces in the complication of reading; as with the gothic, the comic relies on the haunting installation of undecidability. This comes to be particularly troubling when the traces of humour, of a comedic knowingness related to fantasy, excess, and irony, project themselves through the body, the image and the very idea of youth, with all its supposed innocence and purity. Comedy thus unveils that which haunts our own phantasies of the child, those uncanny oscillations of alterity.

The question of Englishness, the constitution and constant policing of national identity, finds a peculiarly intense focus where the gothic and the comic come together. It is not simply the case that Dickens is sometimes gothic and sometimes comic. Frequently both emerge as the disruptive troping phantoms of the narrative, rather than being the defining parameters of narrative form. Constantly disturbing, both humour and the gothic haunt the most typically English scenes in Dickens' writing and have their haunting half-lives through those figures of children and adolescents which are the concern of this chapter. Moreover, it is not the case that the comic and the gothic figure some neat, stable binary opposition; around and through the youthful body both return and refigure themselves and each other constantly, making the identification of undifferentiated identity problematic at the least, undecidable at the most. Comedy and gothic exceed themselves, overflowing the limits we seek to assign them and becoming this other apparition which we are naming here the comic-gothic.

## THE FAT BOY

The title of this essay is well known. It comes from that most famous of narcoleptics (literary or otherwise), the Fat Boy, also called 'young opium eater' (*PP* 345) no doubt in deference to Thomas de Quincey, from *The Pickwick Papers*. The scene from which the lines come is equally well known, but no less comical and worth repeating for all that.

It was the old lady's habit on the fine summer mornings to repair
to the arbour in which Mr. Tupman had already signalised himself,
in form and manner following: – first, the fat boy fetched from a
peg behind the old lady's bed-room door, a close black satin bonnet,
a warm cotton shawl, and a thick stick with a capacious handle; and
the old lady having put on the bonnet and shawl at her leisure, would
lean one hand on the stick and the other on the fat boy's shoulder,
and walk leisurely to the arbour, where the fat boy would leave her
to enjoy the fresh air for the space of half an hour; at the expiration
of which time he would return and reconduct her back to the house.

The old lady was very precise and very particular; and as this
ceremony had been observed for three successive summers without
the slightest deviation from the accustomed form, she was not a
little surprised on this particular morning, to see the fat boy, instead
of leaving the arbour, walk a few paces out of it, look carefully
around him in every direction, and return towards her with great
stealth and an air of the most profound mystery.

The old lady was timorous – most old ladies are – and her first
impression was that the bloated lad was about to do her some grievous
bodily harm with the view of possessing himself of her loose coin.
She would have cried for assistance, but age and infirmity had long
ago deprived her of the power of screaming; she, therefore, watched
his motions with feelings of intense terror, which were in no degree
diminished by his coming up close to her, and shouting in her ear in
an agitated, and as it seemed to her, a threatening tone, –

'Missus!'

Now it so happened that Mr. Jingle was walking in the garden
close to the arbour at this moment. He too heard the shout of 'Missus',
and stopped to hear more. There were three reasons for his doing
so. In the first place; he was idle and curious; secondly, he was by
no means scrupulous, thirdly, and lastly, he was concealed from view
by some flowering shrubs. So there he stood, and there he listened.

'Missus,' shouted the fat boy.

'Well Joe,' said the trembling old lady. 'I'm sure I have been a
very good mistress to you Joe. You have invariably been treated
very kindly. You have never had too much to do; and you have
always had enough to eat.'

This last was an appeal to the fat boy's most sensitive feelings.
He seemed touched as he replied, emphatically, –

'I knows I has.'

'Then what do you want now?' said the old lady, gaining courage.
'I wants to make your flesh creep,' replied the boy.

This sounded like a very blood-thirsty mode of showing one's gratitude; and as the old lady did not precisely understand the process by which such a result was to be attained, all her former horrors returned. (*PP* 92–3)

The scene is stage-comic and in its stage management provides the would-be gothic writer – or scourge of timid old ladies everywhere – with a textbook example of how to bring off a scene that is at once both gothic, potentially terrifying in its eventual outcome as all good scenes of gothic tension should be and, simultaneously, unremittingly comic. Although all is soon revealed after the last moment described above, as is usually the case in the novels of, for example, Anne Radcliffe, when the rational explanation arrives to calm down the unbearable agitation of being (for both the reader and the principal subject), Dickens works the scene in at least two different directions at once. The scene relies for both its gothic tension and its knowing comic solicitation of that tension on producing the simultaneity, the doubling of feeling, while also providing the reader with a Hitchcock-like view from above down onto the terrorstricken old lady, similar also to the elevation permitted the reader over Catherine Morland by Jane Austen in *Northanger Abbey*.

We know, because we have been told repeatedly, that the old lady is deaf. This is why the Fat Boy bellows. Nonetheless, the information and the manner in which it is delivered does nothing to allay the old lady's fear. If anything, it is increased. The information, the performance, the anticipation and effect: all are radically incommensurate. Joe's bellowing in anticipation of the revelation of a secret goes directly contrary to the laws of gothic. He shouts when he should be whispering, and it is a summer's day at a country cottage, and not the dead of night or dead of winter in some far-off chateau, castle or monastery. We might even suggest that the scene is knowingly anti-gothic, that Dickens is just having a laugh at the expense of tired form, a form he loved as a child and continues to embrace throughout his career, were it not for the fact that the deaf old lady is genuinely terrified. She is made even more an abject figure by her being unable to scream. The comedy of the scene only works because there is such a departure from routine as Dickens makes quite clear, and because the force of the old lady's emotions is not to be denied. It is in part the cruelty of this scene which makes us laugh, whether or not we choose to admit it. And it is in the results of the cruelty that we glimpse the fleeting ghost of the gothic. For the old lady responds not to any particular object or event, but to the invisible shadows which she has phantasized, and which we can only imagine at a double remove.

The moment in the garden is exemplary of the comic-gothic then. The reader works – and is expected to work – in a number of ways at once here, not least in accommodating the ludic oscillation between comedy and cruelty, the latter as the necessity for the former, the former the outcome of what happens when you get close enough to the gothic to see how the special effects work (which is precisely what Dickens does). At the same time, the scene sets for us all sorts of normal patterns of behaviour, which we are asked to take for granted, solely for the purpose of departing from them so excessively. Yet something remains unsettling in this scene, two things to be precise, moments when the gothic never quite resolves itself away. The first is the Fat Boy's own agitation, that nervousness of demeanour as he prepares himself for his greatest performance (walking in and out of the arbour is merely for the purposes of warming up). The second is the Fat Boy's outburst, which serves as the title for this essay: 'I wants to make your flesh creep'. Why the Fat Boy should wish to do this is a mystery, unless he is merely relishing the effect like all good stage villains. Also, the news he has to impart is hardly the sort to make the flesh creep. The gothic is quite exploded, though the uncanny remains, thereby intimating the return, if not of the repressed then, at least, of that which cannot be described. Quite.

To make someone's flesh creep is, we might say, Young Opium Eater's desire. Anyone less like Thomas de Quincey, the man who made even Wordsworth gothic, is hard to imagine. But the Fat Boy's desire finds its target in the terrified old lady. The Fat Boy understands that creeping flesh is a necessity if the narrative he wishes to unfold is to be deemed successful. He relishes his role, his performative status in the whole event. It is participation that is important. The Fat Boy is thus exemplary of the domestic gothic. He no longer is content, like so many good British subjects, with sitting back and enjoying being scared. He wants to take part. The English, no longer afraid – temporarily – of Catholics and foreigners (the Irish of course are always an exception, but that has to do with proximity to home, as all good cultural historians will acknowledge) need to scare themselves, to cut a caper at home, put on a sheet and run around going 'hoo,

hoo' for their own delight and terror. There are no bogeymen abroad, so why not pretend to be a little spooky in one's own back yard? As Sam Weller's knowing sobriquet for the Fat Boy attests, the other is within us, in this case in the possible form of the drug addict. And of course it doesn't really matter if the Fat Boy is addicted, what matters is that he might be. The perceived drug addict as the most gothic of figures then, haunted from within, tremulous without. Right in our own gardens. This is what we are witness to and the Fat Boy plays it up unmercifully. As James Kincaid notes, the Fat Boy is double, both 'harmless toy and raging demon' ('Designing Gourmet Children', 8). Doubleness is of course a feature of the uncanny, as Freud acknowledges (*U* 234).[3] It is this doubleness which Dickens remarks through the ambivalence, if not the undecidability, of the comic-gothic.

Kincaid also raises the issue of the boy's appetite, his constant desire to consume flesh and to turn whatever he consumes into flesh. It is interesting to speculate, in the light of Kincaid's remarks, on a possible connection between the Fat Boy and the then contemporary concern with cannibalism in relation to the distrust of medical science's advocacy of anatomy, as H. L. Malchow discusses.[4] As Malchow suggests, there were growing worries about 'domestic, if metaphoric, cannibalism' as a manifestation of the gothic in the form of anatomical dissections in the 1830s given voice in places both high and low, in *The Lancet* and in popular songs of the day (110). Perhaps from a fear of the anatomist's knife and its implied relation to 'barbaric' practices, a grim humour, a '[d]issection-room humor', arose during the period, and 'Dickens made much use of this kind of humor' from *Pickwick* to *Our Mutual Friend*, as Malchow acknowledges (114–15). Malchow cites the dinner scene between the medical students Bob Sawyer and Ben Allen, who joke about the 'source' of their meat (a child's leg), terrifying Mr Pickwick. He also recalls the meal consumed by Wegg and Mr Venus in *Our Mutual Friend*, in the taxidermist's shop where the two men are surrounded by jars containing the pickled remains of 'Indian and African infants', along with scenes from *Bleak House* (115). Harry Stone also notes the frequency of the 'comic mode' in relation to the theme of cannibalism, citing the example of the Fat Boy.[5] As Stone makes clear, Young Opium Eater makes little if any distinction between animal and human flesh (78). Such comedic business succeeds, argues Stone, in banishing the gothic quality of such moments. However, I would argue that gothic elements remain potent as haunting effects precisely because, while neither are these are banished absolutely nor are they absolutely commensurate with the identity of gothic. Instead, they operate at the limits of gothic because of their immanence and promise, laying below the surface and getting under our skins, waiting suggestively to make our flesh creep. As with many instances of alterity, the comic-gothic operates through proximity and intimacy.

The scenes with the Fat Boy and other scenes in Dickens' writing clearly revel in the comic-gothic as it pertains particularly to children, where the young become the source of sustenance and comedy. There is the grimly comic moment in *Great Expectations* when Magwitch hungrily begins to eye Pip's fat cheeks, saying 'Darn Me if I couldn't eat 'em . . . and if I han't half a mind to 't!' (*GE* 5). Eating young boys is much on Magwitch's mind, for he conjures the spectral young man who, Pip is promised, will find a way to Pip's heart and liver, in order that they may be torn out and roasted (*GE* 6). As fascinating as such moments of potential cannibalism are, and departing from Malchow's study, Dickens is, we would suggest, not so much interested in bringing the foreign, gothic other home, as finding it already at home, at the dinner table, locating the gothic *within* English humour. The grotesque is a necessary component of such comedy. In turn, comedy devours, it feeds off the other, often to hilariously ghoulish effect. The Fat Boy is, in a figurative if not literal sense, the embodiment of comic canni-balism (again, see Stone's argument). Consuming flesh and fowl, he also has digested the gothic sensibility, incorporating the incorporeal which ghosts his appetites, to regurgitate it in a particularly stagy and English manner.

## WRITTEN ON THE BODY

The Fat Boy impresses us of course because, not to put it too coyly, he is *fat*.[6] His excessive, grotesque, quivering corporeality names him. This mountain of flesh, who consumes more flesh and sleeps, is known by his body, by the excessiveness he embodies. Were he not fat, could we laugh at him, could he provide us with comic and gothic moments? Probably not. The flesh is everything, it makes the act believable, and it is his size, as well as his creepy proximity, which terrifies the old lady. Dickens knows this no doubt, and relishes the blubbery mon-strousness of the boy, seeing in it not only a good turn but also a sure-fire commercial winner, guaranteed to keep us coming back for more. It is almost as if one can imagine Dickens advertising the Fat

Boy in the words reserved for Mr Whackford Squeers, speaking of his son: "'Here's flesh!'" cried Squeers, turning the boy about, and indenting the plumpest parts of his figure with divers pokes and punches. . . . "Here's firmness, here's solidity'" (*NN* 517). There is a slight difference between the boys however, it should be noted. While the Fat Boy provides comedy by inflicting (metaphorical and psychological) pain, here it is the almost equally rotund Master Squeers who feels the pain while being part of the comedy. Fatness is not the bodily articulation of comic pain and gothic, grotesque excess, so much as it is the medium through which such discourses may be expressed, and onto which they may be inscribed. What we as readers comprehend, from one fat boy to another, is the use to which the child's corpulence may be put, the abuse which it endures for the sake of the joke, at a moment where pain and pleasure are inextricably linked. The experience of both and their simultaneity is, for the reader, of the flesh made word and the word fleshed out, embodied. It is, as with so many gothic narratives, an 'experience rooted in the body', as Steven Bruhm puts it (*Gothic Bodies* xv). And for all the comedy, both the Fat Boy and young Whackford perform for us as gothic bodies, in Bruhm's definition of this corporeal and textual phenomenon, for it is principally their bodies which are 'put on display' in all their 'violent, vulnerable immediacy' (xvii).

It is through the figure of the figure, the troping of the body, that Dickens reinscribes the discourse of the gothic, a form of writing which 'needs to be regarded', as Robert Miles argues, 'as a series of contemporaneously understood forms, devices, codes, figurations, for the expression of the "fragmented subject"' (*Gothic Writing* 3). Young Opium Eater and Young Whackford overflow their limits, their identities breaking down to become excessive and grotesque articulations. They are exploited and made to work. Dickens understands therefore, in the words of José Gil, that the body 'carries the symbolic exchanges and correspondences between the different codes that are in play'. He continues: '[t]he body is the exchanger of codes . . . on its own the body signifies nothing, says nothing. It always speaks only the language of the other (codes) that come and inscribe themselves on it.'[7] It is precisely the transport of codes, the symbolic rhythm of exchanges, which traces the boy's body as haunted, the locus of phantasmic projection and revenance. Thus the Fat Boy as spectralized body, as a materiality through which spectral substitution takes place figuring that ghostly dismantling described by Slavoj Žižek (and cited in the introduction), where '[o]n

the one hand, there is the *spiritual element of corporeality* . . . [while]
On the other hand, there is the *corporeal element of spirituality*: the
materialization of the spirit . . . in substanceless apparitions', presented
by an 'incomplete-failed symbolization' whereby 'spectral apparitions
emerge' (SI 20–1). Caricature relies on the materialization and concomitant destabilization which takes place in the boy's body through
the comic and gothic exchanges, which, in being apparitional, may be
read as addressing the fear that narrative modes and discursive models
are themselves inescapably haunted. Yet how does Dickens achieve
this in so clearly corporeal a figure?

Despite his corpulence, his idleness and gluttony, the Fat Boy is, as
James Kincaid puts it, hollow, this hollowness in all its gothic splen-
dour being 'the mysterious hollowness of fascinating caverns'.[8] Dickens
writes the boy as hollow in order to fill him from other places; the
boy's size is of a paradoxically disembodied kind: the more there is of
him, the more space there is to fill, the more we witness the projection
of fantasy and excess. Dickens writes Joe as fat in order to write large
the apparitional conjunction and cross-contamination of comic and gothic
discourses which find their meeting place in the particular scene already
considered. It is not that the Fat Boy is always in gothic mode although,
arguably, his constant state of being narcoleptic is suggestive of zom-
bies or the undead, albeit of a carnivalesque order. We might even
suggest, given his often death-like state – extending the performative
aspect further – that the Fat Boy's performance is analogous to an act
of mesmerism on Dickens' part,[9] as well as an act of ventriloquism
through the mesmerized boy by the author. Dickens puts on a theatrical
turn by having the Fat Boy adopt a gothic mode of discourse, arriving
with the promise of a tale to harrow the old woman, in a low, comic
parody of Hamlet's father (both, after all, involve gardens in one way
or another).

But is it possible to find the conjunction of the comic and the gothic
in bodies which are decidedly not obese? One possible example of
this is worked through in the scene leading up to Oliver asking for
more food, as Harry Stone discusses (81; for more concerning Stone's
discussion, see below). Another example comes from *The Uncommercial Traveller*. In the article entitled 'Wapping Workhouse', the narrator,
on his way to that institution, encounters a rather strange boy who is
referred to four times in two pages as an *apparition* (UT 19–20). The
ghastly and grotesquely comic come together in the bodily form and
voice whose most noticeable features are 'a ghastly grin and a [voice]

like gurgling water' (*UT* 19). The unnerved narrator remarks of the locks by which they are standing '"A common place for suicide"', to which the uncanny figure returns in a possible jest (which may just be a misheard response), '"Sue?" returned the ghost with a stare' (*UT* 19). With music-hall timing, not missing a beat, the proper name of one of the dead comes back, not as a presence but in the apparitional trace of the name. And this is achieved with that gallows humour to be found everywhere in Dickens' writing. Utterance calls up the return of that which has never been there. Yet it is not merely the pun which is important, the joke at the expense of self-slaughter. Importantly, the scene is set up through the body of this ghostly, liminal creature, especially in that humorous rictus and in the voice of the drowned. The body of the dead-alive apparition is, once more, expressly written as an empty figure on which are traced the comic and the uncanny. Everything about the young man is uncanny, uncomfortable, especially his wit, which insists on disrupting the meaning of words.

Thus Dickens, again, abusing identity in order to entertain, raising a laugh as well as raising the dead. We may turn for our next example of the empty body across whom the language of the other is inscribed to that favourite turn from *Martin Chuzzlewit*, Bailey Jr.

## BAILEY JR.

Bailey Jr.'s name and person offer the reader a constantly redoubled figure traced by the return of spectres and phantoms. Like the Fat Boy and Whackford, he is in the food line of business. Bailey is first encountered in the kitchen area of Todgers', illuminated by a frequent gleaming *of mysterious lights* in the area' (*MC* 199; emphasis added).[10] This is a small detail, so small in fact that the reader might ignore it altogether, yet it is significant in preparing the stage for the boy's entrance. The boy, who is a 'conspicuous feature among the peculiar incidents of the last day of the week at Todgers's' (*MC* 200), bursts in on the Miss Pecksniffs who are working by the fire, suitably lit as gothic moments should be only by a single candle. Bailey's purpose is to carry news of tomorrow's dinner to the sisters, which he does by adjuring them not to eat the fish. This, we are told, is delivered as a 'spectral warning', after which he 'vanished again' (*MC* 200). Later in the evening, Bailey returns briefly, 'squinting hideously behind the back of the unconscious Mrs Todgers' (*MC* 201). The comic scene is punctuated by the merest hints of the gothic as we can read in Dickens' choice of words, while it is also equally staged, rather than simply described. First made visible by mysterious lights, this strange apparition intrudes unexpectedly in dimly lit places, in best gothic fashion, to make portentous utterances only to disappear, then to return figured synecdochally by the disturbing squint.

Bailey's appearance is thus written according to a range of discursive effects, already discussed above, his identity traced in this manner, his subjectivity constituted by the comic, the gothic and the theatrical. Even as it signifies nothing, the fragmented gothic body is nonetheless the material place in Dickens' text where contemporaneous codes are exchanged and overwritten, to recall Gil. The scene itself is also coherent and consistent in terms of the gothic: mystery is suggested, events are startling and remain unexplained fully, atmosphere is established, and the harbinger of calamity vanishes. Dickens is careful to determine the comic moment according to gothic convention, so that the overwriting of Bailey Jr.'s body overflows the limits of that body onto the form and the representation of the scene itself. Saturday night supper is expressed through the gothic mode, while the ludicrous nature of Todgers' boarding house reciprocally impresses itself onto the gothic, not exactly domesticating it but transforming it into a peculiarly English moment.[11] This process is, arguably, itself gothic and, more especially, spectral, inasmuch as there is the intimation of an excess overspreading particular identities, spreading from form to scene to character and back again, 'extending by contiguity, a particular chain of attributes', to borrow Eve Kosofsky Sedgwick's definition of a particular gothic convention (*Coherence* 149).

The overwriting effect – itself a process of apparitional disinterrance – extends to naming, which also operates in the example of Bailey Jr. as a 'particular chain of attributes' and of which the temporary renaming of the Fat Boy may well be one more sign. Bailey Jr. is known by several names, all of which are given by the lodgers at Todgers, and all of which reveal a melodramatic and gothic pedigree. Dickens tells us that the boy's name may have been Benjamin, although this is merely gossip rather than fact (*MC* 201). This is changed to Uncle Ben, or just Uncle. In turn, the boy's name is transformed into Barnwell. He is also named Young Brownrigg, or otherwise given the names of 'any notorious malefactor or minister' (*MC* 201). Even the name 'Bailey Jr.' appears to be a name provided with reference to the law court, rather than the boy's real name. This is not certain however. For the reader is informed that the name of Bailey invokes a somewhat gothic tale, involving 'the recollection of an unfortunate lady of the same name, who perished by her own hand early in life, and [who] has been immortalised in a ballad' (*MC* 202). The ballad of the female suicide notwithstanding – who unwittingly provided posterity with the comic, though grim, spectacle of hanging herself with her garters, and who subsequently returns to haunt Bailey and through his slightly uncanny nature, the proprieties of Victorian narrative – Bailey is established by his various names as having an impeccably scurrilous literary and cultural pedigree. The names inscribed on the boy mark him with a history of violent spectacle and morbidity belonging to the city of London. In fact, his identity is haunted by the city's otherness. Dickens uses the boy to recall various eighteenth-century grotesqueries and *grand guignol* events, fictional and real, which the various names counter-sign against the propriety of nineteenth-century society. George Barnwell is an apprentice in Lillo's play *The History of George Barnwell, or the London Merchant*, who murders his uncle and robs his employer. Mother Brownrigg whipped three apprentices to death, subsequently hiding the bodies in the coal-hole, before being caught and hanged. Moreover, while not particularly gothic in itself, at least two acts of renaming mark Bailey with a certain female otherness, as though the grotesque and the feminine were somehow aligned (of which more in the discussion of Jenny Wren, below). The space filled by Bailey is also a screen on which gothic-comic phantasms are projected. There is, in the haunting of Bailey through the play of names, a phantasmal succession of spectral traces as a dark, alternative history of London.

As with the Fat Boy then, the propriety and property of the proper name hardly appears to matter with regard to Bailey. As far as these two characters are concerned, the proper name is decidedly improper. It is erased, as if to make the figure either hollow or blank, fresh for further inscription. Identity becomes the function of a series of performative personae read from some other place, rather than being intrinsic to the self. In the case of Bailey Jr., his identity is all too often deemed villainous and mysterious, good for nothing except hanging (*MC* 201), even though, simultaneously, this appears to be the source of comedy rather than horror. Strictly speaking though, this moment is all the more uncanny in its doubling motion, thereby remaining undecidable.

However, it appears that Bailey enjoys a joke as much as the next person, for he consciously performs in a comic-gothic register for the members of the lodging house, and most especially for Merry and Cherry

Pecksniff, as the scene described attests. At another moment, almost immediately after the spectral warning concerning the inedibility of fish, Bailey frightens *and* amuses the young ladies in an act of gothic pantomime:

> He entertained them on this occasion by thrusting a lighted candle into his mouth, and exhibiting his face in a state of transparency; after the performance of which feat, he went on with his professional duties. (*MC* 200)

It is all but impossible to imagine the performance of this act without imagining the pain which Bailey inflicts upon himself for the amusement of the sisters, but the moment is striking in its effective rendering of the boy as nothing but an illuminated head, as though he were a spectre or Jack-o'-Lantern. While this term today suggests more immediately a pumpkin carved to resemble a face (and Bailey inverts the conceit, making his head resemble the Halloween pumpkin), the phrase has more fantastic origins, being a term dating back to the latter part of the seventeenth century, and being synonymous with *ignus fatuus* or will-o'-the-wisp. Thus Bailey's act is, like his various names, indebted to and haunted by a tradition of popular narrative concerned with ghosts and phantoms.

Furthermore, the very pain involved in thrusting a lighted candle into his mouth suggests an unnerving irrationality about the boy, which disturbs precisely because the infliction of pain on the self cannot be explained.[12] What we can suggest is that the act is theatrical and spectacular. Dickens side-steps the internal coherence of the scene to present the reader with the moment of comic, yet at some level terrifying melodrama, of what John David Moore describes in his work on early nineteenth-century theatre as 'vulgar popular art'.[13] We might suggest in passing that it is the very question of vulgarity and popularity as otherness which is potentially terrifying as spectacle for certain members of Dickens' audience. Such low instances of intrusive alterity are frequent in Dickens, and it is particularly important to recognize in Bailey Jr. the coming together of various, heterogeneous forms of otherness, through naming, speech and performance. Moreover, in making himself suffer for the amusement of others Bailey brings together the supernatural with the murderous criminality that his various names authorize. (It is as if, we might say, Bailey embodies or incorporates the ghosts of narrative, figured as phantasms of the imagination projected onto Bailey, as the multiplication of his names implies. The comedy of the performance is doubled from within by a dark alterity.) This is, itself, another gothic narrative convention, as E. J. Clery points out.[14] However, it is clearly an internalized Gothic – and in this Dickens is haunted by a spectre from the future. He unwittingly (unconsciously?) pre-empts Freud, who took, in the words of Mark Edmundson, the 'props and passions of terror Gothic . . . to [relocate] them inside the self'.[15] For it is as if, in miming the consumption of the candle, Bailey Jr. promises to illuminate the darkness inside us all.

For such a revelation and a willingness to play the part Bailey Jr. must of course be punished, if only so that he can figure as a pantomimic version of the return of the repressed – or, in Bailey's case, the return of the irrepressible. In one of *Martin Chuzzlewit*'s several notable violent scenes, the carriage in which Bailey travels, with Montague and the gothic Jonas, is overturned (*MC* 723–7). To all intents and purposes it appears that Bailey is injured mortally. Indeed we are told this on more than one occasion: 'the boy was past holding up, or being held up, or giving any other sign of life than a faint and fitful beating of the heart' (*MC* 726); then, 'but [the surgeon] gave it as his opinion that the boy was labouring under a severe concussion of the brain, and that Mr Bailey's mortal course was run' (*MC* 727). Finally, the news of the alleged death is relayed by Poll Sweedlepipe: '"Bailey, young Bailey!" . . . "He hasn't been adoing anything! . . . He'll never do anything again. He's done for. He's killed . . . and if you was to crowd all the steam-engines and electric fluids that ever was, into this shop, and set 'em every one to work their hardest, they couldn't square the account, though it's only a ha-penny"' (*MC* 827). It is not too fanciful perhaps to read that reference on Sweedlepipe's part to 'electric fluids' as an acknowledgement of the much vaunted powers of galvanism in the nineteenth century and through that, indirectly, to *Frankenstein*, to acknowledge once again how Dickens recalls the gothic through the slightest of touches. However, despite the reassurances of mortality, as with all good gothic tales, the hero-villain in the shape of Bailey does return. Shortly after Pecksniff is both reviled and revealed by Old Martin, Sweedlepipe, a '*monstrously-excited* little man', comes 'bursting up the stairs, and straight into the chambers of Mr Chuzzlewit, as if he were *deranged*' (*MC* 892; emphases added). Such comedic grotesquerie is counterposed by Dickens against the ironically labelled 'sublime address' of the departing Pecksniff. In what amounts to an hysterical state, Sweedlepipe rushes in and out, repeating himself, until

'a *something* in top-boots, with its head bandaged up, staggered into
the room, and began going round and round, apparently under the
impression that he was walking straight forward' (*MC* 893; emphasis
added). Bailey appears finally, providing both those in the room and
the reader with a comic rendition of bodily monstrosity and spectacular
pain, so common to the gothic. Reduced to a 'something', an 'it' no
longer human yet raised from the dead – we're not told how – Bailey
Jr. manifests himself once more, his body abused for the sake of the
comic entrance.

## SCARING CHILDREN IS FUN

If children are constructed socially and through various cultural narratives as different from adult, rational human beings, this is no doubt a
self-sustaining process which, in fearing the otherness of the child, the
adolescent or the teenager rewrites the narrative of childhood being in
order to maintain its alterity, precisely for the purpose of punishment.
The child's world is, as James Kincaid says, 'unnecessary, useless'
strictly speaking, it is a made-up world, creative rather than mimetic
(*Child-Loving* 221). In recognizing this, the adult may recognize a certain
lost world, and seek to punish its other for the loss of that which we
failed to keep within our grasp. The adult, haunted by the spectres of
the child and childhood, seeks revenge on its corporeal counterpart, as
that counterpart figures that corporeal place onto which the adult's
anachronic, phantasmatic otherness is projected. So, we might say what
the adult says when confronted by the uncanny figure of childhood,
what we want is facts, not fantasy or, indeed, phantasms. And what
better way at getting back at the childlike delight in the gothic – that
which scares us because we have grown ever so sensible, rational –
than to punish it with that mode of representation by which the child
can create laughter? Even while children may triumph occasionally in
the text of Dickens it remains a fact nonetheless that, at some point,
they are punished in some fashion for their difference. All too frequently the writing of punishment in Dickens' novels takes a gothic
turn (which is never comical), as in the process of 'education' at
Dotheboys Hall, in the death of Paul Dombey, or in the manifestation
of a schoolmaster named, appropriately, Bradley Headstone.
    There are however other ways of punishing the child in which Dickens

indulges whereby the gothic mode may be maintained, while comedy is reintroduced for the amusement of the (no doubt) adult reader who may, like any number of Dickens' adult characters, tend to understand children as 'naturally wicious'. Because at some level the child, adolescent or teenager is perceived in all his or her (frequently gothic) otherness, so fun may be made through the gothic mode. Not all children get to have the last laugh, as does Bailey Jr.[16]

*Oliver Twist* provides one example of comedy – albeit of a very dark variety – at the expense of the child, as Oliver progresses from the workhouse, to the undertaker's, to Fagin's den (all gothic structures), where other children enjoy themselves but not Oliver. (No doubt there is something of the morality tale here; all children, being naturally wicious, have criminal propensities, Oliver's plight is a warning to us all, my dears, concerning the inevitable recidivism of childhood.) Harry Stone offers a fascinating discussion of the well-known moment when Oliver asks for more (79–81). This moment, argues Stone, is equally laughable and fearful:

> the scene in which Oliver asks for more . . . is generated by a bizarre and laughable fear. Everyone is familiar with the scene itself, but how many remember the fear that generates the scene? That fear flows directly from a terrifying cannibalistic threat, but this threat – a threat made by one workhouse boy that he will devour another – is cauterised by its outlandishness and its humour: we chuckle rather than shudder, and we dismiss the threat as a bit of humorous Dickensian grotesquerie; the threat, we feel, has no abiding importance. But Dickens does not dismiss the threat, nor does he discount it or forget it. (81)

This is an admirable reading of the comic-gothic event, though I would argue that it is not a question of dismissing the threat so much as seeking to domesticate it, making it manageable through emphasizing the comic register. This is a precarious moment for, in the potential effect of making manageable, the economy of the workhouse – that which seeks to make children manageable – may become reproduced in and by the textual satire. Dickens will not let us do this however, for his text maintains the fearful and the comic, the revenance of the gothic and the humorous which disrupt the textual economy as they maintain a precarious balance where the seemingly opposing discursive

and psychic poles in question here open between them an uncanny
aporia into which either mode threatens constantly to overflow and
commingle, each to ghost the other.

The other well-known Dickensian scared child is Pip who, like Oliver,
spends much of his early life in gothic surroundings – whether the
marshes, his parents' gravestones, or Miss Havisham's – or in proximity to gothic moments, such as that of the soldiers' arrival at Joe's
door in search of Magwitch, described as an 'apparition' (*GE* 30). Of
such instances, the most comical for the reader, though not for Pip, is
the following:

> It was a rimy morning, and very damp. I had seen the damp lying
> on the outside of my little window, as if some goblin had been
> crying there all night, and using the window for a pocket-handker-
> chief. Now, I saw the damp lying on the bare hedges and spare
> grass, like a coarser sort of spiders' webs . . . The marsh-mist was
> so thick, that the wooden finger on the post . . . was invisible to me
> until I was quite close under it. Then, as I looked up at it, while it
> dripped, it seemed to my oppressed conscience like a phantom de-
> voting me to the Hulks.
>
>   The mist was heavier yet when I got out upon the marshes, so
> that instead of my running at everything, everything seemed to run
> at me. This was very disagreeable to a guilty mind. The gates and
> dykes and banks came bursting at me through the mist, as if they
> cried as plainly as could be, 'A boy with Somebody-else's pork pie!
> Stop him!' The cattle came upon me with a suddenness, staring out
> of their eyes, and steaming out of their nostrils, 'Holloa, young thief!'
> One black ox, with a white cravat on – who had to my awakened
> conscience something of a clerical air – fixed me so obstinately with
> his eyes, and moved his blunt head round in such an accusatory
> manner that I blubbered out to him, 'I couldn't help it sir! It wasn't
> for myself I took it!' Upon which he put down his head, blew a
> cloud of smoke out of his nose, and vanished with a kick-up of his
> hind legs and a flourish of his tail. (*GE* 16–17)

Between the pie and the cattle, there is more of gravy than of grave
about this scene,[17] even if, despite its clerical air, the black ox bears
more than a passing resemblance to the devil rather than any clergy-
man, while Pip's behaviour recalls in parodic fashion Hamlet's words
concerning the reaction of guilty creatures, given certain stimuli. As

Pip's phantasms and yet also real, the cattle are doubled and then re-doubled in being both comic and gothic, humorous and terrifying. Furthermore, there is a subtle distance between Pip's older, narrating self, and his younger, other identity, by whom he is haunted. While the elder Pip may well be able to construct the narrative comically at his other's expense, his younger self clearly is not in on the joke, and is terrified by the spectral cattle and the animated features of the land-scape. The goblins, spiders' webs and the dripping phantom finger-post operate within a gothic mode, as the supernatural scene displaces the real world in leading to the comedy of frightened childhood.

That there is a discernible gap between the older and the younger Pip suggests to what extent the child as other has to be punished by its older manifestation. There is a double movement here in imagina-tion and memory for, while the elder Pip remembers the scene, he is also shaping its narration in a particular gothic fashion. His younger self's terror is transformed into a medium for entertainment. And this is not the only example of Pip's comic-gothic abilities at the expense of the young. His manipulation of gothic discourse is presented when, in London, he hires a 'boy in boots' (*GE* 216). Invoking *Frankenstein*, Pip remarks that he makes a '*monster*' of the boy, who has 'little to do and a great deal to eat' (notice once more the obsession with chil-dren eating), these being the '*horrible* requirements' with which 'he *haunted* my existence' (*GE* 216; emphases added). Furthermore, Pip refers to the boy as an 'avenging phantom'. Whether or not Pip in-tends to be humorous, his description of the boy in boots is comical even while it is indebted to gothic discourse; more to the point, we can read that the gothic child is inescapable. It is always present and always hungry – for something.


JENNY WREN


Bodily monstrosity and excessiveness when figured or disfigured in writing may be said to be a performance of catachresis, reworked as and, importantly, *through* an image of the subject. Such embodied catachresis is familiarly recognized as the grotesque, and the grotesque is never far from gothic modes of representation. Thus far the comic-gothic examples given have been boys – Joe the Fat Boy and Bailey Jr. In both cases their physical transformation is not natural to them, effected through various abusive processes, whether overeating or violent occurrence. Their bodies may be said therefore to have been written, not only by Dickens but also through the impression on the individual body by social activity. The Fat Boy need not eat so much (although chances are this is idle fantasy), and Bailey, it seems, will recover. At some level then, the grotesque identity of male children is constructed, not essential. (Arguably, even Smike's condition is exacerbated by neglect and abuse to the point of gothic excessiveness; systematic punishment by Squeers has written the boy's body as the reader encounters it, there is no Smike other than the creature whom we read.)

In distinction to the boys and turning to our final example of the comic-gothic, Jenny Wren, we might consider that her misshapen body is a *natural* body. The strangeness of her behaviour, attitudes and identity appears to spring from her physical deformity. As a figure of female, rather than male gothic, she shares certain aspects of her identity with the boys, but is also somewhat different. In this final example, we wish to explore how Jenny's body only *appears* natural from certain perspectives, and that her writing is an altogether more complex affair. Unlike the Fat Boy and Bailey, Jenny Wren is not the passive recipient of uncanny or grotesque names meant to approximate her identity or otherwise provide a fictive identity for her. She names herself twice: as Jenny Wren and also as the person of the house, this later name signalling uncannily the anonymity of a spectral figure which resides in and belongs to the house she so disturbs. Jenny takes it upon herself to reinvent her identity and thus pre-empt, at least in part, the act of gothic determination imposed on the child by the adult. We should also recall at this juncture that Jenny's real name is Fanny Cleaver, which is itself suggestive enough of gothic narratives and potential acts of dismembering.

Also, unlike the Fat Boy and Bailey who create gothic scenarios out of the everyday for the entertainment of others, the dolls' dressmaker engages with the gothic mode, as much for herself as for those with whom she comes into contact. Her gothic performance is an act of self-identification, of psychic reflection and re enforcement. Her sense of humour is not farcical, it is darkly disturbing, frequently satirical, unsettling in its ability to find as a corollary to her own physical deformity the deformity of identity or spirit in others. In this manner, Jenny is able to laugh at the gothic alterity, the psychological monstrosity within all others, hers being an act of reading rather than projection. By comparison, the laughter evoked by our two previous examples is all surface play even if it does bespeak a condition of otherness.

Jenny is the most uncanny of Gothic characters in *Our Mutual Friend* where, as Adrian Poole puts it in his introduction to the novel, '[m]ost of the life . . . tends to a state of suspended animation. Nothing seems certainly dead nor entirely alive'.[18] Jenny's ethereal condition seems part of this certainly, and she invests her dolls with imaginative animation that manages to make the flesh creep with the ease of a seasoned music-hall performer. Even the house in which Jenny lives exists amongst a row of houses in a square, which is described as having a 'deadly kind of repose on it, more as though it had taken laudanum than fallen into a natural rest' (*OMF* 221–2). This is perhaps Dickens' first clue that appearance should not be taken for granted, but should be read as an induced or constructed, rather than as a 'natural' state. Jenny first appears in the second book, when Charlie Hexam and Bradley Headstone come to her house to visit Lizzie Hexam:

> The boy knocked at a door, and the door promptly opened with a spring and a click. A parlour door within a small entry stood open, and disclosed a child – a dwarf – a girl – a something – sitting on a little low old-fashioned arm-chair, which had a kind of working bench before it. [. . .]
> The queer little figure, and the queer but not ugly little face, with its bright grey eyes, were so sharp, that the sharpness of the manner seemed unavoidable. (*OMF* 222)

These initial descriptions strike us with their instability and undecidability. They engage in a process of supplementation, and are themselves supplemented by others during the puzzling conversation maintained by the dolls' dressmaker, as if to make fun of and so disconcert both Charlie and Headstone:

> The person of the house gave a weird little laugh . . . and gave them another look out of the corners of her eyes. She had an elfin chin that was capable of great expression; and whenever she gave this look, she hitched this chin up. As if her eyes and her chin worked together on the same wires. [. . .]
> It was difficult to guess the age of this strange creature, for her poor figure furnished no clue to it, and her face was at once so young and so old. Twelve, or at the most thirteen, might be near the mark. (*OMF* 224)

Everything about Jenny is sharp, from her pointed comments to her fingers, her chin and the looks she gives the master and his pupil.

Dickens makes no distinction as to a limit or border between physi-
ological sharpness and its counterpart in the girl's personality and manner.
Moreover, this erasure and blurring of borders moves uncannily between notions of the human and inhuman, as well as in the simultaneity
of different ages. As if to erase the divisions between one aspect and
another, Dickens intimates the fantastic possibility of Jenny's being an
automaton of sorts, connected by wires, whether those of a marionette
– thereby aligning her uncannily with her dolls – or some *thing* given
artificial life by galvanic current. Her uncanniness, amounting to a
daemonic spriteliness, is inscribed by a number of undecidables and
ambiguities. Trope gives way to trope in a process of spectralization
of identity which is resistant to and exceeds any governing taxonomy
or epistemology. The success of reading is suspended by the phantastic
rhythm while what we do read is, in the words of Paul de Man, the
'unsettling of mimesis' (*RR* 274)[19] as the spectralization of identity
and text puts Dickens' narrative *en abyme*.

   This daemonic condition is hinted at by the later description of her
as 'of the earth, earthy' (*OMF* 243). Her age is indeterminate, she
appears 'queer' though not ugly, and it is impossible to tell exactly
what she is, so that the final definition must be indefinite of necessity –
she is a *something*. Like Bailey Jr., although in an altogether different
register, Jenny is not human, not quite. Yet while Bailey is a comic
monstrosity, Jenny is an abject figure. Jenny is configured by Dickens
as a figure for the uncanny, for that which is unknowable. Defying
definition or identification, she is the figure in gothic narrative which
Joseph Andriano terms the 'daemonic feminine'[20] (139), troubling the
masculine self through an address to the blind-spots within masculinity
while resisting recuperation.

   And even while she haunts the story she provides mischievous laughter
often at the expense of men, and especially at the expense of her father.
As Rosemary Jackson, Joseph Andriano and Barbara Warren all suggest
in different ways, the 'haunting Other may be a projection of the haunted
Self . . . [the]inner daemon, [is] a psychic entity unrecognized as such
by the male ego' (Andriano 2).[21] As such, Jenny Wren can be read as
the externalized, gothic other of the self, who deploys her pointed comedy
to hold up the distorted mirror of the psyche to her male victims. One
example of this is Jenny's relationship to her drunken father. Her humour
is to reinvent her father as her child, as is well known. Her transformation of him is both gothic and caustically comical, as he becomes a
'wretched spectacle', a '"naughty, wicked creature"', while her scolding

turns him into a 'shaking figure, unnerved and disjointed from head to foot' (*OMF* 239). Though deformed, Jenny has the narrative and symbolic ability to re-form, if not reform, others, to create the male subject and thereby exert control through the verbal punishment of her humour.

Of all Dickens' comic-gothic characters Jenny is then, arguably, the most complex of figures. 'Compounded of opposites', as Malcolm Andrews suggests, she is apparently marked by both physical and psychic inconsistencies.[22] Yet the inconsistencies of which Andrews speaks are only such if Jenny Wren is read within normative or realist parameters. She only appears as natural. Her inconsistencies are wholly consistent within a certain representation of the grotesque, and she is written by Dickens with a wholly symbolic function in mind. Mary Russo's eloquent introduction to the female grotesque serves usefully in helping to come to terms with Jenny Wren. Drawing on the work of Geoffrey Galt Harpham, Russo discusses the figuration of the grotesque in Renaissance art, with its 'combination of the fantastic with . . . [the] rendering [of] realistic detail',[23] an ability which 'so astounded and even infuriated critics like John Ruskin' (5). Such combination is clearly at work in Dickens' articulation of Jenny, with her queer, though not ugly face, her weird laugh, and her beautiful hair. Also, as Russo points out, the grotesque is in itself 'suggestive of a certain construction of the feminine' (5). Jenny's deformity and her marginal relationship to the narrative of *Our Mutual Friend* bespeak this construction and also its cultural necessity, for 'subjectivity', as Russo argues, 'requires the image of the grotesque body' (9), even as masculine identity requires the marginalized feminine for the purposes of self-fashioning. Dickens may be read as inscribing physical deformity onto Jenny, making her a comic grotesque in order to foreground from the margins, wherein such identity is written and to which it is consigned, the cultural projection of the female in general. Marginalized and yet necessary to what Russo terms the psychic register, woman is always deformed within and by patriarchal discourse.

Yet, as Jenny's example shows, she returns to haunt the very place of containment as a spectral and uncanny figure located at the centre of, and as other to, the shaping fictions of the feminine. Confined within the patriarchal house and within its symbolic register, she returns as its repressed, a vengeful ghost who exploits her parent's infantilized condition. The ambiguity, the undecidability, the 'inconsistencies' of Jenny are merely the traces of the 'uncanny grotesque body as . . . monstrous, deformed, excessive' constructed through the 'discursive fictions' of nineteenth-century bourgeois culture (Russo 9). What appears 'natural' in Jenny is revealed by Dickens through the deployment of undecidability and irresolution as the tireless work of construction, and Jenny's revenge is that she is able, through her satirical reformulations, to bring out the gothic monstrosity of men, which had been hidden all along inside them, and not in the foreign or female, or indeed the child.

Jenny's gothic mode is not merely an effect of the grotesque. She combines those elements of grotesquerie with the uncanny, which manifests itself not only in the unresolvable ambiguities which write Jenny but also in Jenny's own sense of an 'individualized, interiorized space of fantasy and introspection' (8). As much as Jenny jokingly toys, often viciously, with the men with whom she comes into contact, she also performs for their troubled perplexity her own psychic life. She refers to herself in the third person, calling herself the 'person of the house' as already noted, or else the 'child'; she projects imagined lives for her dolls, and speaks in conundrums (*OMF* 222–3). She imagines various fantasy scenarios worthy of the Brothers Grimm or as a strange parody of gothic narrative, such as locking children in the vault of a church and blowing pepper at them through the keyhole (*OMF* 224). She has visions of fantastic and cruel empowerment with regard to her father (mentioned above), imagining, as Harry Stone puts it, 'punishing and tormenting him, even . . . torturing him' (501). Her flights of fantasy take a particularly gothic turn when, as Stone reminds us, 'she envisions ravenous creatures battening upon' her father (501). Such narratives are not only strange; they *estrange* both the subject and the reader and render the person of the house distinctly unhomely. It is important at this juncture that we do not forget that Jenny Wren is herself a child (despite the fact that she rails against children), and one who was, as she herself seems to imply, at one time 'chilled, anxious, ragged [and] beaten' (*OMF* 238). Like the idea of the female (of which we have spoken above), the child in Victorian culture was constructed in a position of passive centrality *and* simultaneously marginalized, rendered monstrous. Jenny's gothic narrative concerning her father transformed into a child serves to remind us of the abject fate of the child, while pointing to the ways in which marginalization and punishment originate as a form of psychic projection manifested in material conditions.

Her uncanniness is given its strangest and most eloquent expression in Chapter Five of Book Two (*OMF* 266–80). Sitting on the roof with Lizzie, the person of the house, now no longer in the house but above it, imagines disturbing yet transcendent possibilities which she expresses thus, to Riah and Fledgeby: 'But it's so high. And you see the clouds rushing on above the narrow streets, not minding them, and you see the golden arrows pointing at the mountains in the sky from which the wind comes, and you feel as if you were dead' (*OMF* 279). As the two men leave, Jenny calls out repeatedly in a sing-song voice 'Come back and be dead, Come back and be dead!' (*OMF* 279). At one level this may be read as yet one more example of Jenny's sense of humour, an uncanny humour no doubt, but imbued with a playfulness all the same. However, in another manner Jenny's gothic lyricism imagines or desires a space beyond abjection. The fantasy of shared death is a response to the unspeakable freedom of death imagined beyond the house. Jenny's discourse operates vertically away from the streets, away from the internal and confined space of the house and towards the immanence of her identity freed from its body, doubled and projected onto what Mary Russo describes as the 'aerial sublime' (29). Sublimity is of course a correlative to the grotesque and gothic. Not so much a binary or polar opposite, the sublime is the imagined configuration of the 'high', to the grotesque's 'low other'. Jenny's discourse figures the movement towards the sublime, from low to high, from materiality and mortality to spirituality and immortality, from excessive and deformed details of the material conditions of existence to the ethereal and inexpressible possibilities of a place 'beyond' or 'to-come'. Thus Jenny Wren articulates the possibility of movement which leads nowhere in true gothic form, as Fiona Robertson makes plain.[24] From the all too material terror of existence, there is envisioned the immaterial terror of the absolutely other, the unspeakable, which produces anxiety in the face of mystery and, ultimately, suspense.

## THE PERFORMATIVE IN-JOKE OR, RAISING A LAUGH AND RAISING THE DEAD

To return to an earlier moment. Sam Weller gives away more than perhaps even he knows when he describes the Fat Boy as 'young opium eater'. He writes onto the Fat Boy's body a gothic identity *par excellence*, and yet one which is also knowingly constructed, given as a textual performance by its own author, Thomas De Quincey. Weller provides Joe with a narrative that self-consciously has already involved itself in a knowing act of fictional performance. This gothic identity is not a simply comprehended subject, but a complex textual performance. The name which Sam appropriates requires a recognition to make it work; like a literary in-joke, if you don't know the reference you won't find the moment tellingly comical, and the gothic is misunderstood. In a different manner the various names imposed on Bailey Jr. operate according to the same logic. The humour of intertextual reference relies upon a knowledgeable audience, a community of readers within a common cultural frame. Sam Weller brings it home to us then that the gothic is not out there, not far afield, not in a foreign and exotic place but right here, with us and in us, ingested and inscribed, and actively regenerated. To reiterate the point, the gothic is troped as that which haunts our shared identity. The melodramatic seriousness of De Quincey's gothic self-haunting becomes transformed from one of unending desire to a figure of local, recognizable plenitude and excess.

And let us not forget that the full title of De Quincey's most famous text provides a national identity for the opium eater. There is the very question of Englishness at work, as if to unsettle several identities at once, as if to make plain that the uncanny is already here, that the repressed didn't have to return from very far at all. This is a point made by De Quincey himself, early on in the *Confessions* when he slyly suggests that more public figures in English political life are addicts than either they, or we, would care to acknowledge. Joe is one such barely disguised affront to bourgeois guilt and secrecy, exposing himself in all his adipose and somnambulant glory.

However, to come back to the question of textual acknowledgement. What Dickens' young comic-gothic characters share is a certain knowledge regarding their textuality. This is not to say that they knowingly imitate or impersonate other characters, so much as they are written according to particular textual models, ghosted by them. They are given an ironic spectral reflexivity by Dickens so as to speak beyond themselves, beyond their own individual cognizance about the ways in which children and adolescents are constructed in nineteenth-century culture. Parents did not necessarily see their children in a gothic light, at least not at any conscious level which they would willingly have acknowledged. But what we may read from Dickens' text, glancing at it from a rather odd angle of parallax, is a recognition on Dickens' part of the gothic aspects of childhood's construction, and his willingness to engage this construction against the grain, so as to shed light on the very practices of cultural configuration.

To return to De Quincey: following Margaret Russett's argument from the first chapter of her *De Quincey's Romanticism* (14–52), Thomas De Quincey knowingly constructs his other self in his memoir within a recognizable gothic paradigm, while locating this addicted subjectivity as distinct from the narrating subject. Particularly, he produces his childhood other as a gothic child, an interpreted figure, somewhat like Bailey Jr., founded, as Russett puts it 'on strictly textual antecedents' (16). Dickens, we suggest, pursues a similar act of identity formation for certain of his children and adolescents, exploiting the conventions of the gothic by making them figures from a gothic tale, yet nudging the reader into a position of recognition through the comic self-consciousness of such a ploy.

If, as Russett argues, De Quincey knowingly 'adumbrates reader-response . . . more explicitly than . . . the novels of Ann Radcliffe do' (17), then arguably Dickens brings his ensemble of effects to an even greater pitch. It is as if Dickens, recognizing the unintentionally humorous aspect of gothic narrative, turns to the comedic mode in order to fashion a strength from an aesthetic weakness. Comedy knows what the gothic does not, it knows itself and understands that it returns from within rather than being merely the monstrous without. Comedy has the ability to sneak up on its audience, and to take them hostage through an uncanny moment of comparison and identification – of similarity – in the very same moment when the audience believes itself to be set apart from the subject of comedic discourse. Comedy is predicated on reader-response and Dickens connects the comic – whether the belly-laugh and excessiveness or the pointed dark satire at the expense of masculinity – to the gothic in order to manipulate the reader beyond even De Quincey's imagination.

However, it is not a question of manipulation for its own sake, whether it is a question of the manipulation of the character, the scene, or the reader. In each example considered the work of manipulation involves a ceaseless movement between form and content, between character or subject and scene. Furthermore, this is not a simple question of appropriating the various nervous tics of the gothic mode. The very act of knowing intertextual contamination is, itself, gothic. To show how this works, let's remain with De Quincey a moment more, this time through J. Hillis Miller's reading of the older Opium Eater. In *The Disappearance of God: Five Nineteenth-Century Writers*, Miller describes De Quincey's acts of opium-induced memory in the following manner: 'The dreamer who is endowed with the power of resurrecting the past is a *vampire* who drinks the fountains of his own vitality' (emphasis added).[25] The image of De Quincey as a self-consuming member of the undead is one of the earliest recognitions in criticism of the extent to which the *Confessions* are, in part, gothic. Miller's delineation of the gothic-ness of his subject, and the ways in which writing manifests the act of vampirism by feeding on an other self for the purposes of production, suggests a practice of inscription as consumption through memory or, perhaps more specifically, re-membering as an act of dis-membering.

Dickens performs similar acts in his creation of comic-gothic adolescents. Dickens turns vampire on his own memory of narratives heard or read in childhood, infusing the bodies of his literary children with the life-force of others' texts. His act is, moreover, a vampiric manifestation in that it feeds off the literary and dramatic corpses which haunt the Victorian psyche in general and, perhaps, the lower-middle and working classes in particular. If proof were necessary, one final example might be the double occurrence, the return of *Timour the Tartar*, in both *Great Expectations* and *Nicholas Nickleby*. In the former the play – written, by the way, by Matthew 'Monk' Lewis – is chosen as entertainment by Mr Wopsle, while in the latter Vincent Crummles recalls its performance with great fondness. Dickens' use of intertextual reference has the power to transcend time and space (as De Quincey's opium dreams do, to recall Miller's argument once more). Returning from the past, such spectral moments step outside their own otherwise historically identifiable identities while transforming also the present moment and with that the present identity. Dickens thus recognizes the ability of the gothic mode to exceed formal limits, to transgress the limits of identity across time, and thereby to suggest through such play the transgressive continuation of transgression. In overwriting his comic-gothic children with the spectral traces of prior discursive and textual formations, the author acknowledges an already fragmented body, which is nothing less than an alternative and dissident tradition within English culture and literature. For the Fat Boy, Bailey Jr., and Jenny Wren each speak to us of other identities, of the otherness within English identity, without the constant melodramatic and occasionally anarchic eruption of which there can be neither sense nor sensibility concerning Englishness at all.

Gothic narrative at the end of the eighteenth century sought to assert a sense of national identity in response to fears of the foreign. Such irrational fears sought to identify and marginalize the other and all that was not-English, as is well known. Perhaps closest to home in the nineteenth century is the equally well-known representation of the Irish as monstrous.[26] What we may come to understand from Dickens however is that the gothic, the monstrous, the other, is a lot closer than we are comfortable in acknowledging. Taking the vestiges of gothic and exploring its tropes comically, tracing those tropes' manifestations in the comic, is one method of assuming haunting proximity, if not intimacy with the subject (the phantom knows more about us than we do). Comic discourse and performance brings down the defences of the psyche. It allows the connection to be made between high and low, self and other. In so doing, it seeks to make us face the 'monstrous' within ourselves, so to make our flesh creep, making us tremble simultaneously with laughter *and* fear, just enough so as to allow us a view of ourselves we had always striven to deny and to project onto others. Always multiple, the comic-gothic haunts at precisely the limits of the identification of any straightforwardly representational discourse, bringing into question the authority and efficacy of representation. It delegitimizes narrative's pretensions to speak in a single voice. The comic-gothic, never a single genre as such but always identifiable in its multiplicity through the constitutive workings of double, haunted, haunting tropological *clinamen* within, counter-signs the Dickensian text as the incorporeal phantasms arising from the child's body. Those phantasms constitute a heterogeneous idiom. Such an idiom, to quote Jean-François Lyotard, 'is the idiom that is spoken in the idiom I speak.'

> It speaks more softly than I do. It means to say something I do not mean to say. The phantasm is a peculiarity at once more familiar and more strange than my point of sensibility. It commands that point; it makes me blind and deaf to what is otherwise visible and audible . . .[27]

Dickens' comic-gothic reduplicates the enunciation of idiomatic alterity. Bringing with it the traces of laughter and the uncanny, both partially dressed in the guise of the other, it oscillates with that simultaneous familiarity and the power of estrangement noticed by Lyotard.

# 2
# Tennyson's Faith:
# *In Memoriam A. H. H.*

The 'unknown' is not the negative limit of a knowledge. This non-knowledge is the element of friendship or hospitality for the transcendence of the stranger, the infinite distance of the other.

Jacques Derrida, *Adieu*

I should consider that a liberty had been taken with me if I were made simply a means of ushering in something higher than myself.

Tennyson to John Tyndall

That in all ages, individuals who have directed their meditations and their studies to the nobler characters of our nature, to the cultivation of these powers and instincts which constitute the man . . . and distinguish the nobler from the animal part of his own being, will be led by the *supernatural* in themselves to the contemplation of a power which is likewise super-*human*; that science, and especially moral science, will lead to religion and remain blended with it.

Samuel Taylor Coleridge, *On the Constitution of the Church and State*

A slightly uncanny anecdote, to begin.

Rereading *In Memoriam* as part of the process of preparing to write this chapter, I was, at the same time, listening to the radio. To be precise, I was listening to a 'live' webcast of BBC Radio 4, on 29 April 2000. The programme being broadcast concerned the ways in which archived sound recordings have altered our understanding and reception of the past, and addressed also how the past could return, however indistinctly or scratchily, not only into our present but also, as long as the archive was maintained, the recordings preserved, into any number of presents to come. Amongst the various recordings played there had been the voice of Florence Nightingale, and someone intro-

54

ducing Robert Schumann playing the piano. I had just finished reading Lyric LXXVII, in which Tennyson speculates on what is to become of 'modern rhyme', once the poet, 'a long-forgotten mind' (*IM* 12), has passed away. (He consoles himself by suggesting that utterance is better than recognition.) At this point – I had drifted from paying any attention to the broadcast – I caught the sound of a thin, slightly high-pitched, restricted voice reciting 'half a league, half a league, half a league onward'. It was Tennyson recorded just two years before his death in May 1890. Almost exactly 110 years later and through a relay of recording, radio and the internet, the ghost of the poet had returned, creating a distinctly eerie sensation, as if to answer the concern of that lyric. This almost certainly was not what Tennyson meant when he wrote of 'this electric force, that keeps / A thousand pulses dancing' (*IM* CXXV 15–16). However – and isn't this the point? – we have no control over the oscillations of the afterlife, which is why the question of faith as marked by the trace of the spectral can be taken to be so significant.

When considered in the light of the question of faith, Tennyson's relationship to the conventions of Christianity in *In Memoriam* is revealed as being both complex and complexly encrypted. Articulated through irregular and intermittent, though frequently recurring tropes, Tennyson's discourse on Christianity and his personal negotiation between the systems of Broad Church belief and Christian Typology on the one hand, and his own highly idiosyncratic comprehension of the nature of faith and belief on the other, resists as much as it encourages inquiry and analysis. Yet in Tennyson's 'imaginative act of mourning' (*FF* 23) peopled and figured by countless phantoms, not only are the various tropes by which faith is expressed endless substitutions for one another; every trope is supplemented within itself. Becoming other, tropes trope themselves to the extent that one cannot speak with any confidence of originary figures from which troping is an act of transfiguration.

As one such trope, faith is never simply faith in the possibility of the representation of Christ and thus a figure for such representation. Nor is it a controlling trope, a centre around which all other figures orbit. The poet resists the normative grounding of faith in institutionally orthodox and therefore familiar representations of Christ, and thereby a lapse into unthinking acceptance. In doing so, he struggles to come to terms with the appropriate language, as Kant puts it, for 'a faith that ought to represent what God is in himself' in an onto-theological consideration of being which maintains both mystery and revelation (*IM* XLIV 8: 'A little flash, a mystic hint').[1] What becomes apparent in reading the indirect embodiment of Christ and Christian faith in the poem through lines such as the one just quoted is that one would be more accurate in speaking of Tennyson's faith as the manifestation of an apophatic discourse driven by a poetics of difference and non-synonymous substitution. In the context of Christian faith such a poetics becomes discernible in the text as a constant pre-phenomenal marking whereby faith is articulated through an implicit comprehension of the immanence of incarnation everywhere, yet impossible to represent.

Religious truth as a matter of faith is then only ever '"darkly" or obscurely apprehended', as Isabel Armstrong correctly asserts.[2] *In Memoriam*'s faith is made manifest through indirection, processes of archival memorialization, anamnesis[3] and a specifically Christian 'analogy of apperception or appresentation',[4] rather than through conventional or canonical Christological modes of representation predicated on the promise of presence or the locatability of some logocentric origin, which will either return or to which we will return. To qualify this however: it is not a matter of dialectical choice in Tennyon's verse, it is not a question of, on the one hand, representation and mimesis, or, on the other, the analogy of apperception or appresentation. Instead, the analogical and apophatic are the signs of the apparitional other incorporated and incarnated within Tennyson's borrowings from conventional Christological representation and theological discourse.

Tennyson's is not a negative theology however, even though so many of the lyrics proceed by negation. Indeed, given the poet's resistance to and distrust of philosophical systems, it cannot, properly speaking, be described as a theology at all. Donald Hair has remarked that 'Tennyson's faith [is] unsystematic' (122), while William Brashear, on the same subject, argues for a 'non-rational' articulation of faith: '[t]he truth would seem that Tennyson "would not formulate" his creed, because he had no creed that could be conceptualized or reduced to principles' (96). At best, Tennyson's faith is expressed through something like a quasi-theology which comes from within and yet exceeds theology in its comprehension of the limits of language to express the unknown, the other, and to allow the other to manifest itself as a haunting spirit through a language expressing the limit. Of negation, Elaine Jordan suggests that the poem is 'perversely rich in negative qualifiers – nameless, fruitless, countless, sightless' (115). Thus, negation is not merely denial, it is also the affirmative marking of boundary in language, to which language can go. There are limits after all to what can be expressed in words: 'But there is more than I can see / And what I see I leave unsaid' (*IM* LXXIV 9–10); 'I leave thy praises unexpress'd / ... / ... / I leave thy greatness to be guess'd' (*IM* LXXV 13, 16). Words halt on the brink of representation, choosing instead to bear witness to the unrepresentable as that which is other. Thus the poet halts, saying that he cannot say. *In Memoriam* is a fragmented, self-fragmenting text which seeks to find ways of speaking the word of God indirectly, and attempting to do so, what is more, through the constant recourse to the spectral undecidability haunting even the most assured figures of speech pertaining to the matter of faith, as though speech were itself the constant remarking of the border of apperception. Admitting that one cannot see, that one cannot put into words what one can see, and that one's responsibility is to leave the other 'unexpress'd' and 'to be guess'd' is to articulate one's faith absolutely and in other words; it is to give oneself over to the incorporate, immanent spirit within which one dwells, which haunts one from within and which is yet to come.

Tennyson makes this clear in the following qualification: 'No visual shade of some one lost, / But he, the Spirit himself, may come' (*IM* XCIII 5–6). The distinction is made between the ghost and the Spirit though not explained. At most, one might comprehend the limit at which Tennyson speaks through a fragmenting temporality within the line. The ghost, the revenant, is not our concern here Tennyson tells us. That is merely the phenomenal, anthropomorphized (and therefore normalized) representation of 'some one' returning from the past. The Spirit is different from the ghost in that it is remarked as the haunting possibility of something other which may or may not make itself apparent from a temporal moment to come. The analogy of apperception makes the two forms of haunting distinct, broken off from one another by the play on similarity or resemblance which is itself negated as the limit of representation, and further disjointed through the temporal distinction formally marked between the two lines. And the distinction, the fragmentation, is enforced further in that implicit rejection of what may be seen in favour of what may be hoped for; or, in other words, that possibility, the articulation of which expresses faith.

The fragmented condition of the poem extends from verse organization and subject to its syntax, and is observed by a number of critics.[5] Its concomitant resistance to readerly unity is, I would suggest, Tennyson's formal recognition that one cannot come face to face with

God, but one must articulate the incarnation of Christ indirectly (as in the lines just considered), and always in terms which promise to give way to the trace of alterity or haunting in the moment of their utterance. Analogy is, again, one particular modality for admitting the spectral operation its play, as we have seen and will consider further. To quote Donald Hair on this, whose reading is developed from the ecclesiastical source of Bishop Butler's theory of analogy: '[the] theory rests upon the assumptions that language and nature are analogous because both proceed from God; that nature gives imperfect evidence of providence; that language is likewise ambiguous and inadequate; and that these inadequacies in both nature and language make necessary our judgement, which sorts out degrees of probability where clear and unequivocal evidence is not to be had. Such assertions of probability are statements of faith' (101). However, faith itself, to be faith, has also to be spirited away from within itself if it is to operate for Tennyson within the ruined structure of *In Memoriam*.

It therefore seems necessary to pause momentarily to make the following claim: while faith is the principal focus of this essay, it is not to be mistaken as some metaphysical guarantor, the figure *par excellence* of figurality and tropological play in *In Memoriam* any more than are the names of either Arthur Hallam or Christ for that matter. To allow this implication to remain unchallenged would be to place the reading of the poem back into the search for a centre or unifying principle which would, in turn, still the 'instrumental possibility of [the] production' (*AF* 17) of faith's fragmentary revelation *and* mystery. As we have said, faith is but one of many figures which operate the troping machinery of the text[6] according to a paradoxical 'disseminating fission' peculiar to the 'spectral motif' (*AF* 84) and the spectral logic of which the figure of faith is exemplary. It is possible only to name some of these tropological devices at this point: haunting, light, illumination, dust, veil, ghosts, phantoms, flashes, spirit, spectre, love, tract, type. None of the figures in question remain stable in Tennyson's use, even as they all serve in the illumination of faith, even as they enlighten the reader as to faith's power to illuminate, addressing also faith's spectrality and the ghostly effects of incarnation whereby, paradoxically, it is precisely as a matter of haunting that Christ comes to be embodied through the poet's attention to faith and love (which two, though not the same, are inseparable). With this in mind, we may observe that it is no accident that 'the dark church [is] like a ghost' (*IM* LXVII 15), a configuration of the spectral motif through a variation on the conventional image of the haunted house which also relies for its cogency on a markedly gothic resonance.[7] The analogy in this line is all the more uncannily haunting and haunted in that it figures the architecture of the church, and through this the figure of the church as metonymy for faith, as spectral. The church is not haunted by some anthropomorphic ghost. Rather, it is a phantomatic structure, a structuring phantasm, through and through.

This essay concerns itself then with certain tensions pertaining to matters of Christianity and theological discourse as these operate in *In Memoriam* in general and, specifically, through the spectral troping of faith. Such tensions are readable, arguably, not simply as those of Alfred Tennyson, as the working through of personal grief following the death of Arthur Hallam. Rather, they are tensions peculiar to matters of representation and its limits in the context of early nineteenth-century Christianity. Such tensions are installed throughout *In Memoriam* and are irreducible to a unified semantic or theological horizon concerning the question of Christian belief or the role and parameters of either Christian typology or Christology in early Victorian England. Being irreducible – and, often, irreconcilable or otherwise paradoxical – such discursive and philosophical tensions open within the poem itself, and as a necessary condition of its structures, the aporetic trace which is conventionally termed 'doubt' in criticism of the poem, the reading of which has been determined in large part throughout the twentieth century by T. S. Eliot's comment on the poem that '[i]ts faith is a poor thing, but its doubt is a very intense experience'.[8]

Things are not so unequivocal. Although the poet's 'prospect and horizon' (*IM* XXXVIII 4) has vanished, there remains a 'doubtful gleam of solace' (*IM* 8) in the songs he loves to sing. It is significant in the context of Tennysonian tropes relating to the question of faith that the adjectival form ('doubtful') modifies, and is modified by, a questionable illumination ('gleam'), which is both figurative *and* literal. While the effect of the line is to put doubt into doubt even as it is expressed, the undecidability of the figure puts into doubt the certainty of the reading to decide how the trope's movement may be calmed. Elsewhere 'doubt' is again related to the disappearance of light, a conventional enough Christian, specifically Broad Church configuration for the loss of faith (*IM* XLI 19; XCV 49). Yet this is rendered complicated by the repeated insistence on the spectrality of doubt. We read of 'a spectral doubt' (*IM* XLI 19), the 'slender shade of doubt' (*IM* XLVIII 7) and 'doubts', we are told, are 'spectres of the mind' (*IM* XCVI 13, 15). Doubt is therefore doubtful and difficult to read. What is interesting in these figures is that the phantom of doubt arises from within the subject, illuminated as it were by the disappearance of light, whether literal or metaphorical (or both simultaneously). Doubt's intimate relationship with illumination and haunting is traced in the second of the three quotations, not in the figure of doubt itself but in the play in the word 'shade', suggestive of both shadows and ghosts. However, the play does not stop in this oscillation. Shade and its cognate shadow are used by Tennyson as poetic terms for spectres (*IM* XXII, XXIII, XXX, XXXIII, XCIII), as euphemistic projections of Death (already spirited as an anthropomorphic trope haunting the poet: *IM* XXXV, LXVII, LXXIV). They are, furthermore, haunted internally in that which is cast by illumination, a graduated darkness appearing, so to speak, as a result of light. All of which is to cast a shadow on the unequivocal projection of doubt as that which is absolutely distinguishable from faith. Light and shade are both the orbs of the 'Strong Son of God, immortal love' as the 'Prologue' informs us; they inform and incorporate one another. So too, doubt is cognate with faith and not its polar opposite.

Tennyson makes this plain when he remarks: 'There lives more faith in honest doubt / Believe we, than in half the creeds' (*IM* XCVI 11–12). Faith is incorporate: a spectral figure without presence, it nonetheless *lives on*, incarnate in doubt itself. And this is a matter of faith ('Believe we'). Faith persists uncannily in the articulation of doubt with more vitality than in any theological system or programme. Tennyson's affirmation of doubt is also, at the same time, an affirmation of faith, of faith in doubt and faith in faith's immanence in the manifestation of doubt. To go back to the argument concerning Tennyson's tropes then, doubt does not in itself offer some metaphysical or logocentric valence albeit of a negative kind, as Eliot's reading implies, nor is it separable from faith. It is, once more, one rhetorical and tropological figure among others by which Tennyson maintains the tensions of the text in his consideration of being, and in the disruption implicit between transformation and transcendence (translation opposed to sublation), and between a personal a-systematic expression of belief ('There lives more faith in honest doubt') and a more conventional Christian metaphysics of Broad Church discourse. There is in Tennyson's figures the reading of faith's survival as a process of transformations *within* and perhaps even *despite* systems predicated on metaphysics.

The tension between translation and transcendence which opens onto the aporia of faith can be read in the second epigraph above from Samuel Taylor Coleridge.[9] Coleridge's language is marked, albeit indirectly, by the onto-theological concerns to which I will have recourse to allude with regard to *In Memoriam*. Coleridge addresses the transcendent possibility of 'man' while locating this *supernatural* spectre *in themselves*. There is thus described a transition which is both sublation – the elevation of 'man' – and incarnation as haunting – the *supernatural*. However, this movement is also partly circular, or perhaps more accurately reiterative. For where this leads is 'to religion' while 'moral science' will 'remain *blended* with religion' (emphasis added). The imagined Coleridgean notion is internally disturbed within itself, its transcendent promise interrupted by a translation not necessarily figured by transcendence (even while the translation-effect is inscribed specifically within the metaphysical horizon), and this internal crossing, from one state to another, is also a blending, a moment of incarnation. This double movement is described by Tennyson in the poem as 'the same, but not the same' (*IM* LXXXVII 14). Coleridge's 'cultivation' of the 'nobler characters of our nature' anticipates and finds its echo in Tennyson's assessment of the progression of humankind who moves 'Within himself, from more to more' (*IM* CXVIII, 17).

However, Tennyson is not content to offer one such echo. Instead, he takes this formula (*IM*: 'from more to more', 'from man to man', [Prologue] 25, 35; 'from world to world', XXI 19; 'from high to higher', XLI 2; 'from high to higher', XLIV 14; 'from marge to marge', XLVI 1.7; 'from state to state', LXXII 6; 'from theme to theme', LXXXIX 33; 'From form to form', CXXIII 6, 'from place to place' CXXVI 10) as a transformative trope which, reworked some thirty or more times, incorporates not only the human condition, but also refigures itself as the articulation of belief in natural, spatial, geographical, geological, intellectual, temporal and mortal transition, establishing as it does so a figurative echolalia of faith's faith in that which is simultaneously unrepresentable, unprogrammable and yet which is immanent in all forms, all phenomena.

Furthermore, these reiterated figures, which establish a performative technicity resistant to any but the most basic systematization, recirculate, redouble and move elsewhere. They speak to a constant disinterrance within the same while remaining outside any properly formalizable apprehension. Can we say, for instance, that the speculation on metaphysical transfer has anything other than a syntactical resemblance to

the temporal movement from one year to the next, or the passage from
one country to another? And is there not in this figural play an echo
or reiteration, albeit of a wholly different kind, of the rhythm and
movement of the abba rhyme scheme? To put this another way, is not
Tennyson's most profound expression of the transition of humankind
to be found in the most basic structural device of the poem as a whole,
a rhythmic device which, in seeming to turn back upon itself, initiates
and is part of a movement? And is this motion both the figure of
apparent unity and closure, while also being, paradoxically, that which
maintains a poetry of fragments, in ruins, and resistant to a greater
unity? There is, however, another way to comprehend the double work
of this figure, a doubling which interrupts any straightforwardly discernible structure. 'From__to__' is marked by, and remarks, both spatial
and temporal transition, regardless of what comes to fill those blank
spaces. We read the implication of a motion from one place, one event,
one condition, state of being or emotion to another. We also read temporal transition, inasmuch as, conventionally speaking, one may be said
to move from the past to the future. Yet the phrases cited, and those
which are not, all complete the phrase by a kind of figural palindrome,
so that the motion appears to recirculate, to return to its beginning
point, to disrupt and thus paradoxically double itself in its own process. This brings me back to the analogy of apperception or appresentation,
that troping wherein is figured 'the same, but not the same'.

Of analogy, Elaine Jordan remarks: '*In Memoriam* works by metaphysical analogies between the human, the divine and the natural –
analogies which it does not trust except as a way of working, of keeping going. Metaphysical imaginations of what an individual's state might
be after death are matched by a material psychological account of how
an individual self is acquired through language' (123). Jordan's epistemological model of analogical replacement and re-presentation,
addresses 'the constant flux of displacement', as Isobel Armstrong puts
it (254), that interminable work of mourning *and* faith through deferral, relay, and reiteration. Where Jordan's argument is problematic is
in that assumption that the work of analogy is the expression of a lack
of trust in the analogy. Tennyson works with analogy and from within
the metaphysics of Christian analogical convention, but strives for a
more radical process of analogy that moves expression of faith 'beyond
the bounds of Christian orthodoxy' (Wheeler 239), which struggle is
itself the dim comprehension of the materiality of language and its
limits and the understanding, to cite Armstrong once more, that '"man"

is not only a phantasmal classification of "artificial signs" but the very arbitrariness of those signs ensures their instability and collapse' (264). The only way to work with and in response to this 'collapse' – a collapse, we would suggest, which marks not Tennyson's poem so much as the more conventional, supposed, Victorian crisis of faith – is to put the signs to work in another way, or to put both other signs and the other within the signs to work in the performative expression of faith in the onto-theological persistence of being. The metaphysics of being is still readable, but it is a metaphysics of ruins and in ruins. Such a metaphysics is more appropriate to the analogy of apperception.

Tennyson's employment of analogy as an onto-theologically informed modality is the formal taking place of opening oneself to revelation, to a thinking of God. But, it has to be insisted, it is a thinking otherwise. It is an attempt to think the other, the other thought of the other from within and as the sign of the limit of hegemonic ecclesiastical articulations of Christian belief and the representations by which it functions. Like Kant, Tennyson finds it necessary 'to deny *knowledge*, in order to make room for *faith*'.[10] In this, what I have called Tennyson's 'quasi-theology' might also be understood as a non-metaphysical theology, inasmuch as *In Memoriam* relies on the possibility of thinking Christ and God while rejecting the possibility that either can be known. Doubt, as we have seen, is not doubt concerning God or Christ as such, but is that which clears the ground for such a possibility. Analogy maintains the opening through the various replacements and displacements signalled in the syntax of the 'From__to__' formula. There are two further points to be made about this 'formula of transition', one formal, the other onto-theological.

Metaphysical analogy is reliant on 'a metaphoric transfer of predicates from one subject to another', as Kevin Hart reminds us.[11] Each of the figures bound within the formula of transition addresses, often in the most indirect of analogies, the possible resemblance, the family likeness between humans and Christ, a resemblance which relies on anthropo- and theomorphic counter-incarnation, or the immanence of this possibility. Each figure is thus invested with the possibility of a reading which is, in the words of Werner Hamacher, 'still not yet what it already is'.[12] (This, we might also say, is applicable to an understanding of Tennyson's rhyme scheme, wherein the apparent hermeneutic circle implied in the pattern, offering to represent the connection of *arché* with *telos*, also, always already, opens itself out, disjointing its own completion.) Yet, we can only read the process of analogy indirectly through the basic formal resemblance which its reiteration makes possible. The formula of transition is but one example of what Alan Sinfield describes as 'repetition with difference', which, he adds, 'is the primary strategy of the incremental structure of *In Memoriam*' (115). This analogical formula is performative in that it builds as it reiterates, and yet resists unity and coherence. The 'building' if it can be called this, is already disrupted by the dissimilarity on which it also relies. There is none but the most basic structural similarity between 'from state to state' or 'from place to place' and 'From flower to flower, from snow to snow' (*IM* XXII 4) or 'From April to April' (*IM* XXII, 7). Nor could one draw out distinctly that which echoes from these lines to 'From orb to orb, from veil to veil' (*IM* XXX 28).

Furthermore, because the terms by which the transitional motion is mapped are without exception the same, a kind of palindromic mapping as we have already suggested, precisely what increment or transformation can be said or read to take place? How are we to read the difference in 'Spirit to Spirit, Ghost to Ghost' (*IM* XCIII 8)? Clearly there is the question of difference at work, however displaced, but in this the analogy operates by apperception rather than direct representation. There is, once again, a comprehension of that which is the same, but not the same. Formally therefore, Tennyson's reiterations constitute a prephenomenal marking, a material remarking of the text's and language's materiality.[13] Such a materiality belongs to the condition of apophatic discourse signalling the alterity of Christ incorporate, while forestalling a fall into anthropomorphism, the lapse that is, of course, the authorized version of incarnation, typical of Victorian Christology. Faith 'calls for another syntax', to use a phrase of Derrida's. Repetition, reiteration and materiality belong to that syntax, in that they precede and exceed 'even the order of predicative discourse'[14] and yet are also distinguishable from a purely negative discourse in the maintenance of a material sublime on the basis of inscription. Incarnation through the acoherence of Tennyson's analogy of apperception constitutes an interruption of received narratives *qua* incorporation of the spirit. The performative materiality of reiteration effects appropriation *and* effacement, as the very alterity and sublime ineffability of Christian faith. Tennyson's tropology becomes irreversibly performative once perceived in its material efficacity; in doing so, it re-marks itself precisely as that which cannot close itself off and which cannot be closed off through a reading of the tropological as governable system. 'From__to__' names this constant transference while it also enacts the motion, and thus gives expression to faith in that which cannot be represented. Tennyson's twisting of analogy is always a performative enunciation of faith in that it attests to the sublime as 'a different order of experience' (*AI* 75) even as it resists efforts to represent the unrepresentable. Thus, in attending to the materiality of the text through its most fundamental formal properties Tennyson opens the text for the incarnation of the other.

The formal operation of the material marking of the text also constitutes an effort to prevent a fall into what Kant describes as a vulgar mode of analogy, 'when God is thought of in human shape'.[15] However, in thinking God Kant remarks that analogy is indispensable. The danger is that the process of analogy, in becoming a process of what he calls '*object-determination* (as a means of expanding our cognition)', is precisely the lapse into anthropomorphism (*Religion* 107). In employing analogy, Kant warns, we must never 'infer by analogy that what pertains to the sensible must also be attributed to the supersensible' (*Religion* 107). Anthropomorphism in the Kantian scheme is no analogy at all. There is thus a radical separation between like and like, an ineradicable difference by which analogy may be made and yet which cannot be rendered as a unity. Later, as example of 'sublime analogy', whereby the truth is perceived while the mystery of the divine is maintained in the perception, Kant has occasion to refer to Newton's representation of gravity 'as if it were the divine presence in appearance' with the *caveat* that 'this is not an attempt to explain it'. We are involved in an ethical duty, Kant suggests, the obligation to which 'lies outside the bounds of all our insight' (*Religion* 165). The thinking of God belongs to the Kantian category of *anthropmorphismus subtilis* in the consideration of onto-theology, 'where human perfections are ascribed to God but without separating the limitations from them' (*Lectures* 385). It is better, says Kant, 'not to be able to represent something at all than only to be able to think of it confused with errors' (*Lectures* 385). Tennyson's formal materiality recognizes the lapsarian dangers attendant in matters of belief, and so the material marking of the text seeks to affirm the sublime through a resistance to the coherence of anthropomorphic or theomorphic representation and, in particular, those belonging to dominant nineteenth-century ecclesiastical renditions of incarnation.

One last example of the Kantian propositions readable in Tennyson: the first verse of Lyric CXXIV, which might be read as simply what Tennyson calls 'A contradiction on the tongue' (*IM* CXXV 4):

That which we dare invoke to bless;
Our dearest faith; our ghastliest doubt;
He, They, One, All; within, without;
The Power in darkness whom we guess;
                              (*IM* CXXIV 1–4)

The structural symmetry of the punctuation both within and across
lines halts as much as it impels, making the verse forbidding, and yet
a material manifestation of faith. The punctuation also follows the rhyme
scheme, so that lines 1 and 4 and 2 and 3 are marked in the same
fashion, the former with the single semi-colon as end-stop, the latter
doubling the diaeresis. Such division and discontinuity is also inscribed
in the semantic tensions of the verse. That which we 'invoke' is that
at which we can only guess, given its invisibility. 'It' is thus both
what is dearest *and* ghastliest, faith *and* doubt, both within *and* without. The verse thus incorporates its figures each into the other in a
paradoxical enfolding, which yet works through the maintenance of
separation and discontinuity rather than through the positive process
of identificatory equivalence. The materiality of the verse performs
what it wishes to express, revealing in the process the mystery of faith
while maintaining that enigma through sublime analogy. Faith is taken
as greater faith in not appearing to appeal to reason.

Faith is not coherent then, it never can be. Being nothing as such,
and yet, strictly speaking, not being *nothing*, faith is phantomatic. Neither
there nor not there faith persists. One can never speak of faith singular. Always in ruins, already fragmentary, faith returns and recedes, its
traces everywhere. Faith, furthermore, in having no single definition,
cannot by definition be defined, for every instance of faith will necessarily differ from every other. Faith thus maintains itself and its precarious
possibility by always already having moved on, by having spirited itself into an other manifestation whereby faith is recognized in the
embodied yet paradoxically ghostly fragment of the articulation of belief:
' . . . we, that have not seen thy face, / By faith, and faith alone, embrace, / Believing where we cannot prove' (*IM* [Prologue] 2–4).
Embodying and even, as the poet puts it, embracing contradiction (the
absence of proof is taken as 'proof', if not of Christ, but faith's faith
in the other's revenance), faith, distinguished from knowledge in what
Eleanor Bustin Mattes describes as a 'Kantian-Coleridgean distinction',[16]
appears as the result of illumination and as illumination itself, illumination of faith illuminating itself from within the darkness that we

name doubt, and which, mistakenly, we believe to be separate from faith, not a necessary precursor or condition for the revenance of faith.[17] This is made apparent in James R. Kincaid's symmetrical comments. Kincaid first remarks that 'faith lives in and is assured by doubt'. Later, he inverts this in a manner appropriate to Tennyson's own troping displacements, suggesting that 'doubt is contained within faith'. Such a commentary on the intimate interconnectedness of faith and doubt and their mutual and reciprocal cross-incorporation – the one as the ghost of the other – is pertinent to Tennysonian quasi-theological tropology and anticipates the reciprocity and deconstructive iterability pertaining to incarnation.

Kincaid's fleeting analysis illustrates Tennyson's understanding of, on the one hand, the immanent power of tropes when one opens oneself to the fundamental instability which their haunting motion installs, and on the other, the necessity of being open to such oscillation if one is to recognize faith as the *arrivant*. Tennyson, it can be suggested, comprehends and reveals repeatedly to both himself and the reader that what haunts him is not Arthur Hallam, nor the possible loss of Christ, but faith itself, as phantom or phantasm, as Phosphor (*IM* IX 1.10; CXXI 1.9). Jacques Derrida has remarked on the haunting figure of light, and on the connection between light, the phantom or phantasm articulated in the Greek *Phos* (the root, meaning light or illumination, is common to each of the terms, implicated as it is in *phainesthai*, *phantasma*), in the context of theological discourse as that which institutes an originary taking place and which '*commands or begins discourse and takes the initiative in general . . . in the discourses of revelation . . . or of a revealability*'.[18] Like faith and doubt, illumination and haunting are closely, intimately, interwoven, the one in the other, neither having precedence, and both appearing with such frequency throughout *In Memoriam*, always in terms of faith.

To take this further, it is for this reason that the troping of light, enlightenment, illumination, plays such an important part in *In Memoriam*. Yet light is not stable. Not only does it come and go, it is also always different from itself. The workings of light are irreducible to a single comprehensible concept. There is, for example, the 'Calm and still light on yon great plain' (*IM* XI 10). Is this literal, a simple moment of descriptive narration? A manifestation of the pathetic fallacy in the context of the lyric? Then we read, 'O Father touch the east, and light / The light that shone when Hope was born' (*IM* XXX 31–2). There is clearly a discernible spectral trembling between the certainties of literal and metaphorical, prompted in a destabilizing manner between geographical location as *arché* and personification. God the father brings illumination of a spiritual (metaphorical, figural) nature through the touch, but the touch is already refigured as the literal rising of the sun in the east. Thus the spiritual illumination, which is also a manifestation of sorts of the holy ghost given momentary personification in the figure of the father, is overwritten even as it overwrites the place where the sun always rises (and in this is there the implied figure that the Son always already returns?) in a process which makes undecidable a reading of the figure of light as either unequivocally literal *or* figural. Across the lines the two instances of light suggest how the figure of light is doubled from within itself. Light illuminates its tropological processes, even as there is no 'it' as such but only projection and doubling. Then there is that light in which 'We lose ourselves' (*IM* XLVII 16), which is the same but not the same as 'my light' which 'is low' (*IM* L 1).The former is the Spirit while the latter is also a figure, an apparition, of spirit; the one haunts the other, and it is through the ghost of a chance that difference maintains itself and is barely perceived. What the troping of light illuminates is undecidability, transference and recurrence. Yet faith is arguably discernible if we comprehend to what extent the poem relies on the tropological pushing at the limit of language in the service of radicalized, disembodied incarnation.

Figural recurrence is remarked especially in relation to the subject's reflection upon himself and the embodiment of the disembodied other – whether we momentarily bring such a figure to rest in the desired image of either Arthur Hallam or Christ – through the constant return of faith as that which haunts subjectivity as the spectral possibility of an onto-theology, the incorporation of all beings into a Being to come or, as Tennyson has it, 'to be' (*IM* XXVI 12; CIII 35; CVI 32; CXVI 16; CXXIX 9). The return of the deferred temporal horizon – where, in destabilizing substitutions, 'indifference', 'that great race', 'Christ', 'some strong bond' and the 'Strange friend' refigure the spectral event – intimates the haunting to-come[19] as the event of Christian incarnation or incorporation, illumination or enlightenment within the poetic subject.[20] Michael Wheeler, who suggests that the hope for 'the Christ that is to be' reflects 'the Johanine emphasis upon incarnation in the poem', has argued that Tennyson, developing a 'theomorphic conception of man in the poem' developed from Coleridge, Maurice, Jowett, and, of course, Hallam, saw the question of Christianity in terms of a 'future state, grounded in possibilities, rather than demonstrations or proofs' (223, 224, 228),[21] and the emphasis on faith rather than knowledge in the 'Prologue' bears this out. Yet the movement of incorporation we are reading in the various exchanges and reiterations of 'to be' are not merely the expression of a metaphysical hope, the desire for a future transcendence as the horizon of faith; nor is this simply a one-way spiritual street. For, as we witness, and as the poet bears witness to throughout *In Memoriam*, incarnation, the spectral manifestation of Christ incorporate,[22] always already takes place in an untimely fashion.

For example, the line 'Strange friend, past, present, and to be' is haunted within itself by a destabilizing structural anachrony of dislocation, displacement and redoubling of the friend whose uncanny quality is precisely that of revenance as the incarnation of faith. The ghostly figure of the 'Strange friend' might be stabilized momentarily by reading it as the ghost of Arthur Hallam. However – and this is typical of *In Memoriam's* continuous process of iteration and doubling, where figures are, to use Tennyson's phrase once again, 'the same, but not the same' (LXXXVII 14) – Lyric CXXIX never names Hallam. Instead it partakes of the euphemistic apperception of Christ typical of Victorian hymnody, speaking of the 'Dear friend' and the 'Dear Heavenly friend' (ll. 1, 7). Yet, if the verse does indeed partake of the 'eternal present of Victorian hymnody' (Wheeler 247) it is precisely the ghostly persistence and the polytemporal trace of the 'Strange Friend' which disrupts and makes discontinuous, if not impossible, the very idea of an eternal present which is not fractured from within itself by the constant recurrence of spectral anachrony. At the same time, the quality of strangeness renders strange the humanizing impulse behind the figure of the 'friend'. Tennyson's faith requires that he open himself and remain open to receive the spectre with hospitality; strangeness, however, estranges and thereby resists any inclination to anthropomorphic slippage. Thus a phantomatic force is idiosyncratically installed within early Victorian convention. Of course, as a strategy of normalization critics have argued that Hallam figures in the poem as an incarnation of Christ, that he serves also as an androgynous figure for the typically Victorian representation of the androgynous or feminized Christ, and thus is composed by Tennyson according to conventional nineteenth-century Christological patterns.[23]

While this may be true in part there is still to be read in this representation a resistance to representation of any one figure or a possible stability of representation. The play between the ecclesiastical conventions of hymnody and the intimate appeal to the personal installs an irresolvable aporetic tension. The aporia opens through the stanza's transformative play: between, implicitly, Arthur and Christ and, explicitly, 'human' and 'heavenly' (ll. 6, 7); transition or translation also is to be read between 'far' and 'near' (l. 2), the instances of 'past, present, and to be', and the image of the poet's dream in which he 'mingle[s] all the world in thee' (l. 12), a line which inverts incarnation. The line of Lyric CXXIX which most forcefully performs the taking place of figural disfiguration is that which begins the second of the three verses: 'Known and unknown; human, divine' (l. 5). Tennyson insists on the paradoxical, unending cross-incorporation and counter-incarnation between figures, and does so in the lyric temporally and spatially. He does so moreover in a manner which indirectly reveals, yet again, the limits of conventional, Broad Church representation (implicitly but particularly in relation to the limits of Christological imagery and the representation of Christ's body), while refusing any stable location or privileged position. Thus the articulation of faith works performatively through the visible mutability of the figural architecture of the lyric. Faith is articulated through the subject's ability to let go of the stabilizing referent or image, while at the same time saying – to whom? Christ? Hallam? – 'Mine, mine, for ever, ever mine' (l. 8). If the friend is strange, this response, riddled with proprietorial desire, the formal reiteration of which hints that will never be filled or completed, is equally strange. It resembles nothing so much as a palindrome in ruins. It almost completes itself, it seems to promise a structural symmetry; however, haunted by a loss which its reiterations seek to deny, it remains incomplete, breaking up into its own fragments. Finally, with regard to Lyric CXXIX and the undecidability regarding the 'Strange friend', it should be noted that the unidentifiable figure who haunts this verse is 'Loved deeplier, darklier understood' (l. 10). Recalling the 'Prologue', it should be remembered that both 'love' and 'darkness', unstable figures in themselves which recur throughout *In Memoriam*, are intimately enfolded into the question of faith.

There is, then, always a reciprocal reiterative experience at work in the poem, albeit as a series of discontinuous events which are neither wholly singular nor wholly programmed or systematic, and yet lawlessly partake of the singular and the systematic. While the Son of God may be refigured as love, love, like faith, is never defined or stable. And neither is darkness, which, as with so many other figures in the poem, is at times apparently literal while at others seemingly metaphorical and occasionally and disconcertingly both. Once more, it is important to note how such distinctions themselves (the reading of a figure as unequivocally 'literal' or 'metaphorical') refuse to remain in place and belong to the more general sense of discontinuity and disruption. Thus Tennyson's language operates constantly through transformation, translation and disinterrance in a continuous process of crossing and dissolution of boundaries, whether these belong to subjectivity, time or, as the translation of Christ into love attests, the conventional comprehension of Christianity itself. Hence, to reiterate, the haunted nature of faith, a figure which, despite the modest poverty in which it is presented by Tennyson in what is conventionally called the 'Prologue', exceeds itself throughout *In Memoriam*, and thus remains difficult to comprehend in its true light.

What is revealed in *In Memoriam* is, then, revelation itself, revelation in other words and not as representation or the manifestation of some simple, or simply determinable, anterior presence, originating authority, empirical proof or truth belonging to or otherwise authorizing or guaranteeing 'little systems' (*IM* [Prologue] 17). To cite Michael Wheeler again, '[l]ike Coleridge, Tennyson was weary of Christian evidences' (228). For such evidential, authorized truth would not be that which is revealed but, instead, knowledge, and knowledge Tennyson confidently informs us is empirically grounded, it is 'of things we see' (*IM* [Prologue] 22). *In Memoriam* therefore struggles with the very grounds of any conventional Christology which implicitly operates through mimesis. It struggles at the limit of representation so as to apprehend the Christological spectre, the invisible other within the conventions of form. This invisible, haunting other (by which Tennyson is haunted because it is invisible), is Faith which is precisely that which 'we cannot know' (*IM* [Prologue] 21). The impossibility of knowledge concerning the 'Strong Son of God, immortal Love' (*IM* [Prologue] 1), is exactly the precondition of faith. Faith, like the son of God, cannot be represented because it is not available to sight, it is incorporeal *and* incorporate; and, as already suggested, never single. It is no accident that the 'single church [is] . . . folded in the mist' (*IM* CIV 3–4), folded double as it were. And, as if to make this point as clearly as possible, Tennyson opens the poem with the line just quoted whereby through a process of translation Christ is disembodied, anthropomorphic representation resisted, in being named 'immortal Love'. Thus, from coming to terms with the impossibility of Christological representation, faith grows. It is invisible and yet illuminates, a light emanating from the Son of God as a 'beam in darkness' (*IM* [Prologue] 24). Moreover, in recognizing this, we apprehend how not only is Christ Love, but also illumination. Love illuminates, but invisibly. There is no body of Christ here. Christ illuminates, but faith also illuminates, and what it brings to light is the light of the other. Such enlightenment, while coming from an other place, comes from and dwells within. What therefore has to be negotiated through the revelation of faith-as-incarnation is a kind of spectral onto-theology which, to paraphrase and cite Derrida on onto-theology, is that which dismisses or rejects religion as a 'little system', the 'petty cobwebs we have spun' (*IM* CXXIV 8), while, paradoxically, it is that which also 'perhaps . . . informs . . . the theological and ecclesiastical, even religious, development of faith' (FK 15).

So in conclusion, to return to the Prologue, to its opening line: 'Strong Son of God, immortal love'. As Michael Wheeler and Donald Hair have pointed out, the image of God as love is taken by Tennyson from Arthur Hallam's *Theodicaea Novissima*, an essay first read by Hallam to the Cambridge Apostles in 1831, and in which Hallam both configures God as Love and associates love with incarnation (Wheeler 230; Hair 98). It has been the case, generally, that Tennyson's 'Prologue', written after the rest of *In Memoriam* in 1849 as is well known, is regarded as a somewhat conventional gesture towards the institutionalized discourse of Broad Church theology, and that, more cynically, the lyric was written to appease and thereby win over the future Mrs Tennyson (and, more importantly, her father). Yet, within this seemingly conventional lyric, apparently wholly consonant with Broad Church Anglicanism of the mid-Victorian period, there is this spectral dissonance, a spiritual oscillation or resistance incorporated into the articulation of faith. It is an affirmative resistance, moreover, of the 'faith that comes of self-control, / . . . / . . . / And all we flow from, soul in soul' (*IM* CXXXI 9, 12), which opens constantly to the spirit of Christ as Love, and to the ghost of Arthur Hallam; opens to both, and to the trace of both as the haunting instance of disembodied, yet incarnate alterity at work. The same, but not the same, as the *arché*-origin before the beginning and inscribed at the end of composition as the disruption of orthodoxy and in deference to eschatological deferral and differentiation. Which double motion we find inscribed in the instance that Tennyson appears to take leave of Arthur: 'I hear it now, and o'er and o'er, / Eternal greetings to the dead; And "Ave, Ave, Ave," said, / "Adieu, adieu," for evermore' (*IM* LVII 13–16). The endless act of hearing marks the subject as one who cannot choose but be open, responding and responsive to a mode of communication from the other, itself without end. Indeed the poem is in one sense nothing other than the articulation of the responsibility the living have to the dead. Differing articulations in rhythmic reiteration, different from one another, in three different languages and from different locations give the lie to finality, and thus express the spirit of responsibility. And as Derrida reminds us, invoking Emmanuel Levinas, '[t]he greeting of the *à-Dieu* does not signal the end . . . The *à-Dieu* greets the other beyond being'.[24] In such an insistence, and in the reception and response which informs the radical separation *and* proximity between self and other, are the spectral signs of Tennyson's faith.

# 3
# Phantom Optics: George Eliot's *The Lifted Veil*

Optical signal processing in real time remains a thing of the future.
Friedrich A. Kittler

My inward representation of ... faces ... is so vivid as to make portraits ... unsatisfactory to me.
George Eliot

## I

A man foresees his own death. He begins by expecting an ending, and, later, interrupts himself as the end begins or appears at least on the verge of beginning. As he awaits the scene during the final month of his life, with which his mind has confronted him repeatedly, he recalls the appearance and development of his telepathic powers, narrating to the reader scenes from his past wherein he has had instances of both insight and foresight.

In the narrative which carries the reader back in time even at the same time as it is moving forward toward the eventual end, scenes from a future which is also a past are projected as double phantom moments: as the narrative of the scene told with hindsight, and as the scene which is projected in the narrator's mind (as foresight) in anticipation of its arrival. Then the scene arrives again in the narrative to be reiterated, enacted over again, though still, we should remember, also projected as the return of the past in the first-person narrative of someone moving toward his death, and being moved toward that moment inexorably by the reader every time the page is turned. Thus the narrator and the reader's experience of Prague, seen first in a vision as a city 'doomed to live on in the stale repetition of memories' (*LV* 9), and then subsequently recounted in the narrator's account of his visit (*LV* 22). Eliot's narrator's words concerning Prague resonate as a disturbing commentary on both the haunting of forward moving time by the ghosts of the past and the general condition by which narrative proceeds in *The Lifted Veil*.

However, what is most marked in this reiteration is that it is not simply the scene or details of the scene which come to be replayed, where Prague becomes a 'stale repetition of memories'. Uncannily, words come back almost exactly, doubling themselves in an instance of the rhetoric of haunting. In the vision the narrator 'sees' 'a patch of rainbow light on the pavement, transmitted through a coloured lamp in the shape of a star', a projection all the more uncanny in that the narrator has never seen any pictures of Prague (*LV* 9). Then, on visiting the city and coming as the climax of the first chapter, the narrator sees 'the patch of rainbow light on the pavement transmitted through a lamp in the shape of a star' (*LV* 22).Thus, like a shuttle on a loom, visions and sights move back and forth, time, place, and event doubling and displacing themselves. The instabilities of the narrative's temporal moments jar against and blur into each other, the invisible phantoms of a visionary mind.

But to return to the beginning and end: as the story reaches its conclusion, the moment foreseen from the very first page and anticipated in the very first words – 'The time of my end approaches' (*LV* 3) – so it ends at the moment or, more precisely, in the very instant before the moment of his death in explicitly visual terms: 'the scene of my dying struggle has opened upon me . . .' (*LV* 43). So concludes *The Lifted Veil*. Or so at least it appears to begin to conclude, the story of a death foretold and foreseen but never arriving finally. Death will never have arrived, and this is seen *in writing*: 'It is the 20th of September 1850. I know these figures I have just written, as if they were a long familiar inscription [which of course they are, having been written in anticipation of this last act of inscription on the very first page of the novella]. I have seen them on this page in my desk unnumbered times, when the scene of my dying struggle has opened upon me . . .' There is a doubling, a return and a displacement here, the very complexity of which is dizzying. Latimer, the narrator, finally arrives at that scene of inscription which has haunted him repeatedly. The apparition of this writing has arrived from the future. We know this from the opening page where the words, though then invisible, are anticipated as though his journal entry were a signature, guaranteeing death. On the final page the words finally appear to us apparently for the first time, redoubling themselves in the instant of their inscription.

As with the experience of Prague, words are redoubled, not least in the fact that even as Latimer, as character in his own tale has written them (he tells us he has written them), so they are projected beyond the narrative that we may read them. They become the last page of the story, at once in the story and part of the form of *The Lifted Veil*, seen by us as George Eliot's concluding passage. At the same time as we see them there is another doubling effect having to do with invisibility and visibility, the limit of both and the suspension between the two. For, as we see the words so we read that Latimer sees them also, seeing what he has previously seen 'unnumbered times' without their having ever been visible. We do not see what he sees, for we do not see his handwriting, nor the act of inscription itself; this has already passed ('these figures I have *just* written'). There is thus a structural displacement in the return, the doubling effect. Moreover, even though we do not see exactly what Latimer sees we are still implicated in a phantom dislocation: it is the trace of something which becomes visible, rather than the invisible thing itself to which we are witness. And, most uncannily of all, we see that Latimer sees, but Latimer, of course, remains invisible to us, seeing from some unseen place, in the instant that the apparitional writing, which has been invisible for so long, finally returns as this last inscription, displacing Latimer before us. The spectral writing arrives both for the first time as visible trace *and* as the latest manifestation of the previously invisible revenant. What we thus experience is that it is no true 'first appearance', only an act of inscription as the experience of a ghostly supplement and with that the affirmation of all writing as being articulated by the phantom effect.

Death is to come as this last incomplete paragraph attests, where quasi-eschatologically the death-to-come as a future which will, *can*, never be present in a first-person narrative begins to open, to unveil the condition of one's being. One is always moving towards one's death, and yet one can never experience it as such. Of course, we know rationally that the narrator's death has already taken place, acknowledged in the displacement of the subject which writing makes visible as the trace of the absent subject. If you read *The Lifted Veil* the narrator is already dead. Yet you read the author writing of his own imminent death, inscribing the vision of a scene at once to come and always already past, inscribing the imagined scene of that imagined inscription – a death sentence we might say. Thus there takes place a suspension as the sign of the spectral.

There is in this final moment a discernible, uncanny oscillation. It is 'final' however only in that *there*, there on the page is the final sentence, which itself is never final, never the *last* inscription but – as the narration attests – available for reiteration, doubling, rereading and reinscription again and again. This takes place, reverberating between futures and pasts, between various incommensurable scenes, irreducible to a single moment and, to recollect the discussion of the spectral from the preface, being written at the limits between life and death. For in being doomed to narrate his narrative, Latimer is himself suspended, consigned to the endless reiteration of his fate while never reaching it. He is left only with a kind of ghastly afterlife as he haunts those traces of his narrative to which we are witness.

## II

'Spectrality', remarks Fredric Jameson, 'is not difficult to circumscribe, as what makes the present waver: like the vibrations of a heat wave through which the massiveness of the object world – indeed of matter itself – now shimmers like a mirage.'[1] As a critical approximation of the notion of spectrality, this image has the good fortune of getting at the subject of its comprehension through indirect and, possibly, poetic analogy. In this instance definition requires the emergence of an alternative modality within and to its factual articulation. There is readable therefore a certain vibration, a wavering or shimmering, perhaps itself analogous to the flickering of light in cinematic projection, within and as part of the structure of representation.

We have already witnessed this in *The Lifted Veil*'s levels of reiteration: the more general repetition of a scene, explained away as telepathic power, and, stranger still, the iterability of phrases as a formal acknowledgement beyond Latimer of structural vibration. The present moment of reading wavers as instances of the text return. What is immediately pertinent here for the purposes of this chapter is that Jameson's commentary registers the disturbance in the field of vision by something invisible which, though invisible, nonetheless has a material effect, and which one 'sees'. We see the invisible within the visible. A trace registers itself in the field of vision but this trace is not that which causes the registration. Caused by that which affects the visible it is the trace of something else, something which cannot be seen, as such. The apparent solidity of what we take to be reality and its visual representation is solicited. The perception of the real is troubled and

destabilized from within the visual itself, yet this occurs as a result of
something other than what is or can be seen. More than this, there is
noted in this manifestation the disturbance of the present. As already
implied, the certainty of the temporal moment is unseated.

What we come to understand through the example given by Fredric
Jameson is the veracity of a comment made by Jacques Derrida on the
structure of visibility in general. The visible, he writes, 'has an invisible inner framework (*membrure*), and the invisible is the secret
counterpart of the visible, it appears only within it . . . it is inscribed
within it'.[2] Rather than being simply a reading of Eliot's novel from
the perspective of theories of the spectral, this chapter attempts to develop
notions of haunting and the spectral through *The Lifted Veil*. This chapter
seeks to approach the question of the invisible within the visible as a
matter of that which haunts within Eliot's *The Lifted Veil*, providing a
provisional framework or otherwise making it visible as a narrative
concerned with such 'invisible inner frameworks' and their spectral
relation to questions of representation, mimesis, and realism. While
other of Eliot's fictions such as *Middlemarch* concern themselves with
differences 'between individual characters' fields of vision and the differences within them',[3] *The Lifted Veil* concentrates its focus on the
differences of vision in its various literal and metaphorical manifestations within one character, Latimer. As Athena Vrettos suggests, 'Eliot
seems to recognize a potential fluidity in specular roles that applies as
much to authors, narrators, and readers as to the fictions they create'
(110). This is particularly intensified through the figure and fields of
vision of Latimer, the fluidity in question a revelation of the spectral
work in the field of vision as it crosses and recrosses different moments in time, and between the narrator's sight and his insight. As
readers we are implicated in this because we 'see' such transference
take place. Indeed, it is at work in the ghostly motion between the
idea and the limits of the distinction just made between the literal and
metaphorical, so-called. Thus we 'see' the invisible at work within the
visible, as the spatial and temporal frameworks of narrative are caused
to tremble.

One framework brought to shimmer before our eyes in the narrative
is the structure by which narrative prose implicitly makes claims to
being realist. The story's indirect, invisible self-reflexive consideration
of what narrative realism can represent is a condition noted by several
of the novella's critics. In addressing the 'relationship of the story to
Eliot's consciousness of herself as author', Charles Swann has drawn

the reader's attention to *The Lifted Veil*'s fictive self-consciousness, remarking that 'Eliot self-consciously raises the question of what the relationships between art and life are, might be, and should be'.[4] Sally Shuttleworth has argued that Eliot's strangely powerful tale concerning the telepathic powers of foresight and insight of Latimer is 'a text aware of its own fictionality. The life of Latimer ... is synonymous with that of the narrative ... concerning a vision of the end of time which the end of narrative fills ... [It is] a text which seems to exist only to confirm its own death'.[5]

This is, we would do well to remember, Eliot's only first-person narrative, a point which either implicitly or explicitly involves the mediation of the narrator's line of sight or vision in a manner that is both more and less interruptive than that of the traditional omniscient narrator. The so-called first person narrative doubles and returns or projects the narrator as invisible and yet observing, as though speaking from some privileged, ghostly location which cannot be fixed precisely. We appear to 'hear' the voice of someone who, apparently, is dead, and yet who shows us all that he can see, all that he has foreseen, all that he has seen. (In this, again, there may be understood an oblique commentary on the phantomatic and phantasmic projection of narrative form.) There is thus an irresolvable rift, a heterogeneity between the location from which the gaze is projected and that which is seen, and this we should recognize as the fractured premise on which narrative as a phantom structure appears to make the invisible – that which is not visible to us as such – appear. *The Lifted Veil*'s apparent 'explanation' of this uncanny phenomenon, its narrator's telepathic powers of prevision is in fact a narrative feint, a spectro-rhetorical manifestation, oscillating and blurring between different temporalities, making not only the present waver, returning momentarily to Jameson's comment, but resonating in all temporal instances to which Latimer's narrative alludes. More than this, the 'return' of Latimer's vision beyond his death (which we will have cause to question as a final moment) doubles Latimer's visions uncannily, returning in the act of reading so that the matter, the 'massiveness', of realist narrative is caused to shimmer (again, recalling Jameson's remark). Far from being a 'supernatural' element which offers the narrative an 'internal' self-rationalization or coherence all its own, the effect of telepathy, or what Nicholas Royle in his reading of Eliot terms *telepsychology*,[6] lifts the veil on narrative's unsettling power to make appear that which has never been present.

Furthermore, and with reference to the story's self-reflexivity, while commenting on the scientific impossibility of the blood transfusion which Latimer witnesses, Terry Eagleton points to the fact that we are forced to accept the scene due to the conventions of realist fiction and that this aporetic moment, opened between realist convention and the 'flaw' in the account, 'forces us outside the frame of the realist fiction to ponder – as the story has surreptitiously done all along – the theoretical problem of realist fiction as such'.[7] Finally, Kate Flint has argued that *'The Lifted Veil* provokes conjectures about the operations of fiction. Composed at a time when George Eliot was developing her theories concerning realism, the story bends laws of probability in order to investigate questions that are implicit throughout many of her later novels.'[8]

The novella's self-conscious traces highlight its ability to make felt that which is not immediately visible or present. Such is the eerie processing we name, after Freud, the uncanny (which processing is discussed in the Introduction to this book). Clearly, although we comprehend the truth of these statements we have to perceive indirectly the Jamesonian vibrations of narrative referentiality while considering what Flint describes as the 'wider issue' of Eliot's tale, the question of 'more strongly developed powers of vision' (457). Thus the self-reflexion of Eliot's narrative, the mirroring if you will of that which can be traced though not be seen or made available to vision directly in *The Lifted Veil*, draws us into the complex concerns of the novella with sight in all its forms – insight, hindsight, foresight, prevision – and with matters of visibility and invisibility in relation to questions of haunting, the uncanny, and matters of what I describe in the title of this chapter as 'phantom optics'. *The Lifted Veil*, in undoing and complicating the matters of narrative temporality through the troping of sight, vision, illumination and all the coterminous cognates by which the story is invisibly haunted and driven, addresses for us the uncanny mechanics of projection and the invisible manipulations involved in so-called realist narrative. In doing so it 'challenges', as Kate Flint puts it, 'that often-assumed Victorian drive toward making things visible' (472) and, along with this, what George Henry Lewes describes as rendering 'the invisible visible by imagination' (cit. Flint 473).

Of course, we do not 'see' in *The Lifted Veil* any direct discussion of fictive or narrative modalities, such as Eliot's remark, for example, from her essay 'The Natural History of German Life': 'Boundary or outline & visual appearance are modes of form which in music and poetry can only have a metaphorical presence.'[9] The invisibility of the

self-referential frameworks which haunt Latimer's narrative disturbs
the illusory power of narrative claims to re-present to us what is not
in front of us. We have to contend with what might best bc termed a
spectralization of narrative theory. As Terry Eagleton puts it with regard to *The Lifted Veil*'s destabilizing play between past and future
moments (cautiously and correctly bracketing off the figure of sight),
'"[s]eeing" either past or future entails an insuperable contradiction:
if you *do* see them, then they aren't there, since their nature is to
be elsewhere and invisible; if you don't see them, they aren't there
either' (60).

While Eliot never discusses directly the powers of narrative to project
that which is invisible, and while there is furthermore an absence of
any sustained consideration or theorizing of aesthetic or narrative convention, nevertheless this is a tale which everywhere concerns itself
with the limits of such representation and what can or more significantly cannot be seen. As Swann remarks, the 'story could be used to
construct a theory of Eliot's idea of the artist, though it would be a
theory based mainly on negatives' (44). It is neither, we would argue,
a narrative of negatives nor the narrative working-out of a negative
theory. Rather, it is an apophatic discourse, a medium of indirection,
the very strangeness of which is readable in Eliot's efforts to work
with the problematic of sight and vision in relation to narrative representation. This is very much a mode which always relies on the fact
that what it represents *is* invisible, not present even though, as readers,
we enter into a contract with the story-teller that we will not advertise
the invisibility on which representation is predicated. Understanding
this, we comprehend how narrative is truly a modality driven by analogy
rather than mimesis. It is therefore always already a haunted medium
as already stated. We contrive not to see the invisibility as such but,
instead, to pretend to see that which is not there as though it were.
George Eliot thus strives to make the spectral condition of all narrative
along with the temporal anachrony by which spectrality may operate
as 'indirectly visible' as possible through the story of Latimer's visionary
powers. However, such powers not only disrupt the field of vision on
which narrative is reliant. They are not confined to narrative but are
directed, albeit implicitly, beyond aesthetic formal concerns. The effect
of the apparitional gaze and the phantom optics by which it functions
spatially and across time also challenges the virility of nineteenth-century
science, the discourses and institutions of which were almost entirely
dependent within their classical epistemologies on a hermeneutics of

visuality. This is effected through a transference, a translation, which is also the work of an internalizing phantomization common in the nineteenth century.


III


Recollect Fredric Jameson's comment on spectrality. The resonance of Jameson's analogy is figured in a reading of spectrality's material efficacity by George Eliot in *Janet's Repentance*. Somewhat uncannily, Eliot also addresses the relationship between ghostly oscillation, phenomenal apperception, and the disruption of the real in the field of vision:

> Ideas are often poor ghosts; our sun-filled eyes cannot discern them; they pass athwart us in thin vapour, and cannot make themselves felt. But sometimes they are made flesh; they breathe upon us with warm breath, they touch us with soft responsive hands, they look at us with sad sincere eyes, and speak to us in appealing tones; they are clothed in a living human soul, with all its conflicts, its faith, and its love. Then their presence is a power, then they shake us like a passion, and we are drawn after them with gentle compulsion, as flame is drawn to flame.[10]

This passage, on the almost imperceptible transport of ghosts, requires our attention for a number of reasons as a prologue for consideration of Eliot's *The Lifted Veil*. There is, first of all, the not-quite-domesticated image of ideas as those invisible figures which haunt us. Eliot is unequivocal in her registration of the internalized, and therefore invisible, place of haunting, the mind. The opening clause is no mere simile. Ideas are not *like* ghosts, they *are* apparitions. Ghosts do not reside elsewhere, outside ourselves, but are within us and thus have a greater power to haunt, in that they occupy what Terry Castle calls 'the intimate space of the mind' (*FT* 165).

   In describing this haunted condition of thought, Eliot is not alone in the mid-nineteenth century. Indeed, the passage from *Janet's Repentance* is wholly symptomatic of the irreversible shift described by Castle. Castle traces the 'translation' of the term 'phantasmagoria', from its 'literal meaning' pertaining to the technological production and representation of ghosts in 'ghost-shows of late eighteenth-century and early nineteenth-century Europe – illusionistic exhibitions and public entertainments in which "specters" were produced through the use of a magic lantern' (*FT* 141), to the *Oxford English Dictionary* definition as a 'shifting series or succession of phantasms or imaginary figures, as seen in a dream . . . as called up by the imagination, or as created by literary description' (*FT* 141).

Through her pursuit of the transformation of the figure of 'phantasmagoria' from literal to metaphoric meaning (a transformation which, I would argue, is already at work in the word), Castle describes how, in the nineteenth century, there occurs a concomitant shift from 'something external and public . . . to something wholly internal or subjective: the phantasmic imagery of the mind . . . the spectralization or "ghostifying" of mental space . . . [and the] primal internalization of the spectral' (*FT* 141–3). Castle goes on to say: 'By the end of the nineteenth century, ghosts had disappeared from everyday life, but . . . human experience had become more ghost-ridden than ever. Through a strange process of rhetorical displacement, thought itself had become phantasmagorical' (*FT* 144). This rhetorical displacement, registered by Latimer as his 'inward experience' (*LV* 29), is arguably traced in the transport which takes place through the various tropes of sight and vision throughout the story. Eliot's 'phantomization' of narrative structure through the device of her principal character's perceptions and perspectives is comprehensible as a violent and uncanny response to the increasingly ghost-ridden world of the nineteenth century as described by Castle. It is as though the 'Victorian frame of mind', to use such a familiar structural figure, is itself translated into a haunted house. Thus what is seen on the surface of *The Lifted Veil* as Latimer's 'abnormal sensitivity' (*LV* 13) is in fact wholly symptomatic of the relentless interiorization, the spectralization of mental space of which Terry Castle writes. Latimer 'sees' himself in Bertha's thought, 'as she lifted her cutting grey eyes, and looked at me: a miserable ghost-seer, surrounded by phantoms in the noon-day' (*LV* 31), he records inadvertently the spectralization already at work. For what he sees, what is rendered visible in the reciprocity of Bertha's gaze, and from there projected from the invisible space of her mind onto Latimer's own, is the unstoppable traffic of phantoms, the fluidity of which blurs the boundaries between sight and insight, observation and imagination, visible and invisible, and, significantly, self and other.

The transference from the external world of ghosts manufactured in the gothic novel and by the machinery of ghost shows was not a gradual displacement, as both Castle and other critics acknowledge: 'the general tendency in nineteenth-century writing was toward metaphoric displacement. The crucial connection between phantasmagoria and the so-called ghosts of the mind seems to have been made very early on' (*FT* 156). The 'haunting' of the mind and the concomitant spectral apparition to the mind's eye is, as Castle's exhaustive research shows, already at work in various writings throughout the nineteenth century, even if internal ghostly manifestations seem to acquire greater frequency as the century progresses. In 1841, surgeon Walter Cooper Dendy anticipated George Eliot in *Janet's Repentance* when, in *The Philosophy of Mystery*, he stated that ghosts were manifestations of 'nothing more than an *intense idea*' and that, conversely, 'it is not strange that this thought may appear *embodied* . . . if this idea be intensely defined, does it not become a phantom?' (cit. *FT* 164).

Dendy's apprehension of 'Ghosts of the Mind's Eye, or Phantasma' (to borrow the chapter title from which the remark is taken) does, in a certain uncanny manner today, appear to anticipate, at least in part, the Freudian notion of the phantasm (especially as that figure is given powerful figurative force by Louis Althusser[11]); or perhaps it is the case that Dendy's comment is haunted by a spectre of the future, and that the transport from the external to the internal read by Castle is nothing other than the revenance of that which is to come, and is therefore all the more spectral, all the more unsettling. Whether or not this is the possible scenario here, what is noticeable in Dendy's inversion and transposition of ideas and ghosts is a radically unsettling account and oscillation between figures, which Castle's otherwise superlative study does not take fully into account. We also witness the destabilization in Dendy's remark, which is a sign of the spectral effect, at work in that opening clause of Eliot's in *Janet's Repentance*. In distinction to Castle's untroubled rhetorical displacement, I would argue that this metaphor is not completely controlled or controllable, as the rest of the quoted passage attests in its efforts to embody and thereby represent the ghostly. There is not simply a displacement or substitution of one figure for another in this uncannily modern comment. Were this the case, the neutralization would be effected completely and the work of this phrase would be wholly conventionally rhetorical, without disturbance from within.

Rather, the phrase unfixes itself in a movement between the figure of ideas and that of ghosts, a movement of disjointing made all the more forceful by what may be read as the insistence on the literal transference and translation in the phrasal copula: Ideas *are* ghosts, while, conversely, in a barely perceptible, implied motion, ghosts *are* ideas. The phrase performs a doubling, a division *and* displacement of the principle it articulates.[12] It does so performatively: for the remark, the commentary, enacts its own proposition in that very transference of the idea *of the idea* which, though invisible and having no material presence, only comes momentarily to be embodied through the manifestation of the 'poor ghost'. We cannot see the idea and so are asked to imagine it in the form of something which is not a 'thing', yet which apparently has the power to move from invisible to visible, and then to retreat once more. This figure, while materializing the idea of the idea, does not calm down the spectral haunting even if it may be said to familiarize or orient the reader through a momentary glimpse of the gothic. Instead, the appearance of the ghost serves, uncannily, to remind us that the idea *of the idea* is always already spectral and can only come back, if it comes back at all, in a haunting fashion. And that it comes back as always already a phantomization of itself is, in this return, a sign of its uncanniness.

There are other effects here also. The phrase provides a foreshadowing, a prevision, of a disturbing crossing and partial erasure of barriers, most notably between the internal and external, as well as between the invisible and the visible, upon which the rest of Eliot's passage comments and which can be seen at work in *The Lifted Veil*. This is already in operation of course in that first phrase, where the ghost, traditionally a manifestation beyond the self, is now all the more troubling because of its ability to traverse invisibly the psychic structure of our identities. What we come to read here, and which will be discussed in more detail with regard to the title of *The Lifted Veil*, is the idea that the invisible is not simply the dialectic opposite of the visible but is part of the visible, as what makes the visible possible. However, Eliot does not let things rest here. For her 'poor ghosts', the ideas which prove so haunting, appear to move effortlessly from the place of the unseen to a location where they become *flesh*, and where their relationship to us is of a most intimate kind. Despite the apparent difficulty in seeing this – 'our sun-filled eyes cannot discern this' – the question of the gaze is nevertheless paramount here, albeit a gaze of a different order, that of the mind's eye.

Once more we read a transference from and between representation and imagination, between the supposed literality of sight, blinded by the light, to a form of metaphoric vision, given visibility through the 'insight' of this passage as Eliot juxtaposes and inverts sight in the real world as that which establishes and verifies empirically discernible data for the blindness of the mind. This translation effortlessly undoes the binary assumptions we cherish concerning inner and outer, sight and its lack, literality and metaphor, as the implied boundaries which supposedly keep such locations intact are blurred and made to waver, to recollect Fredric Jameson's remark once again, as though there had occurred before our very eyes the manifestation of a spectral crossing. Such a crossing and counter-crossing signals the limits of particular modes of representation. In doing so it shows the limits to which those modalities go. The efficacity of the spectral is readable in the following manner. On the one hand, it opens to experience – the experience of reading, the experience of sight – the aporia between supposedly stable locations. On the other hand, as we have already witnessed, the spectral installs a radical suspension between apparently discrete modalities, even as it overflows their limits.

IV

To what extent does the 'spectralization of the mental space' haunt *The Lifted Veil*? If this were simply a supernatural tale, the concerns with the spectral, with haunting and with phantoms might be rationalized or otherwise explained away as the internal rhetorical devices of the text. Or else, one could read such features as indicators of Latimer's psyche. However, formally and structurally, haunting takes place within the framework of the story itself as we have already seen from brief glimpses, and from the consideration given to matters of anachrony, temporal disjointing, iterability, the movements of revenance and supplementarity. That 'fluidity' and 'oscillation' as signs of the spectral take place is clear enough. I want to pause here, however, to consider another aspect of *The Lifted Veil* suggested by Terry Castle's reading of the spectro-tropological work of phantasmagoria considered in the previous section of this chapter.

Castle's thesis, that there occur throughout the nineteenth century the effects of transport, of transference, and translation from the literal to the metaphorical as the signs of the 'spectralization of the mental space' belonging to an unstoppable internalization, is clearly at work in Eliot's projection of phantom images onto the mind of Latimer. Indeed his 'foresight' brings into focus the power of language to make visible the invisible as part of the general phantomatic quality of the rhetorical effects of metaphor, its haunting power to project representation. We seem to 'see' Prague even as it 'appears' to Eliot's narrator, even though what he sees is, strictly speaking, invisible, a prevision and phantasm. It has, to cite Althusser on the metaphorical status of the phantasm, 'an existent – though nonmaterial – reality' (104).

This revelation is, as we know, not some aberration but what takes place throughout the story. Moreover, to recall the arguments concerning *The Lifted Veil*'s general self-referentiality, here is an example again of the way in which Eliot's text alerts us to the condition of narrative, to the power of narrative to place 'before our imaginative or mental gaze, according to the traditional metaphor [of representation] which can also be interpreted and overdetermined as a representation of representation' (SOR 299). Yet, as we comprehend implicitly from the priority and privilege given groundless vision over reality in the narrative, where the phantasm precedes and thus comments on the very question of re-presenting what has never been present, the phantom, the image or figure, 'returns' to Latimer (and to us) without depending on some originary presence. That we are witness to this uncanny instance unveils the spectral nature of all figural language, not least metaphor, and we find the veil lifted on the abyssal doubling/displacing configuration. For let us recollect that Latimer's visions, so-called, are already redoubled, recalled through narrative and returning as the invisible (the vision) within an existent – though non-material – reality (the narrative) given visible form in the written or printed form. There is thus an overflowing, disfiguring and radical metaphoricity which takes place, that kind of transport or translation always already spectralized within the very framework of representation, and described by Derrida as 'specular reiteration or infinite regress (*renvoi à l'infini*)'.[13] Translation, projection, transmission: all are seen to take place without, before, and in excess of any object, any reality, other than that we describe as the textual, textuality. This is the work of metaphor as the figure for all spectrality.

We can explore this further with regard to Terry Castle's argument. The displacement from the literal to the metaphorical (which apparently straightforward historial movement we will accept, for the moment) identified as spectralization is at work from the first pages of *The Lifted Veil*, and almost invisibly at that, in the most fleeting and mundane of figures of speech. 'I have lately been subject to attacks of *angina pectoris*', Latimer informs us (*LV* 3). Through that Latin identification of a heart condition the reader is offered the certainty, the fact, of scientific truth. What the term signifies, however, is not stable in the period during which Eliot wrote, as Helen Small points out in her gloss on the term (*LV* 88). This aside, though, the figure of the heart pulses irregularly throughout the narrative. Shortly after the opening passage, Latimer remarks '[w]hile the heart beats, bruise it' and '[t]he heart will by-and-by be still – *ubi sæva indignatio ulterius cor lacerare nequit*'[14] (*LV* 4). In both these figures there is already an oscillation, a translation between the literal and the metaphorical which occurs, we are tempted to say, in a heartbeat. The figure of the heart, neither solely literal nor metaphorical and yet both, trembles before us. In both examples, the hidden organ is made visible and, in being so, is in its visibility already translated, spirited away from itself. The heart made visible becomes other, the visible trace the phantasmic figure or metaphor of something else. Thereby transplanted, its metaphoricity – being already what it is not yet – appears, a figure in these examples for both life and the human spirit. This takes place because the text lifts the veil on that which we cannot see, through an internalization which is both a spectralization and a revelation. It is not simply that we see into the human body or comprehend life as the result of the functioning of organs as Latimer's friend, Meunier, would have us do. Rather, the inscription of the figure of the heart as simultaneously itself and something other, as literal *and* real *and* yet not solely, places us between the real and the fictional, even as its palpitations mark the limit between life and death, to return once more to the exploration of the spectral in the preface. Latimer is not speaking literally of bruising the heart, and the Latin epigraph 'translates' the 'literal' heart in the first part of the phrase into another haunting metaphor.

What is thus revealed through the figure of the heart is that, with regard to Eliot's tale at least, the motion described by Terry Castle is not merely in one direction from literal to figural as a motion of internalization. Instead, as Eliot makes clear, the spectralization of the figure is already at work here as elsewhere in the text. While Latimer's heart palpitates 'violently' (*LV* 7), there is also the 'madness of the human heart under the influence of its immediate desires' (*LV* 18). While Meunier seeks to bring the heart back to life (*LV* 39), Latimer's heart goes out, finally, to others around him (*LV* 40). When Latimer is emotionally scarred by Bertha, he speaks of this as a 'sort of crushing of the heart' (*LV* 28), thereby metaphorizing the physical effects of the *angina*. Of Bertha and his father, Latimer remarks that he could *see* into their hearts (*LV* 18, 25).

These final two examples bring us back to the question of sight or, to be more precise, the spectrality of sight which persists throughout *The Lifted Veil*. As with the heart sight never stays in place, it is never sight singular but names a plurality of incommensurate modes of perception, as we know. While we can insist that, rationally, we know that Latimer cannot *see* into the hearts of his father or Bertha, and that, furthermore, when he speaks of *seeing* into their *hearts* he does not mean the organ, nonetheless we overlook the fact that such images play with the very idea of representation and its impossibility. Simultaneously, indirectly, Latimer's language unveils for the reader the uncanny, spectral analysis of the invisible inscribed within the visible.

V

One of the most conventional, yet disturbing aspects of the passage from *Janet's Repentance* and pertinent to *The Lifted Veil* is that of the image of ghosts in intimate contact with us, touching us, breathing on us, speaking to us, *seeing us*. The other gazes unseen. There is always some invisible place from which we are observed, as Jacques Lacan makes clear in his discussion of vision: 'I see only from one point, but in my existence I am looked at from all sides'.[15] Latimer's inner visions and previsions express the multiplicity of invisible perspectives and exceed the purely human limit of single perspective. This optical process is spectral precisely because it does not await the phenomenal, subjective response, and nor is it limited by this. At one moment, in an attempted representation of what he calls 'superadded consciousness' (*LV* 13), Latimer speaks of the uncanny power of the other's gaze to unveil the invisible traces of people's characters: 'the web of their characters . . . were seen as if thrust asunder by a microscopic vision' (*LV* 14). There is a forensic impersonality in the narrator's description of the optical-processing by which the invisible fabric of the psyche is made visible. In this very impersonality, in the technology of the gaze, there is revealed that which, other than the narrator, looks on unseen, returning to us as a process of impersonal projection all that is otherwise invisible. This spectral gaze comes to Latimer unbidden. Projected through him, the gaze figures a haunting alterity irreducible to the narrator. Though the medium of this uncanny perspective Latimer has no control, and indeed feels himself to be haunted. The spectral gaze thus takes place everywhere as that which makes narrative possible. There is thus revealed in this virtual, impersonal gaze an unending process of uncanny surveillance, which always takes place in a present without presence. What is seen, when it becomes visible, is always seen *now*, and, then again, *now*. In returning, this phantom gaze thus disrupts the temporal stability of the present. Being neither of the present nor a presence what the gaze brings into view are those phantoms of past and future presents which are returned, neither as themselves nor as representations of places, people, objects, but only as spectral traces. In this, that which wavers or trembles causes the revelation of a frightful secret: that we are always already haunted: for, as Eliot tells us, we are shaken by the invisible gaze of some 'palpable-palpating specter' (which phrase arguably hints at the beating of an invisible heart) (Mavor 80).


VI

We should, in conclusion, return to that liminal site, the title. This title, *The Lifted Veil*, addresses vision and thus deserves a degree of patient attention. Seeing it clearly, or as clearly as possible, will allow us to understand, as Hélène Cixous puts it with regard to Freud's essay *Das Unheimlich*, that '[t]his text proceeds as its own metaphor' (FP 526). The condition of metaphoricity is addressed in the figure of vision and the address to matters of vision and sight, which are approached indirectly. Never specifically naming either sight, vision, natural or mechanical optical matters as *The Lifted Veil*'s concern, nonetheless the narrative implicates within itself and as the disturbing force of its movement and rhythms a question of what is partially hidden and therefore equally, partially visible, while appearing to promise greater visibility, either in the instance of the veil's having been lifted, or as the outcome of the eventual lifting of that veil. Whether one takes the figure of the 'veil' as that representing a literal veil, or whether one understands by this a metaphorical figure for what will come into plain view in the reading of the story but which in the title at least is either wholly or partly obscured from vision, there is inscribed the notion of some aspect of sight. Veils are usually diaphanous. They tease and seduce with the idea that what might be seen in outline can ultimately be seen completely. The title operates in this fashion, for it 'veils' its story as much as it opens our eyes onto what lies behind; that is to say, it seduces in opening our eyes to the promise of what is beyond, if not the 'thing' itself, which remains, in the title at least, both beyond our sight and beyond our comprehension.

The title is thus performative. It enacts the condition of veiling it addresses. It offers enigmatic contour, trace or line without ever making out that figure and enticing with the implied revelation of what it is we hope may come to be delineated, revealed. Playing with the reader, the title plays on the potential for the reader's anticipation of an erotics of visuality which is intimately caught up with the empirical knowledge and therefore mastery or control, which the gaze apparently guarantees. As Kate Flint correctly points out in her reading of *The Lifted Veil* in the context of medical science, veils 'are inescapably associated with eroticism, exoticism and fetishism' (456). However, the lifting of this particular veil suspends precisely the revelation on which the expectation of the erotic is predicated. Because nothing is revealed either as yet or as such, the potential of the veil is also in its hiding and ultimately revealing something terrifying. Sight of the hidden other may well cause the viewing subject to lose control instead of gaining it.

Or it may just be that there is nothing to be seen or understood, that there is nothing to be made visible, whether literally or metaphorically. It may be that all the veil keeps invisible to view is invisibility itself or the absence of anything capable of becoming visible. What the title thus 'reveals' to us, amongst other things, is, on the one hand, a radical instability which only becomes more and more pronounced as the act of reading – which is also an act of seeking to see clearly – strives for greater mastery and clarity. On the other hand, what the idea of the lifted veil makes plain bringing this sharply into focus, is the fact that visibility – what we see – and visuality – the mechanics of making visible – are dependent on that which haunts them as the condition of their possibility: invisibility. What we see in the title is what we cannot see, and we see this unequivocally in the materiality of the title's veiling, enigmatic inscription, which hangs as a veil between us and what might or might not be in the text. All we see, straining at the limit of enabling vision, is that there is that which sight can never finally reveal, a radical invisibility which is never reducible to the dialectical opposite of the visible. As Derrida suggests of the incommensurable difference between the visible and the invisible: '[t]his heterogeneity of the invisible to the visible can haunt the visible as its very possibility' (*MB* 45). The visible, Derrida remarks elsewhere, 'is pregnant with the invisible' (*MB* 216). That which is the 'secret counterpart' of the visible will come forth at some point; the invisible is always imminent within the visible. This too is named in the title. This is what we 'see' *at* and *as* the limits of reading the title, and which the title and, following it, Latimer's narrative, make visible, like the apparition of the trace of the invisible idea in the form of Eliot's 'poor ghost'. For in a sense, and as if in response to Tennyson's assertion in *In Memoriam* that some answer lies 'Behind the veil, behind the veil' (*IM* LVI l. 28), what *The Lifted Veil* shows in its title is that the veil is lifted and there is nothing to be seen. *Nothing* here in this formulation does not name an absence from sight but, more disturbingly, that *nothing* is precisely, albeit paradoxically, what we see. We see and we comprehend that there, *there*, is invisibility.

Sight, vision, hindsight, insight, foresight, prevision, and, concomitantly, blindness, lack of focus, obscured or partial vision, even seeing 'through a glass darkly', are all insistent concerns, interests, tropes and traces in *The Lifted Veil* then, as we have already suggested. They constitute what Darwin described as an 'inextricable web of affinities'.[16] Thus and very visibly, perhaps more so than in any other text by Eliot, they constitute a skein or weave of filaments which, for being so numerous and so visible, speak of the limits of sight throughout the story while reminding us, if not the narrator Latimer, that there is always that which remains invisible within the very condition of sight, and that the power of empirical observation, of rational deduction and analytical reasoning which the act of reading as interpretation promises will always come up against a limit, itself invisible and constituted by the invisibility on which the visible is predicated. It is this invisibility, which, again to make the point, is not some thing, not some presence which if we just look hard enough we can see, which drives the story so relentlessly. This, Eliot's story gives us to see, is the very limit of narrative, of science, and even pseudo-science, with which the story tantalizingly toys. It is as if, in a moment of exhaustion in the face of the plethora of visible traces, which themselves constitute the textual-optical machinery (the story is a form of optical technology productively fragmenting vision even as its modality of operation is concerned with the production of visions, literal and hallucinatory), we might find ourselves tempted to settle on some form of normalizing or neutralizing explanation. *The Lifted Veil* is about telepathy or some other ill-defined, because ill-understood, new means of tele-technological communication. The story may produce a somewhat uncanny effect in the reader, it may appear to rely in small part on the familiar stage machinery of the gothic or supernatural tale, or it may be understood to an extent by suggesting the clairvoyant subject's pathology as a very understandable mid-nineteenth century psychological internalization of previously gothic terrors.

But all such explanations explain away rather than confront the sheer destabilizing undecidability around the troping of sight and vision by which this story operates.

# 4

## *Little Dorrit*'s 'land of fragments'

This chapter takes as part of its title a phrase commonly employed from the late eighteenth century through the first half of the nineteenth to describe the perception of London's institutional, governmental, financial, and other systematic relationships. Specifically, what is of interest is the ways in which Dickens maintains a certain spectral effect of the fragment in order to announce the condition of reading, writing, and representing London differently. Such an act on Dickens' part, which is effected as we will see through the exploration of a spectralized epistemology of urban sound as the traces of a revenance constituting the city, is readable as an act of remembering; thus the tracing of the urban conjures, in Peter Nicholls' words, 'a forgotten history [which] has the power to shake the social and metaphysical forms against which it breaks . . .' With these haunting effects, Dickens arguably projects another city as a resistance to institutional politics in the present, and with that 'the idea of history as a violent intrusion from somewhere else'.[1]

The expression, 'land of fragments', signified the relatively loose organization of the city's institutions such as government offices, civil service departments, banking organizations, the courts and prisons: structures in short such as the Marshalsea, the Circumlocution Office, and the financial organizations presided over by the Mr Merdles of the early nineteenth century. Significantly, at least for this reading of Charles Dickens' eleventh novel, *Little Dorrit*,[2] the phrase began to disappear by the mid-nineteenth century, as recent historiographical research into the languages of urban representation has shown.[3] Replacing the image of the city constituted through the fragment, the concatenation of fragments, and more importantly the discourse of the fragment, were languages stressing, as one city newspaper, the *Citizen*, puts it in 1849, 'firmness and unanimity' (cit. LCC 23), or, as Peter Claus has more recently suggested with regard to the dominant language of representation and relationship in the mid-century, discourses signifying 'umbilical' connections (LCC 23). *Little Dorrit* appears, I wish to suggest, as a testimonial text, remembering and producing the discursive condition of London as site of fragments and often contradictory, perhaps excessive countersignatures irreducible to any 'unanimity' or political consensus. (It is tempting to note in passing that the excess of phantom testimony by which the novel is composed and by which the present of the novel is discomposed disrupts economic circuits and limitable exchange, as exemplified in the monetary 'testimonials' solicited by Mr Dorrit.)

The mid-century language of London's alleged organic unity and architectonic uniformity marks a transition in modalities of representation while announcing, through that transformation, one aspect of hegemonic control over official representations which propagate and disseminate images of a city where there are close ties between institutions, their official discourses, and the discursive, narrative and ideological constitution of civic life. The language of organic unity is itself obviously unified and unifying, or at least apparently so. It assumes and thereby attempts to project a single voice over the potential uncontrollable excess of revenant articulations from the various 'fragments' of the city. The language of uniformity implies close and 'natural' connections between institutional and civic life. The two are figured, at least hypothetically, as reciprocally enmeshed, like the cogs of a well-oiled, self-sustaining machinery. On the one hand, the successful functioning of the former relies on the peaceful co-operation of the latter. On the other hand, the self-maintenance of ordered civic life within a structure incorporating numerous class locations is dependent on keeping the engines of finance, government, and the law running without hindrance.

The 'co-habitation of financial and civic activity' (LCC 23) was a necessary narrative of urban Tory-Liberal equipoise (otherwise well known in Dickensian terms as the Science of Government or, 'How Not to Do it' *LD* I.x. 110); it served the promotion of imagined or desired organicity and the epistemo-ideological denial of the city as a 'land of fragments' following in part as a response to the failures of Chartism in 1848. And, in this, the discursive transition is readable as but one mediation from the 1840s onwards towards what Richard Price has defined as 'the general drift of urban politics', which incorporated in this drift 'expanded town council control'. As Price continues, '[t]he working-class presence in municipal politics had been much diminished by the 1850s'.[4] Civic and financial co-operation and control is, then,

clearly effectively promoted and determined at least in part by a concomitant control over matters of representation.

Before proceeding further, I should state that this language of incorporation and consensus is not my immediate subject. I introduce it in
passing however, in order to orient and shed light on the discussion
of *Little Dorrit* which follows. I should also point out that neither is
the question of mid-Victorian politics narrowly defined my particular
interest here, except, again, obliquely. In announcing this moment of
transition, and its 'translation effects' if you will, I wish merely to
mark a certain transformation in particular manifestations of London's
languages with an eye on the mimetico-political effect which advances
the occlusion of representational difference in its operations, silencing
and making invisible a large proportion of Londoners. What I am concerned with is an attempt to read the possible ways Dickens' text
maintains the very idea of London as a 'land of fragments' and, in
doing so, to comprehend the Dickensian text as maintaining the otherwise invisible who haunt the structures of power and law on which
the city is built, as London's silent inhabitants.

It should also be remarked that this maintenance on the part of
Dickens' novel is not to be comprehended as part of some simple or
simply conceived polemical or dialectical opposition to the hegemonic
political and discursive structures of the 1850s (which opposition is
then recuperated into the positions it supposedly challenges, as some
critics, Sylvia Manning for example, have suggested[5]). Nor should we
necessarily understand the Dickensian project as unproblematically
nostalgic or sentimental. Rather, I would argue, *Little Dorrit*'s 'land
of fragments' is a complex historical-temporal affirmation and engage-
ment with the heterogeneity of the urban, while at the same time exposing,
even as it exceeds, the limits of any organic, mimetic or monocular
representation of the city. Such affirmation, I wish to contend, is, in
being foreign to the logic of dialectic, never available as unequivocally
nostalgic or not nostalgic, sentimental or not sentimental, oppositional
or not oppositional. It is, strictly speaking, a registration of that which
is other in the city, the reading of which is undecidable except as *just*
this enunciation of the urban. For example, we read such assertion
through the brief description of the '[c]ourtly', 'costly', 'picturesque',
'desolate', and 'teeming ideas' of Covent Garden: 'Covent Garden . . .
a place of past and present mystery, romance, abundance, want, beauty,
ugliness, fair country gardens, and foul street gutters; all confused together' (*LD* I.xiv. 167–8). Here is the city spatially and temporally,

the excess, fragmentation and confusion incommensurate with any ordering system or programme. 'Past' and 'present' disrupt the idea of a
single temporal moment, while suggestive of the return of an unfixable
seriality of past moments persisting in the very idea of the present as
that which, invisible within in the field of vision, nonetheless makes
the present waver, to paraphrase Fredric Jameson on the idea of
spectrality, and cited in the chapter on George Eliot. Moreover, each
term in Dickens' urban taxonomy is doubled by the temporal trace
even as each term is, of course, placed so as to disturb the burden of
identification in its other. The result is that any meeting for the city is
undecidable as a result of Dickens' attempted fidelity to the condition
of London.

Published initially in monthly parts from 1855 to 1857, *Little Dorrit*
may be read then, however provisionally, as a text of affirmative resistance: paradoxically resisting the language of *either* unity *or* occlusion,
it affirms London as a 'land of fragments'. The text maps this comprehension by remembering its inhabitants as intrinsic both *to* the city
and *as* the city, through what Andrew Sanders has recently described
as 'Dickens's focus on the multiple blurrings, gradations and confusions
of nineteenth-century London'.[6] Moreover, it is through the concerns
with memory and forgetting – the memories of characters as well as
those of the narratorial voice – that the city's fragmented, excessive
condition is returned as so many phantasms of remembrance belonging
to a Dickensian mnemotechnic, by which the experience of the city is
encountered. As Sanders comments, in reading *Little Dorrit* one experiences a 'revisiting [of] emotions and memories' (*DSA* 142), while William
Palmer has commented that the novel involves the 'plundering of memory'.[7]

It is not that we are dealing directly with memories *of* the city, so
much as we are asked to understand this novel and the city of London
as places of memory. Memory takes place as so many secretive and
encrypted fragments as the necessary corrective to the institutional and
discursive work of government. It is thus through the very operation
of the loose assemblage of haunting remembrance – as distinct from
the excessive frequency of official *memoranda* issued by the Circumlocution Office – by which the 'free city' (*LD* I.vii.86), as Dickens
calls it, is traced. Indeed, one need only pause to consider that, while
the Circumlocution Office is involved in 'the work of . . . memorandum-
making' (*LD* II.viii.497), producing 'several sacks of official memoranda'
(*LD* I.x.110) and, elsewhere, 'thirty-two thousand five hundred and
seventeen memoranda' (*LD* II.viii.497), the work and play of 'unofficial',

unsystematic memory in the production of the city beyond the confining machinery of institutions is incalculable. As an example of why we should be wary of reducing the text to a dialectical formation, it is not that memory is opposed in any direct or obvious manner to the mechanical production of memoranda; instead, it is necessary to comprehend the former in its fragmentary, unstoppable drifting and blurring as that which no system or institution can contain, or for which it can account. We see this when Mrs Clennam enters the Marshalsea in search of Little Dorrit and an ineluctable aurality is related to remembrance: 'The air was heavy and hot; the closeness of the place, oppressive; and from without there arose a rush of free sounds, like the jarring memory of such things in a headache and a heartache' (*LD* II.xxxi. 752–3). Like the city outside the prison, sound is free. More than this sound *is* the city; like the bells at the beginning of Chapter Three (of which more, shortly), sound-memory or memory-sound is jarring; yet this 'intrusion' is not opposed in any direct or obvious manner to the prison. It is simply *there*, invisible, immaterial, a haunting surplus or excess announcing a somewhat spectralized urban alterity irreducible to any institutional or carceral structure.

Of course, criticism of *Little Dorrit* has already commented at length on the trope and work of memory. As Anny Sadrin puts it, the novel's 'issues' are 'memory, atonement and vindictiveness . . . "Do not forget" is . . . the formula that best seems to describe the author's intentions and the narrator's method, that merciless way he has of hoarding up evidence'.[8] However, the performative aspect of impersonal memory as constitutive of the city has yet to be acknowledged. Take, for example, this description of the monotonous routine of Mrs Clennam's confined life and the function of her chair as particular to the memory of the city:

The house in the city preserved its heavy dullness through all these transactions, and the invalid within it turned the same unvarying round of life. Morning, noon, and night, morning, noon, and night, each recurring with its accompanying monotony, always the same reluctant return of the same sequences of machinery, like a dragging piece of clockwork.

The wheeled chair had its associated remembrances and reveries, one may suppose, as every place that is made the station of a human being has. Pictures of demolished streets and altered houses, as they formerly were when the occupant of the chair was familiar with them, images of people as they too used to be, with little or no allowance for the lapse of time since they were seen. (*LD* I.xxix.331)

The two paragraphs map precisely the different languages of *Little Dorrit*. The first, in its depiction of the stasis of Mrs Clennam's life, speaks tellingly to the 'holding patterns' of the economic programme. There is readable the institutional and programmatic condition which elsewhere is writ large in the structures and discourses of the Circumlocution Office and the Marshalsea, the programme articulated in that phrase, the 'return of the same', as the marking of or desire for a repetition without difference, defined appropriately as a machinery, by which the invalid becomes subsumed, becoming part of the business 'transactions' belonging typically to a 'house in the city'. (What is interesting in this particular phrase, by the way, is the way in which the domestic space is occluded by the rhetoric of the phrase itself: it was a commonplace of the period, and still persists today, to refer to offices and banks as 'houses'. For example, it is reported that Pancks is destined to become a partner 'in the house' of Doyce and Clennam [*LD* II.xxxiv.785]. Domestic economy slides into, or is always already apprehended by, capitalist economics, quite economically we might say; and we would do well to recall the etymology of 'economy' with its meaning of 'control of the house' when considering the struggle between Arthur, his mother and Flintwinch.) Yet, while the first paragraph structures itself in this way, rendering Mrs Clennam as a willing, complicit figure in the invalidation of her individual responsibility, the second paragraph affirms impersonal memory. In doing so, it attests to the motion, the rhythmic and temporal change of London, and thereby asks us to bear witness to the difference of the city, and to the memorial reiterations which take place *as* the experience of the urban event. As a counterpoint to the machinery or programme of business which, because learnt by rote requires no active memory, the machine of the 'wheeled chair' becomes the conduit for remembrance. The traces of 'demolished streets' return, ghosts of themselves undoubtedly, unreadable ruins which, along with those phantasms the 'images' of people, disorder strictly conceived time and the efficiency of clockwork in this act of anachronistic, imaginary restitution. Or, perhaps it is a matter of a haunting testimonial 'reparation', to recall one of Mrs Clennam's favourite words.

Acts of memory may then be situated indirectly as they enact a tension against inflexible or organized notions of time or history on

the one hand, while bringing occasionally into focus the flows of the
city as a nonplace in relation to the rigidly defined institutional structures such as the Marshalsea and the Circumlocution Office (and also
Clennam's family house, of which more below). Thus London as 'land
of fragments', as a site constructed through various institutions and
their discourses, is readable as contested internally by other rhythms,
other fragmentary surges and motions.

There is, it has to be stressed then, not a dominant form of memory
by which the shaping of the novel or, more significantly, the configuration of city is governed or controlled; rather, it is a question of multiple
memories, of numerous fragmentary acts and surges of remembrance,
as those phantom traces which contend with one another and jostle in
the articulation of the urban. For example, while Amy Dorrit's role is
'to secure collective memory: to make sure that past people and places
are accorded the right weight', as Hilary Schor puts it,[9] Flora Casby's
speech is performative, her hurried articulations an addict's version
of remembrance of things past projecting an undifferentiated flow of
the past.

Such a flow disrupts dialogue in various unmanageable and irreducible ways when Flora visits Arthur Clennam at the business premises
of Doyce and Clennam:

'Pray say nothing in the way of apology,' Arthur entreated. 'You
are always welcome.'

'Very polite of you to say so Arthur – cannot remember Mr Clennam
until the word is out, such is the habit of times for ever fled, and so
true it is that oft in the stilly night ere slumber's chain has bound
people, fond memory brings the light of other days around people –
very polite but more polite than true I am afraid, for to go into the
machinery business without so much as sending a line or a card to
papa – I don't say me though there was a time but that is past and
stern reality has now my gracious never mind – does not look like
it you must confess.'

Even Flora's commas seemed to have fled on this occasion; she
was so much more disjointed and voluble than in the preceding
interview.

'Though indeed,' she hurried on, 'nothing else is to be expected
and why should it be expected and if it's not to be expected why
should it be, and I am far from blaming you or any one, when your
mama and my papa worried us to death and severed the golden bowl

– I mean bond but I dare say you know what I mean and if you
don't you don't lose much and care just as little I will venture to
add – when they severed the golden bond that bound us and threw
us into fits of crying on the sofa nearly choked at least myself everything was changed and in giving my hand to Mr F I know I did so
with my eyes open but he was so very unsettled and in such low
spirits that he had distractedly alluded to the river if not oil of something from the chemist's and I did it for the best.' (*LD* I.xxiii, 265)

In a telling eruption of the traces of the past as so many fragments of
ruined grammar and syntax, Flora acts as a medium for all that questions of economics and business cannot account. Her upbraiding of
Arthur's entering into the 'machinery business' in the recent past of
the novel is situated in relation to Arthur's own forgetfulness of polite
form. However, the uncanny power of her remonstrance is that she
projects this critique as the place from which, seamlessly, the haunting
moments of the past sacrificed to the economic figure of the house of
business flow. The tension between the figures of the house of business
on one hand and the domestic space on the other (once anticipated as
the marriage of Arthur and Flora but subsequently displaced onto the
marriage with 'Mr F') reverberate in the dissidence of memory as the
haunted reality of Flora's speech, emerging from within and yet in
excess of any purely economic exchange.

Thus, if we consider the difference of the work of memory between
two of the four principal daughters in the text as it pulses through
them it is clearly not the case that the daughter's role is unequivocally to act as 'a kind of narrative last testament', as Schor somewhat
idealistically and reductively puts it (129). In the figure of Amy, small
and compact, memory is gathered, a restricted economy so to speak;
in that of Flora, 'grown to be very broad' (*LD* I.xiii.152), memories
are disseminated through profligate speech. (And, it has to be suggested,
as does Dickens, that Flora's return gives the lie to, or makes equivocal
at least, Clennam's powers of memory; 152.) Flora overflows with 'fond
memory' and 'old remembrances', and more than 'a word about the
dear old days gone for ever', as she puts it (*LD* I.xxiii.153), engendered
as an inadvertent and unwilled response every time she encounters
Clennam. Thus, it may be said that Amy's role is to restrict the economy
of memory, while Flora's is to emphasize performatively a blurring
contest of memories' fragments. While Patriarch Casby's daughter may
be a figure of comic fun, that for which she is the medium is the spirit

of a burlesque, if not carnivalesque other space of memory, typical of the energies of the city, as haunted by the stories of the past, a past which Clennam cannot be allowed to forget.

John Glavin has suggested that *Little Dorrit* is constituted through these fragments of competing narrative, comprising 'this underworld of lost and haunting stories . . . about remembering, [and] repeating',[10] while Soultana Maglavera has commented on 'the intense preoccupation . . . with memory and time past'.[11] Old Nandy offers us an important figure apropos these matters. First introduced, appropriately in the chapter titled 'Spirit' as someone who 'knew some pale and vapid little songs, long out of date' (*LD* I.xxxi.355), he is one figure of this urban 'underworld'. Through him the snatches of song about 'Chloe, and Phyllis, and Strephon', anachronistic popular fragments, return from the London pleasure gardens of the eighteenth century, where they were first performed. His songs are thus instances of performative revenance. And we are asked to respond to Nandy not as idiosyncratic but, as the beginning of the chapter indicates, as typically a 'meagre, wrinkled, yellow old man . . . creeping along with a scared air, as though bewildered and a little frightened by the noise and bustle', who '[a]nybody may pass, any day, in the thronged thoroughfares of the metropolis' (*LD* I.xxxi.353). While the textual focus narrows to produce Old Nandy, the initial emphasis of the chapter is on a 'London type' who, for all his typical anonymity, we should, *must*, not forget, and whose affirmative persistence is registered barely in that phrase 'any day'.

Thus *Little Dorrit* does double service here, announcing its remembrance of the otherwise anonymous urban poor, while intimating, through Old Nandy as a figure for the city's countless others, memory-through-reiteration of the city's pleasures. Not simply 'memories' but articulated through and as the interanimation of a tropological assemblage, the traces of the city inform the reader's perception even as, however immaterially (as in the example of Old Nandy's song), they bear the material experience of London, which we in turn are asked to witness, even while, because of their fragmentary nature, they remain at least partially unreadable. Old Nandy's song-fragments, uncanny, poignant instances of irreducible revenance, return as the enactment of one of several fragmentary states. There is remarked in them what Hans-Jost Frey, in a discussion of the status of the fragmentary text, describes as an 'anonymous, posthumous endlessness'.[12] The songs are all the more haunting for being fragmentary, and they are fragments to the extent that, according to Frey's definition, they do not speak of an event;

rather, they 'just happen';[13] this is our experience of the fragment, a neutral experience of the unreadable, and so we have to deal with what is not there, we have to negotiate with the nonplace from which the song returns as that phantom site's memory. Such memories speak, however indirectly, to a series of unstable and drifting tropes in *Little Dorrit* as the responsibility of the text in remembering other Londons. We might provisionally identify these tropes as belonging to the poetics of the constellated urban imaginary: iterability, time or, rather, temporality, and the related figures to which I have been alluding and will turn, ghosts, phantoms, and the processes of haunting in general. Such troping figures, so many non-synonymous substitutions, fold and unfold themselves in various ways and, in doing so, drift within themselves and from themselves, even as they disinter the idea of a definable or finite location.

The novel and the city are therefore available to us as being composed from what Pierre Nora calls *lieux de mémoire*: places or sites of memory. Such sites, Nora argues, are 'the ultimate embodiments of a memorial consciousness that has barely survived in a historical age that calls out for memory because it has abandoned it. They make their appearance by virtue of the deritualizing of our world.'[14] Mrs Clennam's wheeled chair recalls the past to the present and invites us also not to forget as its remembrances deritualize the place and patterns of business. The deritualization is clearly in operation *as* the work of remembrance and the call of conscience – Do not forget (*LD* I.xxx.347) – which memory invokes in *Little Dorrit* as it struggles against the official forgetting necessary to a world of business and government. Such forgetting is actively willed in Dickens' original and abandoned title for the novel, 'Nobody's Fault' and subsequently by the doxical, anonymous ritual repetition of the comment that it – whatever 'it' may happen to signify – is 'nobody's fault' in Christine Edzard's film of *Little Dorrit*. Indeed, Dickens makes clear the amnesiac imperative of the abandoned title not only through the repetition of 'nobody' in the novel but also in a well-known article from 1856, published in *Household Words*, 'Nobody, Somebody, Everybody', in which the ritual utterance of Nobody amounts to its power to avoid responsibility for the past, to forget it and thereby remain always in an illusory present.[15]

However, while there is the insistence on ritualization also in the form of form-filling as the proper procedure before the law of the Circumlocution Office, by going through the 'mechanical' procedure of 'memorialising' the Department 'for leave to memorialise the Department' (*LD* I.x.121), there is also the reiterated effort to disrupt ritual *in the name of* remembrance. Arthur Clennam, for example, implores his mother repeatedly to remember: 'I have habitually submitted, and I only ask you to remember it . . . Remember I was with my father. Remember, I saw his face . . . Remember, I saw him at the last' (*LD* I.v.57, 58–9). Habitual submission and the mechanics of form-filling are but two aspects of the attempted obliteration of memory in the novel. Within these impersonal and ritual processes we witness the will to remember as the articulation of Nora's 'memorial consciousness'.

Arthur Clennam's demand upon his mother is not, of course, originary, and we should remember *this*. It arises within the Clennam house, which is also a house of business, as a response itself to the haunting injunction, *do not forget*, which is all the more haunting for not having yet been uttered when Arthur and his mother first speak and yet is already, silently there. This call, encrypted as the fragment *D.N.F.* and secreted within Clennam's father's watch, arrives – arriving before it arrives, as it were – as the call of the other. With all the silent dislocating force of a diacritical mark, the disembodied abbreviated inscription remarks time in an untimely fashion, returning every time the owner of the watch seeks to know the arbitrarily determined and absolutely regular, regulated moment in time in any given present. These initials arrive therefore in a disruptive uncanny fashion, always from another time as a ghostly call. The inscription calls for memory and Arthur's response is to reiterate the demand, to enjoin responsibility as the articulation of an ethical relay which calls for the act of memory as bearing witness. While therefore readable as personal, Clennam's desire for remembrance is, strictly speaking, part of what I call elsewhere the architexture of Dickens' London; Clennam's call – but which one? for both he and his father are 'Arthur Clennam'[16] – is symptomatic of the work of the novel as a whole, he and the house of Clennam being merely 'switches', if you will, in a circuitry of impersonal memory, bringing into sight the invisible flow already underway.

Clennam's guilt brings with it so many other haunting returns of remembrance, such as the phantasms and memories of childhood, parental dispute, and the tediousness of London Sundays (*LD* I.iii.40–52). And again, these memories are not originary; they announce a certain inescapable 'relation to locations'[17] whether spatial or temporal, returning unbidden as a response to the city itself, to the '[m]addening church bells of all degrees of dissonance . . . In every thoroughfare, up almost every alley, and down almost every turning, some doleful bell was throbbing, jerking, tolling . . .' (*LD* I.iii.40–1). Through Arthur the city returns, not once but twice at least: for the bells which simultaneously compose and discompose, which fragment and blur, announce the city of the narrative's present moment, 1827, as well as that of nearly forty years before, the London of the 1790s, *and*, I would contend, that time of the novel's publication in the mid-century. Disrupting the present, the bells enact the city as so many places and displacements of memory in both timely and untimely fashion. (A brief parenthesis: in this, *Little Dorrit* appears to anticipate, uncannily, the play of London's bells in *Mrs Dalloway*.) Arthur Clennam is thus called to remember before entering his house by the city itself.

The temporal disjunction invoked here suggestively announces the 'free city', an ambivalent identity at best, as a nonplace distinct from those architectural, systematic and institutionally constricting sites of the Circumlocution Office and the Marshalsea. The bells, as Dickens makes clear, invoke city memories for countless anonymous others beyond the example of Clennam. Indeed, like Old Nandy's song, the bells are *just* the fragment-memories of the city. In general, bells define both the city and the Londoner at least since the Early Modern period, as both Bruce Smith and Peter Ackroyd have acknowledged, and as is remarked by John Stow in his 1598 *The Survey of London*.[18] A Cockney is of course defined as one born within the sound of the bell of St Mary-le-Bow, in Cheapside, and the sound of bells reiterates through the centuries as intrinsic to the city's identity. As Ackroyd comments, the 'monstrousness' and 'unnaturalness' of the sound of bells have informed the texture and memory of the city for over seven hundred years: 'secular bells, church bells, convent bells, the bell of the curfew and the bell of the watchman' (*L: TB,* 71). So, the 'maddening' 'dissonance' of the ringing and the 'hideous' echoes of which Dickens speaks (*LD* I.iii.40) need not be necessarily available to us in some way as a symbolic foreshadowing of the more materially oppressive structures of the Marshalsea or the Circumlocution Office. Indeed, I would argue that the bells are undecidable, merely the acoustic articulation, marking *and* disordering the time and returning across time (as well as across the novel) as part of the fabric of London. Specifically in *Little Dorrit*, the bells mark two immediate purposes in Chapter Three: on the one hand, the chimes announce the endlessness of 'streets, streets, streets' (*LD* I.iii.41). On the other, and as part of the irreducible and unresolvable tension of which the novel partakes between the official and institutional and the nameless and unquantifiable, the chimes ring out the call to church *and* the fact that the people won't come (*LD*

I.iii.41). They therefore constitute one particular *lieu de mémoire*, or what Ulrich Baer defines as a 'memory site in a time when communal settings or collectively shared symbolic contexts for experience and memory . . . have all but disappeared'. The bells, in their relationship to impersonal London memory 'wash up', to quote Baer again, 'as remnants of real and symbolic sites where memories may now cluster'.[19] This suggestion of the clustering of memory might be an appropriate figure for the ways in which the city is experienced as that which takes place over and against any simple sense of place. It is, certainly, a figure for the gathering and unstoppable revenance of ghosts, phantoms, phantasms and the work of spectrality in general.

If we consider the work of memory as response, as an opening to acts of spectral revenance, then the haunt of memory is comprehended best not only as analepsis, a restoration of the past through vision generated by the subject, but as a kind of anastamosis, a process of inter- or even telecommunication: Dickens' London as one particular configuration in the city's network, where 'invisible' signals leave their traces, emerging *in* and *as* barely discernible fragments. The Clennam family house is the most obvious site of haunting in the novel, though by no means the only one. Obviously, the ghost of Arthur's father is the most persistent figure to return without ever being there as such. His force is such that Arthur cannot but help imagine that his father inhabits his old room in the house 'invisibly' (*LD* I.v.65). Affery dreams that the house is haunted, she seeks to make connection to the living of the city 'beyond and outside the haunted house', while in her dreams she is 'impelled . . . by ghosts and curiosity' (*LD* I.xv.181, 183). Arguably, Dickens' use of zeugma announces a ghostly destabilization at work in narrative structure. Within this house even Mrs Clennam's figure eventually assumes a 'ghostly' condition (*LD* II.xxx.748), a condition which becomes fully 'spectral', after the house has collapsed and she is freed from it to drift through the streets, amidst 'the turbulent irruption of this multitude of staring faces' which anonymously announce the city, in search of the Marshalsea (*LD* II.xxxi.751). Of course those haunting figures which appear without appearing in the minds of Clennam and Affery, awake or asleep, are the unbidden phantasms of belated memory, their own uncanny remembrances as responses to the secrets of the house. We might even suggest, in passing, that in *Little Dorrit*'s silent recirculating passage from the late eighteenth to the mid-nineteenth century Dickens plays on the figure of the ghost, responding to its haunting power and playing between earlier understandings of the phantom as an apparition external to the mind and the developing comprehension of the relentless interiorization of the phantom as psychic projection, as Terry Castle has shown in *The Female Thermometer*.[20]

Be that as it may, the Clennam house's gradual fragmentation and disintegration results as the haunting power of memory persistently asserts itself. Indeed, the destruction of structure comes about as the imaginative result of accumulated revenance where, in the ultimate process of blurring, the house as place of economic transaction, trade, secrecy and the arrest of remembrance is seen to be reclaimed as nonplace in and by the city. More than this, the collapse of the house signals the end of that other instance of blurring where the supposedly discrete private and public spheres of 'family' and 'business' have reciprocally informed one another. Moreover, there is such a 'surplus of responsibility'[21] within the house, to use a phrase of Derrida's, that the economy and law of the house must give way within and to the free city. Furthermore, to continue the quotation from Derrida, the spectral surplus calls forth 'the deconstructive gesture' (EW 117); and there can be, perhaps, no more deconstructive gesture than that the structure, the institution, the economy, and the law of the house collapse as a result of the return of all that is invisible, hidden and forgotten within it. This strange, so-called 'literal' collapse, seemingly so 'symbolically' overdetermined and yet never quite readable, appears to appear in the text as what might be described, following the title of Thomas Keenan's recent book, a 'fable of responsibility'.[22]

It may be suggested that the novel's climax in the form of the fall of the house of Clennam is excessive. If we are to be true, however, to the responsibility which the ghosts of the city and the various memories which, in returning, remind us not to forget, then it has to be admitted, after Derrida, that the 'surplus of responsibility . . . will never authorize any silence'. Derrida continues: 'responsibility is excessive or it is not a responsibility. A limited, measured, calculable, rationally distributed responsibility is already the becoming-right of morality' (EW 118). I would argue that the figures of the city of London, its fragments, traces and ruins, a few of which I have sought to acknowledge here, are, to reiterate the necessary point already made, irreducible to any straightforwardly 'political' reading which either counters the idea of the system or else sees nothing other than the systematic oppressions of institutional mechanics at work. In figuring the irreducible and undecidable, the excess of the city that the work of haunting and memory unveils

demands an unlimited, immeasurable, and incalculable responsibility
on the part of the reader. Were we to seek to measure, to limit and to
calculate, we would find ourselves back with Mr Meagles's scales,
back at the Marshalsea or Circumlocution Office, back with Flintwinch's
accounts, or even, it has to be admitted, Amy Dorrit's desire to manage
(in which we might read the limit in the Dickensian text; for is it not
through Amy that we might read a 'rationally distributed responsibility'
which is 'already the becoming-right of morality'?).

Instead, we have to remain with the risk which responsibility entails.
It is this risk and this responsibility which are articulated in the preface to the novel, from 1857. In his preface, Dickens goes in search of
the Marshalsea or, rather, what remains, finding only ruins, fragments,
remnants of structure incorporated into newer buildings (*LD* 'Preface',
5–6). Here, he insists, 'whosoever goes into Marshalsea Place . . . will
stand among the crowding ghosts of many miserable years' (*LD* 'Preface', 5–6). The ghosts of the city are those belonging, to recall the
words of Peter Nicholls with which we began, to that 'forgotten history
[which] has the power to shake the social and metaphysical forms'.
Dickens' crowding ghosts waver in the present time and liminal space
of the preface (to recall Jameson, once more), in the remnants of the
Marshalsea and into the future of the novel's reception, as part of the
forgotten history of Londoners. The ghosts of urban memory whose
irreducibility I have sought to insist on, 'are public, and private, and
neither', to borrow from Thomas Keenan (*FR* 188). Haunting is but
one instance of this uncontrollable, excessive return which issues an
impossible claim, and belongs more generally to the work of memory
in its most powerful and spectral effects. The function of reiteration,
temporal displacement, haunting and memory as these operate in *Little
Dorrit* is to open and disclose that which is the writing of the city's
secret but which had been there all along, whether in plain sight or as
the barely visible trace of some phantom inscription.

In conclusion, then, and in the light of this response to the idea of
London as a 'land of fragments', let us turn to the final passages of
the novel: the marriage of Arthur and Amy, and beyond. I am tempted
to read the marriage scene as the 'end of the book and the beginning
of writing' to borrow a well-known phrase. However, what I would
like to propose is that the end of *Little Dorrit* resists closure as much
as it appears to invite that reading through the conventional trope of
the marriage. Indeed, a final reading is precisely what appears to be
suspended. The marriage register is signed (*LD* II.xxxiv.785), the clerk

referring to the three volumes of Amy's life: those in which her birth and marriage are registered, and the death register which she had used as a pillow. Somewhat uncannily, a London life is transformed into an authorized triple-decker, institutionally approved and located. (Perhaps not *too* fancifully, we might imagine the clerk as one Charles Dickens, author of Little Dorrit, and the three-volume novel which bears her name.) However, following this – and, curiously, it should be noted that Clennam's name is never mentioned following the marriage, except in brief parenthesis as part of the public name of a business, Doyce and Clennam – 'Little Dorrit and her husband walked out of the church alone.'

> They paused for a moment on the steps of the portico, looking at the fresh perspective of the street in the autumn sun's bright rays, and then went down. . . . They went quietly down into the roaring streets . . . and as they passed along in sunshine and in shade, the noisy and the eager, and the arrogant and the froward and the vain, fretted, and chafed, and made their usual uproar. (*LD* II.xxxiv.787)

The novel does not lead us into the house, into the home, exactly, even though it promises such a future of care and management. Instead, with its chiming reiteration of 'went down', it absorbs the happy couple into the streets of the city, into its constant noise and ceaseless activity. Little Dorrit ends with the endlessness of an irresistible urban inscription and articulation, which ineluctably remains with us and through which, I would propose, we are asked to remember, the 'sound of London', as Peter Ackroyd puts it, 'transmitted through' the silent, and increasingly invisible pair (*L:TB*, 78). Noise is also invisible, of course, and it is important that it remains as that which remains after the city's immediacy has been left behind, because Little Dorrit, in being a novel concerned with urban invisibility, insists that good reading comes down to acts of listening, of responding to the excess of the 'land of fragments', without seeking to calm down that play.

# 5

# 'The persistence of the unforeseen': *The Mayor of Casterbridge*

Having reached the analytical stage [novel writing] must transcend it... Why not by rendering as visible essences, spectres, &c. the most abstract thoughts of the analytic school.

Thomas Hardy, *The Life and Work of Thomas Hardy*

We two kept house, the Past and I.

Thomas Hardy, 'The Ghost of the Past'


## INTRODUCTION

*The Mayor of Casterbridge* is haunted. Spectres are everywhere, even in the faces or actions of the living. The town of Casterbridge is a haunted place, its topographical, architectural and archaeological structures resonating with the traces of the spectral. The ghosts of other textual forms, of which the tragic is only the most persistent or obvious, haunt the very structure of the novel. Michael Henchard particularly is troubled by the past, by a certain spectral revenance. The Mayor of Casterbridge is haunted.


## HAUNTING

From one perspective, haunting might best be described as the ability of forces that remain unseen to make themselves felt in everyday life. Such an oscillation causes us to anticipate, to fear, to act or to respond in ways which we do not fully comprehend, supposing that we understand them at all. As Keith Wilson suggests of the novel, 'all the major characters reveal a capacity ... of responding to experience as the

110

working-out of inevitable courses'.[1] While we might quibble over the term 'courses' as projecting too simple and linear a model, nonetheless this assessment does catch the sense of a spectral movement of the invisible within the visible, discussed in the previous chapter. Such haunting can also cause us to feel unsafe, uneasy, in places where we had always felt at home. Avery Gordon describes haunting in the following way:

> If haunting describes how that which appears to be not there is often a seething presence, acting on and often meddling with taken-for-granted realities, the ghost is just the sign . . . that tells you a haunting is taking place . . . The ghost or the apparition is one form by which something barely visible, or seemingly not there . . . makes itself known to us, in its own way, of course. The way of the ghost is haunting, and haunting is a very particular way of knowing what has happened or is happening.[2]

Perhaps presence is not the right word in this passage, and this is acknowledged when, in the same sentence, Gordon speaks of the ghost as a sign. Importantly, it is not a sign of some absent, deferred or prior presence. The sign is the sign of haunting: it signifies the event of haunting, its habitation within a certain structure.

Haunting creates the sense of the unfamiliar within the familiar. Its operation is thus a structural disturbance, as we have seen in the Introduction and elsewhere (if you recollect, for example, the remark of Fredric Jameson's and the discussion of this remark in the chapter on George Eliot). Haunting inhabits and, in creating an uncanny response, manifests itself not as arriving from elsewhere but instead making itself felt, as Mark Wigley suggests, in an effect of 'surfacing . . . in a return of the repressed as a foreign element that strangely seems to belong to the very domain that renders it foreign' (*AD* 108).[3] As we shall see, haunting, ghosting, and spectrality are all necessary traces in the structures of *The Mayor of Casterbridge*. Barely comprehensible and supplementary to the logic of the narrative, they nonetheless inhere, haunting the very places, narratives and forms they make possible. Haunting is written into the novel's constant concern with economy, households, architecture and habitation.

## CRITICAL APPARITIONS

The persistence of the past in the present of *The Mayor of Casterbridge*, that unsettling or uncanny recurrence described by Ned Lukacher as 'a strange peculiarity in the presence of the present',[4] is accepted by several critics of the novel, even if the ghostly peculiarity is not recognized in full.[5] J. Hillis Miller, Bruce Johnson, and Tess O'Toole in particular consider in interesting ways the question of what returns from the past to disturb the calm sense of the present.[6] Thus there is commonly acknowledged the configuration of universal recurrence, the sense that events leave their imprint on time only to recur, albeit it in a different manifestation. Also, there is figured that Freudian spectre, the return of the repressed, which creates in the disturbed subject the sense of the uncanny, described appropriately by Mark Wigley as that 'uneasy sense of the unfamiliar within the familiar, the unhomely within the home' (*AD* 108). Most recently amongst Hardy critics, Suzanne Keen has offered a sustained consideration of 'the return of the repressed' in relation to 'centuries-old tradition'. She considers also the persistence of 'residual' customs and forms, along with the 'archaic survival' of equally 'archaic practices' as a temporal trace within the social spaces of Casterbridge and its environs in the novel's present.[7] And Keen's sense of the return moves in the direction of the spectral when she suggests that Newson is 'merely a ghost, or a memory' before his undeniable reappearance (133, 140).

Other brief moments of spectral recognition are to be found in criticism of *The Mayor of Casterbridge*. The question of uncanny resonance is considered, albeit in passing, by Raymond O'Dea, in an essay which focuses on Elizabeth-Jane's 'role in the moral struggle she has imposed to some extent upon others'.[8] Tess O'Toole's study of genealogical patterns and familial structures in Hardy also acknowledges the haunting trace: 'as a "spectre", the genetic product is at once the reincarnation of a figure from the past and an image that has been raised by a guilty party's imagination' (18–19). In reading the images of ghosts and the ghostly trace of heredity from Hardy's poem 'San Sebastian', O'Toole connects subjective perception and external manifestation, as does Miller in his reading of Hardy's poetry, making it clear the spectral is no mere subjective invention (97). Robert Langbaum emphasizes Susan Henchard's lack of sexuality by acknowledging the doubleness of her ghostly quality. She is 'the ghost of a past crime, the wife sale, [and] . . . ghostly in her lack of sexual vitality'.[9]

Despite these tantalizing apparitions of critical acknowledgement of the spectral, however, no critic of Hardy, to my knowledge, has offered an extended analysis of the spectral in *The Mayor of Casterbridge*. This is, in part, doubtless because, as Jacques Derrida suggests, 'Ghosts always pass quickly . . . in an instant without duration, presence without presence of a present which, coming back only *haunts*. The ghost . . . appears only by means of figure or fiction, but its appearance is not nothing, nor is it mere semblance.'[10] The ghost is not a likeness, not a simple copy or representation. It has an explicitly textual relationship to that which it haunts. To reiterate and return to a point made earlier, the spectral is that which inhabits structure or identity in such a way as to displace or disrupt the propriety of the form from within.

Both J. Hillis Miller and Jim Reilly acknowledge this quality of Hardy's writing. Stating that, 'Hardy's is a haunted art . . . [in which] material reality is displaced as the goal of representation by shadowy and spectral unrealities',[11] Reilly reads Hardy as working within a fictional paradigm that is not indebted to a form of mimetic realism. Both Reilly and Miller comprehend the world of Hardy's novels, in the latter's words, as a world 'not of copies but of what Deleuze calls "simulacra" or "phantasms"'.[12] This is hardly a new or modish discovery reflecting the interests of literary theory, given the instances of spectral persistence in Hardy's own poetry, and the novelist's own desire for the manifestation of the spectral as a development in the art of novel writing, cited in the first epigraph of this essay.[13] What it suggests, however, is that it is important that we begin to take the spectral in Hardy seriously, if for no other reason than that the novelist appears to anticipate the interests of theory, and thus to haunt the critical text.


## THAT WHICH RETURNS

Another aspect of the spectral to which we have previously turned our attention is that manifestation or persistence of the past in the present, though never as a presence as such. Instead, the ghost of and from the past leaves its trace in the structures of the present of *The Mayor of Casterbridge*. When we speak of the 'past' in relation to *The Mayor of Casterbridge* this might signal equally a number of traces, none with any precedence over any others. Of personal returns and manifestations of the past there are those who come back from Henchard's personal past: Susan, Lucetta, Elizabeth-Jane, even Newson. There is also the furmity woman, through whom the wife-sale returns to haunt Henchard's public identity, even as it has perpetually haunted his private sense of self. The impersonal past of Casterbridge is acknowledged in a number of ways, not least in the history of the mayoral office and the surrounding land (the Ring, Mai Dun, Diana Multimammia). A rural past is acknowledged through and traced in the return of events such as the fair at Weydon Priors or the skimmington ride. Then there are the 'past' texts which inform the structure of the novel – Greek and Shakespearean tragedy, the Old Testament, references to French novels, to Miltonic monsters, or the novels of Walter Scott, and gothic fiction (we will return to these). This is to name merely a few. Such traces, or 'remains' as Nicholas Royle describes them, are not 'the remains of something that was once present'; they are that which, in being spectral, prevents 'any present, and any experience of the presence, from being completely itself'.[14] This ghostly trace has the ability to disrupt not only the present moment but also any sense of identity. It may even write itself as 'dead men's traits' in the sleeping face of Elizabeth-Jane (*MC* 126).

This is not a simple or single instance in itself. It reiterates in part an earlier moment in the novel, when Susan and her daughter return to Weydon Priors, the mother's features being figured imperfectly in the daughter's as the manifestation of 'Nature's powers of continuity' (*MC* 21). Thus, ghosting returns, while the return is always ghostly. Furthermore, the earlier scene which anticipates the haunting of Elizabeth-Jane, is itself a return. The question of the return is not limited to the reiteration noted between the faces of the two women, as the text suggests. For as Hardy tells the reader, '[t]he scene in its broad aspect had so much of its previous character . . . that it might . . . have been the afternoon following the previously recorded episode' (*MC* 21). This is but one instance of what Dale Kramer describes as the persistence of return as evidenced through 'particularities within a continuum', which in turn establishes 'the anthropology of a location . . . explicitly relating the behaviour of present individuals to that of countless predecessors'.[15]

In that we can read a doubling movement of revenance, where movement haunts moment, we can suggest that the entire order of the novel is predicated on the troping of return as the spectral persistence disordering order and identity from within, as an otherness within the text. Even as Elizabeth-Jane's face is haunted by Susan's, and even as this recalls the earlier moment of return on the part of the two women, so that moment of return, in recalling the supposedly 'initial' scene of arrival at the Fair and the subsequent wife-sale, implies the continuous structural movement of displacement and disjointing. To this can be added a reading of the wife-sale, not as some originary event generating the unfolding of the narrative but as itself a moment of what Suzanne Keen calls a form of 'archaic survival' which, in turn, belongs to forms of economic 'traffic' which 'structure the novel' (140). This 'structuring' is also at the same time a disturbance which inhabits the structure, disordering as the necessity of an ordered form, as an internal 'other' which haunts and makes possible the very form itself. It disturbs the unity or identity of all structures, whether we are speaking of the human subject, an architectural form, the mapping of the town, or the form of the novel.

The spectral can be seen on occasions in acts of uncanny doubling, as one form of return. For example, Elizabeth-Jane, on visiting her mother's grave, encounters a figure 'in mourning like herself . . . [who] might have been her wraith or double' (*MC* 134). Lucetta – she is the 'wraith' – is also an uncanny double of Susan Newson/Henchard on one occasion, the 'double of the first' (*MC* 250). Elizabeth-Jane is herself a double of sorts. Not Henchard's but Newson's Elizabeth-Jane, she doubles even as she is haunted by the dead child whose place she has taken, whose identity is signed and simultaneously displaced in the reiteration of the name. That 'Elizabeth-Jane' is a proper name given to two characters sharing the same mother (whose features 'ghost' the second daughter's face) is important. For it alerts us to the importance of textual haunting, of haunting as textual, where even the act of writing can return, though never quite signifying that which it had done. This is a sign of repetition *and* displacement, return *and* disturbance. In addition, Henchard sees in Farfrae's face the double of his dead brother, as is well known (*MC* 49).[16] Finally, Henchard is doubled (as is Lucetta) by the skimmington ride effigy which, as Suzanne Keen so appositely suggests, comes 'back to haunt him' (140).

Keith Wilson speaks of the effects and figures of doubling in his introduction to the novel (xxviii). Such patterns and the 'phantasms' of which they are composed (for all involve the images and memories of the dead) do nothing so much as signify the operations of each other, rather than intimating either a 'reality' beyond the text or an origin or source of which the text is a copy. Indeed, the uncanny mo(ve)ment of revenance and disturbing reiteration comes from within a figure or face to disturb identity and disconcert the subject. In this operation, the ghostly trace, which in reiterating constantly operates in a manner similar to the simulacrum, 'calls into question the authority and legitimacy of its model'.[17] Such doubling and the rhythm of return of which it is a part destabilize more than the identity of particular characters. It is disruptive of what Scott Durham calls, in his study of the phantasmatic condition of simulacra, 'distinct domains and temporalities . . . [to] the extent to which they increasingly appear as the echoes of doubles of one another' (16). To put this another way, with direct reference to *The Mayor of Casterbridge*, it is not only a question of particular characters being haunted. The various spatial and temporal boundaries of the novel that are found increasingly to be permeable and capable of being transgressed (as Marjorie Garson makes clear[18]) signify one another's functions and potential interpretative roles in the novel.

This is the case whether one is speaking of the 'haunting' of the present by the past, signalled in the numerous returns discussed above, all of which permeate arbitrarily defined temporal boundaries. This can be read at the level of particular words themselves. Through archaic, untimely words such as 'burgh and champaign' (*MC* 30), the present of the narrative is disrupted. Words such as 'furmity' and 'skimmington' also signify an anachronic haunting; traces of other times and other modes of expression, they remain ruinous and fragmentary giving no access to some originary discourse.[19] There is also spatial movement across boundaries, which involves a temporal emergence of residual archaic practices, as in the eruption of Mixen Lane into the 'proper' or familiar space of Casterbridge, as Suzanne Keen argues (132).[20]

Keen successfully reads the structure and space of Mixen Lane as the 'other' of Casterbridge. Structurally internal to the town, part of it, this liminal site haunts the town and yet returns itself through the manifestation of what Keen discerns as 'archaic practices of an ancient environ' (132). Its return is untimely and therefore uncanny, displacing the familiarity and domesticity of Casterbridge which Hardy has worked so hard to project. Yet Mixen Lane is but one figure in the novel simultaneously 'at once removed from and infinitely proximate to' (Durham 17) what we consider to be the novel's present moment and its present action. Thus the worlds of Michael Henchard and of Casterbridge are disturbed in their identities from within by the articulation of alternative structures which signify, and thereby double, the operations of each other. Hardy's 'use of place resonates with personal and social significance' as William Greenslade puts it (55), but such resonance is unstable, even as it is destabilizing.

Such haunting, therefore, while a form of return, is not simply a straightforward temporal arrival from some identifiable prior past. As J. Hillis Miller puts it, '[t]hese are underground doublings which arise from differential interrelations among elements which are all on the same plane. This lack of ground in some paradigm or archetype means that there is something ghostly about the effects of this... type of repetition' (*Fiction and Repetition* 6). Speaking of Hardy's fiction in general, Miller motions towards a reading which acknowledges the reiterative, the reciprocally interanimated, and the effect of doubling that articulates Hardy's text. There is that which returns, though never as itself. In its untimely, not to say anachronistic fashion, this spectral trace articulates – or, rather, disarticulates ahead of either our comprehension or ability to see this disturbance[21] – a dissymmetry, to borrow from Jacques Derrida, or non-identity within identity, which complicates everything, signifying what he calls the irreducible singularity of the other (*É* 138, 139).

## THE GOTHIC

If *The Mayor of Casterbridge* is haunted by the trace of the tragic text, it is also disturbed by manifestations of another textual form: the gothic. Gothic, which might be described as the 'low other' to tragedy's high portentousness, involves the arrival of some apparently external figure which disturbs and makes abject the subject, through the subject's registration of fear and even terror. The gothic relies on making apparent those effects which are often only imminent or otherwise underplayed in tragedy, or which in some manner 'vulgarizes' them, according to the gothic context. There is a question here of a certain spectral trace read as a discursive and structural slippage between supposedly discrete forms, a haunting transference across boundaries.

This slippage is, of course, perpetually at work in Hardy's novel, but it is interesting to observe the extent to which Hardy relies on the discourse of the gothic throughout the novel. The ghosting of *The Mayor* with the traces of gothic textuality serves to produce what Derrida calls a 'ghost-text'. It is not simply a question of the ghost of another text haunting and inhabiting the familiar structure of the nineteenth-century novel. Rather, the very identity of the novel, its familiar shape, and the reader's familiarity with that, is disturbed from within as the traces of the gothic 'phantomize the text itself' for, as Derrida suggests, a phantom-text is that in which 'references, or citations . . . leave only traces' (*MPdM* 80).

The phantom-text is everywhere. Not particularly gothic in itself, though nonetheless appearing as the trace of a reference, there is the doxical acknowledgement of Susan as '"The Ghost"' (*MC* 83), a 'mere skellinton . . .' (*MC* 85). Almost immediately upon her death, Susan is reported as having something of a headstone-appearance by Mrs Cuxsom: 'And she was as white as marble-stone' (*MC* 120). Susan is immediately replaced in this comment, her face equated with – and ghosted by – the second- or third-hand signification of a material which will form the architectural symbol of her being dead. Of Henchard, Nance Mockridge comments, in that knowing, prescient manner peculiar to working women in gothic novels, 'There's a bluebeardy look about en; and 'twill out in time' (*MC* 86). Not, of course, that the Mayor has a dungeon, nor does he chain Susan in it, yet his figure is haunted by a powerful figure drawn from the gothic.[22] Moreover, Nance's prediction points to the 'persistence of the unforeseen' (*MC* 334), as Hardy will put it on almost the final page (which statement, I would argue, is where all the spectral traces return from and to where they might be read as leading us). Her phrase is both economical and excessive: it is an utterance belonging to the cheapest of gothic thrills, while also resonating in a somewhat uncanny, if not haunted fashion. Structurally, therefore, her phrase, having to do with time, is disturbed from within, being both timely and untimely, having to do with the persistence of unreadable traces as a condition of temporal disturbance with which the novel is so concerned.

Other characters are also marked in ways which suggest gothic convention. Newson is given a ghostly quality in relation to the question of the return (see Keen, above). Specifically, he disturbs Henchard: '[t]he apparition of Newson haunted him. He would surely return' (*MC* 300). Conjuror Fall lives outside the town, and therefore outside the boundaries of society, as is typical of figures associated with alchemy and the black arts. His habitation and narrative preparation for the encounter between Henchard and Fall confuse discursive boundaries, intermixing the gothic, the folkloric and fairy-tale. The way to Fall's house is 'crooked and miry' (*MC* 185), and Henchard's approach to Fall's home is suggestively eerie: 'One evening when it was raining . . . heavily . . . a shrouded figure on foot might have been perceived travelling in the direction of the hazel copse which dripped over the prophet's cot' (*MC* 185–6). Even the furmity woman gets in on the gothic act, for, upon her return, it is remarked that she 'had mysteriously hinted . . . that she knew a queer thing or two' (*MC* 202). Of course, what she knows is merely the information concerning Henchard's past, but her return is part of the general movement of return in the text, while Hardy carefully frames her ominous comment in a manner designed to amplify its portentous aspect.

What will return in this instance is the narrative which already haunts Henchard, embodied in the furmity dealer's citation. While the old woman returns, what returns through her is the trace of the past and, with that, the suppressed truth as that which haunts. As Derrida makes clear in reading the spectral in Freud, repressed or suppressed, the truth-as-hauntedness nonetheless 'exists and *returns*, as such'; what returns 'comes down to spectral truth . . . The truth is spectral, and this is its part of truth which is irreducible by explanation' (*AF* 87). The gothic is one mode of production that allows for an economy of explanation, a logic of representation, to order and rationalize, even as it relies on the non-rational. Yet, within that mechanism, there is always the spectral element. Gothic convention is precisely this: convention, structure and law. Within such convention however is that which is irreducible by explanation, as Derrida puts it. What cannot be explained is that the return happens, and that it happens moreover not as the return of some presence to the present, but as the haunted trace. The truth of Henchard's past is coincidental to the general movement of spectral revenance, which the Mayor of Casterbridge is incapable of reading, and which *The Mayor of Casterbridge* barely glimpses.

The technique of repetition at work throughout the novel provides this barely seen spectral condition, even while, within the structures of the text, such reiteration is locally domesticated through the recourse to particularly familiar textual forms, such as the gothic. Not only are characters read and written as if in a gothic context, therefore. They behave as though they were characters from a gothic novel, even as the narrative voice mimics or is haunted by the trace of the gothic. Elizabeth-Jane is 'startled by the apparition of Farfrae' (*MC* 136). Lucetta's face is altered by an encounter with Farfrae also: her face 'became – as a woman's face becomes when the man she loves rises upon her gaze like an apparition' (*MC* 178). There is something decidedly strange, *uncanny*, about Farfrae, that his appearance to two women should be described as an apparition on both occasions. It even disturbs

Hardy in the act of writing, for notice that pause signalled silently in the dash as the writer seeks the most appropriate simile. However, we will have to leave the Scot for a moment.

There are other gothic traces too, improper references and ghostly citations without specific origins. The keystone-mask above Lucetta's door (*MC* 142) and the decaying sign of the Three Mariners (*MC* 42–3) have a certain gothic appeal.[23] Furthermore, their ruined decaying qualities hint at the uncanny, the unfamiliar within the familiar. Suggesting forms of temporal persistence, of the past's ability to return and to disturb, they both signify a certain sinister ineffability which gives the lie to the familiarity and homeliness of the structures – the public house and Lucetta's home – of which they are synecdochic figures. Both serve economically in tracing that 'structural slippage from *heimlich* [homely] to *unheimlich* [unhomely] [in which] that which supposedly lies outside the familiar comfort of the home turns out to be inhabiting it all along' (*AD* 108).[24] (We will return to the uncanny in the next section of this essay, below.) Most immediately however, their function is to create that *frisson* so typically desired in the gothic. Both the sign and the keystone serve a textual, haunting function in that they remind us that a 'house is not simply an object that may be represented, but is itself a mechanism of representation' (*AD* 163),[25] or what Derrida calls 'a structure of reproduction' which is linked to the 'perception of an image' (*GD* 61).

We can read such effects at work when we are told how Jopp's cottage is 'built of old stones from the long-dismantled priory, scraps of tracery, moulded window-jambs, and arch-labels, being mixed in with the rubble of the walls' (*MC* 221). Those scraps, the ruins of the priory, long since gone, operate as references in a number of ways. Priories are, of course, favourite ruined sites, often haunted, in gothic discourse. There is in this image, with its fragments of clauses, the return of the past in the present structure once more, the structure of the cottage and the structure of the sentence. The former is structurally (dis-)composed by the material traces of a former structure; the latter is structurally (dis-)composed by the haunting traces of gothic discourse which in their phantomatic inscription enact a ghostly transference in the image of the cottage, from its being simply an object to be represented, to being a mechanism of representation, as Mark Wigley puts it, or a 'structure of reproduction', to recall Derrida's words. In this, the text does nothing so much as displace itself, endlessly. For the operation of haunting signals not simply a prior moment, if that is

even the purpose. Instead, it serves to signal a certain spectral dislocation that belongs to the novel as a whole, signalling the ruins of other
ruins, the keystone, the decaying sign, the Ring (Ch. XI), even as they
in turn signify other traces, and the other of the trace.

We must develop this point further, at the risk of reiteration. This
movement, the gothic 'oscillation', is not merely an intertextual feature; it is of a different – spectral – order. This order is summed up in
a discussion of Hardy's use of topography by J. Hillis Miller. Miller
notes that reading the novel as a map of a series of places articulates
a chain-like structure, any link of which 'may be placed at any position in the sequence. Any link presupposes the others as its determining
causes, but in its turn is cause of the others'.[26] There is no stable or
stabilizing locus, no originary or central feature, event, character or
textual referent (tragedy, the gothic), by which the reading of the novel
can be calmed, or from which can be generated the idea of a meaning
or identity. Each figure can be substituted for any other, maintaining
both the process of signification and the concomitant disorganization
of the process, prohibiting its coming to rest.

The priory stones are therefore readable, as are other structural and
architectonic features, in a manner similar to more explicitly narrowly
textual referents, such as those from the Old Testament or tragedy, as
we have already suggested. The 'stones', in being the traces of an
absent discourse, being performative fragments and ruins, are not there
to suggest that the reader simply turn back to the literary past, to some
prior form as the novel's inheritance or what might, too blithely, be
described as 'context'. Instead, they acknowledge an inescapably haunted
quality within the structure of any textual form. In this, they may be
read as signifying those other momentary, fleeting textual traces, such
as Hardy's reference to '[t]he *misérables* who would pause on the re-
moter bridge' (*MC* 224). There is also that reference to Henchard's
face and the 'rich *rouge et noir* of his countenance' (*MC* 67). *The
Mayor of Casterbridge* is peppered with French words and phrases,
enough certainly that criticism of the 1950s and 60s would doubtless
have read such usage as part of Hardy's overreaching pretensions and
a sign of the text's lack of coherence. However, such 'foreign' elements, while disjointing the text by their obvious, fragmentary 'return'
(they come to us from somewhere that is neither Hardy's Wessex, nor
his English), also, in the two examples above, appear to signal other
novels, albeit in the most fleeting and undecidable manner. Are these
references to Hugo and Stendhal? Can we tell, can we be certain? The

answer cannot be an unequivocal rejection of such a notion, any more than it can be an affirmative response. The momentary inscription of another language appears to install possible textual reference but, equally, remains undecidable as to its purpose, and thus haunts the structure of the text. Both references do, however, have a somewhat gothic resonance. The *misérables* are those who *haunt* the marginally located bridges, already mentioned above. *Rouge et noir*, the colouring of red and black, is 'Satanic' and is associated with Henchard throughout the novel, as Dale Kramer points out (*MC* 351 n.67).

More obviously gothic *and* textual, but no less haunting for all that, are Hardy's strategic references to Milton and Scott. The 'effigies, donkey, lanterns, band' who appear out of Mixen Lane to instigate the skimming-ton ride, disappear 'like the crew of Comus' (*MC* 282), described by Milton as a 'rout of Monsters' (cited by Kramer in his notes to the novel, *MC* 393). Of course, Milton's does not belong to the gothic genre, strictly speaking, being historically prior to the cultural moment of gothic as narrative form. Hardy's allusion does, however, reinscribe or counter-sign the text of Milton in the more general gothic mechanism of representation to which the skimmington ride may be said to belong. (However, as with all other forms of signification in Hardy, the skimmington ride is not simply gothic in its identity. It too belongs to that more general sense of the haunting of the present, understood as the traces of residual and archaic rural ritual, which allows the novelist to read the ride as part of a 'Demonic Sabbath' [*MC* 279].) The allusion to Scott is more directly, obviously gothic in its tenor:

> A pedestrian would be seen abstractedly passing along Mixen Lane; and then, in a moment, he would vanish, causing the gazer to blink like Ashton at the disappearance of Ravenswood. (*MC* 256)

As part of the author's general introduction of Mixen Lane into the novel as an unsettling topographical feature within the familiar structure of Casterbridge, the sentence is heavy with eerie potential, relating directly to that which remains unseen within any perceived structure. As if to make the disturbance more obvious however, Hardy then alludes to *The Bride of Lammermoor*, in which Ashton 'rubbed his eyes, as if he had witnessed an apparition' (Ch. XXXV; cited by Kramer in his notes, *MC* 390). The movement here is, again, double. For while Scott is not a gothic novelist *per se* he nonetheless draws heavily on the gothic in his writing; or, to put this another way, recalling the discussion of the gothic in the Introduction and the reading of Dickens from Chapter 1, the gothic is spectralized in its returns to nineteenth-century prose narrative. Hardy's indirect reference operates through the more obvious intertextuality as well as through its own second-hand citationality. In this we read the trace, the phantom-text, and what Derrida calls (to recall our own citation) the act of phantomizing the text, as the haunting disturbance within the textual mechanics of representation. The illusion of representation is made possible not by writerly acts of verisimilitude or faithful mimesis grounded on the assumption that writing refers to some anterior reality. Instead, writing is always already haunted by the spectres of other inscriptions.

There still remains though a question pertaining to the trace of the gothic, which we can only acknowledge for the moment before moving on to that of the uncanny. Why does the gothic persist in Hardy's text? This may well be undecidable and thus belong to that order of disturbance within the structure of identity which the haunting trace, its general untimeliness, puts to work within the time of the novel. In true ghostly fashion, it causes questions to proliferate. Why the revenance of the gothic and *as* gothic? Does Hardy apprehend the unsettling condition of the spectral? Does he try to calm that through the deliberate, even obvious application of the gothic as the imposition of a familiar discursive and narrative structure, whereby the effects of the spectral might be limited? Is the imposition of the gothic, like that of tragedy, an effort to make the unfamiliar familiar once again, to keep the ghosts at bay, to give haunting a familiar, even a proper identity? Do the literary allusions and gothic moments seek to impose a limit on that which haunts, that which will not be forgotten but which nags at the memory and thereby becomes an obsession? In addition, who is haunted precisely? Is it Casterbridge? Is it Henchard? Or is it Hardy himself, who, having returned home to Dorchester in 1883, to build himself a home with the help of his family – Max Gate – begins to be haunted in the very moment of being at home? What causes Hardy to dig into local archives, seeking stories of wife-sales, even as the laying of foundations for Max Gate reveals the bones of the long dead? What returns for Hardy, even as Hardy returns?[27]

## THE UNCANNY

Gothic discourse relies on the external sign – decaying ruins, mad monks, skeletons, ghosts – disturbing the subject internally. The gothic is in part a structure of representation which generates unease, discomfort and foreboding as part of what Scott Durham describes as the narrative's immanent interpretative events (18). One's self is disturbed, haunted, by that which appears outside the self. Nevertheless, as in any good gothic tale, the frightened subject, for all the unsettling sensations, frequently becomes obsessed with finding what might be behind those apparitions, those manifestations. We might suggest that this in part is the gothic tale behind the composition of *The Mayor of Casterbridge*, that Hardy's return, a return home which also marks a return to particular narrative interests, is also a story of uncanny obsession. Without pursuing this further, merely to hint at a possible way of reading events, it is important nonetheless to register the internal disturbance, the production of the uncanny precisely in the place where one should feel most like oneself – at home.

There has already been discussion in the Introduction of Freud's essay 'The "Uncanny"' and particular features pertinent to the present volume as a whole. However, it is necessary to return to this essay, albeit briefly, in the context of this reading of Hardy's novel. Already mentioned is the movement in German between *heimlich* and *unheimlich*, discussed by Mark Wigley (see above). In reading the ways in which the sensation of the uncanny is produced, Freud demonstrates how the supposedly separate terms in German are always already deconstructed by that internal slippage (*U* 195–201). What this makes apparent for Freud is that the uncanny is structural in nature, and that the uncanny, moreover, is that sense of the unfamiliar, the disturbing, which is not caused by some external phenomenon but rather arises as something indefinable from within the self. Identity is thus always already haunted from within so that haunting is inextricably connected to habitation.[28]

Other aspects of the uncanny experience are what Freud calls the 'phenomenon of the "double"', which results in a 'doubling, dividing and interchanging of the self' and 'the constant recurrence of the same thing', described by Freud as the 'repetition of the same features or character-traits or vicissitudes . . . or even the same names through several consecutive generations' (*U* 210). We have seen already how devices of doubling and repetition, which are intrinsic to the novel's structure and identity, articulate *The Mayor of Casterbridge*, and yet disturb that very form from within. Thus, arguably, the entire novel may be considered as an exploration of the uncanny, of that 'something which is secretly familiar [*heimlich-heimisch*], which has undergone repression and then returned from it' (*U* 222).

In one sense, Hardy's own return to Dorchester, his research of decades-old newspapers, his discovery of Roman burial remains in the land where he was to build Max Gate, is highly suggestive, were we to seek a correlation between the author's desire for home after a serious illness and the subsequent uncanny and haunted persistence manifesting itself in the novel. There is a persuasive psycho-biographical reading hovering here. However, regardless of what may have turned Hardy's attention to these issues, what is apparent in *The Mayor of Casterbridge*, beyond any reading of Henchard as a psychological character study, beyond any character-orientated reading, indeed, beyond a reading of the story or the novelist's intertextual indebtedness, is the uncanny sense that the novel is haunted. Such an impression must, however, remain exactly that, an impression which is uncanny precisely because it cannot be either validated or repudiated.

At more immediate and local levels, however, there are numerous instances of the experience of the uncanny in the novel. Henchard feels haunted by Newson, as we know already. Moreover, the reader is told repeatedly that he is a superstitious man. Henchard is first revealed as 'superstitious' through his decision to visit Conjuror Fall (*MC* 185). Though this moment is not in itself uncanny (though arguably Henchard's trip to Fall is meant to induce an uncanny sensation in the reader), the next instance of Henchard's superstitiousness is, and deliberately so. Henchard is ruminating on his misfortune over the reckless crop selling:

> The movements of his mind seemed to tend to the thought that some power was working within him.
> 'I wonder,' he asked himself with eerie misgiving: 'I wonder if it can be that somebody has been roasting a waxen image of me, or stirring an unholy brew to confound me! I don't believe in such power; and yet – what if they should ha' been doing it!' ... These isolated hours of superstition came to Henchard in time of moody depression ... (*MC* 190–1)

While we may read the passage as remarking the residue of a superstition imbued with the discourse of folkloric mythology, the passage is notable nonetheless for its sense of the uncanny, of that internal power and the sensation of 'eerie misgiving'. Later, following the skimmington ride, we are told that 'the sense of the supernatural was strong in this unhappy man' (*MC* 297). In this assessment of Henchard's response to the effigy there is the sense that Hardy may be read as explaining away the uncanny feeling through recourse to the idea of superstition, even as Henchard experiences it. Yet uncannily, perhaps, that earlier speculation concerning the waxen image may also be read as one more example of the 'persistence of the unforeseen', while the effigy marks a form of return of Henchard's fear even as it physically returns via the river.

Freud acknowledges that the novelist, in creating uncanny effects in a narrative world otherwise predicated on 'common reality' through the use of events which 'never or rarely happen in fact', appeals to the 'superstitiousness' which we have allegedly left behind (*U* 227). In a novel concerned so much with residual forms of haunting however, the very trope of superstition as archaic pre-modern residue is readable as the uncanny manifestation of the haunting trace. Hardy's narrative is constructed so as to reveal Henchard as haunted by superstition, while playing on the possible residue of superstition in the reader, and yet maintaining a distance from such irrational sensations by doubting whether 'anything should be called curious in concatenations of phenomena' (*MC* 204).

There are, however, clearly uncanny moments for Henchard, which have little or nothing to do with superstition. Towards the end of his life Henchard is described thus:

He rose to his feet, and stood like a dark ruin, obscured by 'the shade from his own soul upthrown'. (*MC* 326)

Perhaps one of the most complex and overdetermined of sentences in the novel, this delineation of Henchard addresses both his own being haunted, suffering from the disturbance of the uncanny, and the uncanny haunting to which *The Mayor* is prone. The ghostly citation with which the sentence concludes traces a double movement at least. It comes from Shelley's *Revolt of Islam*, as does the phrase 'dark ruin', though Hardy chooses not to acknowledge this through quotation marks. While reading a citation, and one which in its signifying operation refers us to those other ghostly citations, we are impressed by the figure, not merely of the soul, but of the 'shade' also. Conventionally, the reading of that 'shade' should imply a shadow. However, there is also at work in this image the more archaic sense of 'shade', meaning 'ghost' or 'spectre'. The phrase 'dark ruin' is itself a ruin, a fragment, an improper citation which haunts the sentence and which does service as a simile for Henchard, even as it echoes beyond the image of Henchard, or, indeed, any animate creature, to hint at the Ring and other architectural sites and remnants out of which Casterbridge is composed, and by which it is haunted.

Not long prior to this moment, at which the return of Newson prompts Henchard's sense of being haunted once again, Henchard returns to the place from where the novel begins (*MC* 318–19). In this instance of reciprocal return – Henchard's return is counter-signed by the return of place – Susan's own words return to Henchard, and, uncannily, to the reader also: for her words are reported directly from her own initial utterance, while they are also adrift from her, from the grave as it were, as a disembodied voice, the voice of the other, haunting Henchard's memory (*MC* 319). The sense of the uncanny is quite startling here, for even as we read the words on the page, so we hear and see those words imprinted in the memory, arriving from some other place, and yet from within at the same time. In this, Susan's voice is doubly haunting, for in its movement of return and address which shockingly – uncannily – places the reader in the place of Henchard as addressee, it carries in it the anticipation of Henchard's will, which is reprinted onto the page, and there for every successive generation of reader (*MC* 333).[29] J. Hillis Miller has provided an eloquent reading of the will as a 'terrifying series of negative performances, spoken from the grave',[30] and as a 'kind of ghostly negative that . . . has positive existence' (*Narrative* 112). The will, directly before us, comes back as a fragment of Henchard's voice which, despite its commands to forget him, haunts us all the more.

'That Elizabeth-Jane Farfrae be not told of my death, or made to grieve on account of me.
'& that I be not bury'd in consecrated ground.
'& that no sexton be asked to toll the bell.
'& that nobody is wished to see my dead body.
'& that no mourners walk behind me at my funeral.
'& that no flours be planted on my grave.
'& that no man remember me.
'To this do I put my name.'

'Michael Henchard'

What this act of narration from beyond the grave suggests to Miller, quite correctly in my view, is the ghostly condition of all narrative: 'all narration is a murmur from beyond the grave . . . killing it as living speech and resurrecting it at the same time as ghostly, remembered speech' (*Narrative* 112). Henchard's address provides exemplary and undeniable proof of, on the one hand, the fact of his death and, on the other, the return of his death, the paradoxical iterability of his finitude which also and at the same time turns us back to, and returns to us, as other than itself, the text of *The Mayor of Casterbridge* awaiting the act of reading, while signalling in this movement and spacing (that spacing which is the effect of haunting) that, in the words of Geoffrey Bennington, 'reading has no end, but is always to-come as work of the other' (*JD* 56). It is through this that the sense of the uncanny is produced, the spectre glimpsed. Through this redoubling, displacing and regenerative rhythm the ghost survives, and we as readers are uncannily transformed, destined to be the addressees, the recipients of the will.[31] Miller's reading of this powerful document offers a convincing account of the spectral in the text, and I can only cite him here, allowing his text to haunt my own:

> The citation of these odd performative locutions by the narrator causes exactly the opposite of their intention to occur. Henchard attempts to insure the nonperformance of all those ritual markings . . . This intention is contradicted anew every time Henchard's will is read . . . To read or to quote '& that no man remember me' is to remember what one is commanded to forget . . . The effort of erasure . . . infallibly turns to an iteration. It becomes a monumental perpetuation beyond or over death . . . like a ghost at midday. The 'not' maintains what is obliterated as the verbal phantasm of itself. (*Narrative* 111)

As Miller goes on to argue, the copy, printed in each edition of the novel with its reiterated signature, is the simulacrum of the letter, the ghostly double. Henchard returns, never as himself, but in writing, effectively indicating that all writing is a form of haunting. To this I would only add that there is one other, or rather several other inscriptions of spectral reiteration in the will, and that is that – those – '& that', by which the haunting rhythm of return, reiteration and displacement are all economically performed. In being the same and not the same each reiteration re-enforces as it spaces, economically signalling non-identity, alterity, difference.

There is one other instance of the uncanny to which we should attend relating to Henchard, which troubles him while also resonating beyond the ex-Mayor. This connects us to the relationship between the uncanny and the home, and to the question of economics. As if to make his triumph all the more complete – and all the more galling to Henchard – albeit inadvertently, Farfrae purchases Henchard's home and all the familiar pieces of furniture within that, as told by Jopp:

> 'He and she are gone into their new house to-day,' said Jo.
> 'Oh,' said Henchard absently. 'Which house is that?'
> 'Your old one.'
> 'Gone into my house?' And starting up Henchard added '*My* house of all the others in the town!'
> [ . . .]
> Farfrae, who had already taken the yards and stores, had acquired possession of the house . . . this act of taking up residence within those roomy chambers galled Henchard indescribably.
> Jopp continued: 'And you heard of that fellow who bought all the best furniture at your sale? He was bidding for no other than Farfrae all the while. It has never been moved out of the house, as he'd already got the lease.'
> 'My furniture too! Surely he'll buy my body and soul likewise.'
> 'There's no saying he won't if you be willing to sell.' And having planted these wounds in the heart of his once imperious master Jopp went on his way . . .
> [ . . .]
> The low-land grew blacker, and the sky a deeper grey. (*MC* 225)

Moving towards its apparently ominous conclusion, where even the landscape is haunted by a possible immanence of uncanny meaning, the passage escalates in its consideration of economics and the house. The metaphor of planting used to describe Jopp's malicious intent clearly operates in different directions. Obviously, it draws on an agricultural discourse which runs throughout the text, from the seed in the furmity, to the bread baked of 'growed wheat', to Farfrae's rejuvenation of that seed, and to the principal economic practice of Casterbridge itself by which Henchard falls. Yet, there is also the sense of uncanny alchemical practice in that metaphor also, belonging to the folkloric discourse of witchcraft, also pervasive in the text, and read convincingly by Joe Fisher (115–35).

However, the uncanny is already installed in this passage. It is not simply a question of Henchard's superstitious sense that his soul can be bought, for if it were this could easily be written off simply as one more expression of superstition. The uncanny haunts the passage in that moment when we are told of Farfrae's *possession*. The word is uncannily haunted within itself, concerning equally questions of economics, property, the law, control, and, as the *OED* informs us, 'the action of a spirit or demon possessing a person etc.; the fact or state of being so possessed'. Particularly interesting is the etymological precision of the term. The Latin, from which the Middle English word descends, defines possession according to land rights and the issue of occupancy, as distinct from mere ownership. Thus, possession defines whoever controls the house, the home. Clearly, from the passage above, Henchard regards the house as still his, so the question of possession is one of disturbance within the home. Henchard, we might say, loses possession through not having been enough in possession of himself. Yet, possessed as he is by the idea of Farfrae's possession, he does not understand that he is being erased slowly, transformed by economic transaction into one more figure who haunts Casterbridge, becoming part of its spectral past. This occurs as surely the fact of his name's erasure: 'A smear of decisive lead-coloured paint had been laid on to obliterate Henchard's name [on the barn], though its letters dimly loomed through like ships in the fog. Over these, in fresh white, spread the name of Farfrae' (*MC* 221). The ghostly name of Henchard returns ahead of his death and yet as a sign of his already being dead (for it is transmissible beyond death, endlessly iterable, as we know from Derrida, Miller, Bennington and others) and, in this, anticipates the moment of spectral revenance which haunts the end of the novel through Henchard's will. In this moment of writing's erasure and partial return, the ghost of Henchard returns from the future, *as the future* in which *The Mayor of Casterbridge* will be read. That image of the 'ships in the fog' is merely one more allusive touch of the gothic, simultaneously a moment of displacement *and* an attempted familiarization of the narrative to counter the uncanny echo, even as it is promised. Yet, as we see immediately, Henchard haunts Farfrae, although both men may believe that matters are the other way around.

However, we must return to the question of the house and economics (even if this necessitates a detour, which will become a return eventually), particularly as these are caught up in, possessed by, the matter of possession. The uncanny is, as is now clear, a matter of that which is repressed and thus returns from *within* the familiar, within the family even, and certainly the house or home. At the same time, upon its return and as a condition of the ghostly movement, the uncanny 'exposes the covert operations of the house', as Mark Wigley reminds us (*AD* 109). 'For this reason', Wigley suggests, the uncanny's 'constitutional violation of the ostensible order of the house is itself repressed, domesticated by the very violence it makes possible' (*AD* 109). This act of 'violence' within the familiar, within the space of the domestic as the uncanny instance of haunting is not alien to the home, but is intimately bound up with the 'law of the *oikos*', as Derrida makes plain.[32] As if haunted himself, and as if to re-mark in a spectral fashion the internal displacement effected by haunting, Derrida makes similar remarks elsewhere, insisting on the relationship between spectrality and economy. In 'Living On • Border Lines', Derrida explores, in telegraphic fashion, the persistence of haunting (in the discussion of Blanchot) as/in the (dis)place(ment) of the home through 'economy, the law of the *oikos* (house, room, tomb, crypt), the law of reserves, reserving, savings, saving: inversion, reversion, revolution of values . . . in the law of the *oikos* (*Heimlichkeit/Unheimlichkeit*)'.[33] Finally, there is a more recent remark, made in a commentary on Freud's reading of Jensen's *Gradiva*. Writing of the spectral, and of revenance as displacement within and spacing of the familiar, Derrida comments that a 'phantom can be sensitive to idiom . . . One does not address it in just any language. It is a law of economy, again, a law of the *oikos*, of the transaction of signs and values, but also of some familial domesticity: haunting implies places, a habitation and always a haunted house' (*AF* 86).

In order to return to Henchard and the novel, we would do well to recall at this moment that 'economy', from the Greek *oikos* + *nemein*, means control of the house. The matter of a certain violence is not simply a question of transaction in the social world, beyond the familiar and domestic, as though the house were free of the economic. It is, we understand, intrinsic to the structure of the home from the first. Henchard's appalled response to Farfrae's *possession* unveils this internal necessity, although Henchard himself is never aware of the intimate violence. The possession of what Henchard considers his is uncanny precisely because it unmasks through the act of economic possession and subsequent occupancy the very condition, the violence, which yokes familiarity and domesticity to the control articulated through the economic act, which is suppressed in the name of home and familiarity, of the house and the family, and yet *which belongs to the house*. However, this is in part merely one more instance of uncanny inverse doubling and return, wherein the spectre of the economic returns with force. It is an exemplary moment of economic violence, and also a resurfacing of an earlier act of economic violence in which Henchard had himself indulged – the wife-sale at Weydon Priors fair.

Beginning with this scene, Hardy has been read as creating a narrative precedent from an 'unnatural' act, out of which develop, through a structure of cause and effect, all subsequent actions in the novel, as well as the fate of Henchard. The violence of the sale is seen as generative and symbolic, the sale itself a violent originary event. Bruce Johnson, for example, suggests that the scene 'stands as a symbolic moment in Henchard's life', signalling 'the triumph of social and commercial signification over the more primitive . . . sources of Henchard's being' which plunge Henchard 'into a commercial and social world' (128). Joe Fisher reads in the fair and the wife-sale a 'remarkably transhistorical gesture', as well a volatile transaction between the discourses of witchcraft and residual medieval rural practice on the one hand, and, on the other, the socio-economic structures which inform the modern, civilized world of Casterbridge (119). Yet neither of these readings will quite do. Neither recognizes – and in this they are reiterating Henchard's own misrecognition – to what extent the violence of the wife-sale is, in being an economic transaction, the most typically domestic, familial and familiar expression of the 'law of the *oikos*, of the transaction of signs and values, but also of some familial domesticity', albeit expressed as the inverse of all that is read as familiar in the idea of the house or home, the idea of the family. Henchard's act is horrendously uncanny, *unheimlich*, because he is expelling the family in the name of economics. His act figures a shocking, yet wholly familiar instance of the repressed at work. Through the 'haggish' aspect of the furmity dealer and the assumption of a 'lurid' colouring in her tent (*MC* 8. 14; see n. 36), the text assumes the gothic and uncanny as its obvious identity. If we comprehend the wife-sale in this context, we come to understand that it is uncanny *and* horrendous, not because it is aberrant, deviant, but because it belongs so undeniably to the economic circuitry which returns everywhere in *The Mayor of Casterbridge*.

What is truly uncanny however, is the force with which the return of the repressed erupts through the familiar and familial, homely form of the family itself as an economic sign, subject to the violence of that law. If Henchard is thereafter troubled uncannily, this is only because he has come the closest to revealing the mechanics of reproduction, which are hidden by the normative concepts of 'home' and 'family'. Moreover, Henchard's divesting himself of one aspect of the homely transforms him into an unhomely figure; doomed to fail repeatedly in the reconstitution of family and home, he is equally repeatedly turned out of the home, making himself homeless. In this he is uncanny to himself, though he does not recognize this, inasmuch as he is behaving in a manner wholly typical of humans or, rather, the condition of being in relation to the familiar, for, according to Martin Heidegger 'man [*sic*] departs from his customary, familiar limits . . . he is the violent one, who, tending toward the strange in the sense of the overpowering, surpasses the limit of the familiar . . . he is cast out of every relation to the familiar'.[34] Henchard does not begin or originate what occurs to him throughout the rest of the novel. He merely enters into the violence and strangeness of Being, estranging itself from itself and within itself.

Henchard is not the only one to be troubled uncannily, however. While Henchard may walk 'restlessly, as if some haunting shade . . . hovered round him and troubled his glance' (*MC* 298), Elizabeth-Jane encounters such moments as well: '[t]hen something happened to occur which his step-daughter fancied must really be a hallucination of hers' (*MC* 168). At another moment, Lucetta 'stood transfixed. Her own words greeted her, in Henchard's voice, like spirits from the grave' (*MC* 247). Lucetta's words disturb her because they come back in a particularly haunting fashion, as both her own and not her own. The more disturbing for Lucetta is the fact that her words return to her in her own house as if in ghostly confirmation of Freud, or, to put this another way, as if the ghost of Freud's text were to arrive from the future so as to disrupt the familiar presence of a world understood to be built on the firm foundations of the past, of tradition, of continuity. For, as Mark Wigley suggests in his discussion of Freud, the 'uncanny is literally a "not-being-at-home," an alienation from the house experienced within it' (*AD* 110). In this moment, yet another manifestation of doubling, this time through the recurrence of language via another, Hardy is keen that we should not miss the uncanny oscillation. Lucetta is also disturbed on another occasion: ' . . . a vague uneasiness float[ed] over her joy at seeing him quite at home here' (*MC* 217). This particular instance of the uncanny brings home to us, yet again, how the uncanny (*das unheimlich*) is installed within the homely or familiar (*heimlich-heimische*). Lucetta's strange experience is wholly consonant with Heidegger's assessment of the *unheimlich*, as 'that which casts us out of the "homely" i.e. the customary, familiar, secure' (150).

Hardy does not limit, however, the expression of the uncanny to the experience of particular characters as their identity is disturbed in places where they feel themselves at home. The familiarity of Casterbridge so carefully constructed by Hardy for the reader is itself disturbed. Not only does this happen with the sudden introduction of Mixen Lane. There are also occasions when the customary comfort and familiarity of the town find themselves disturbed at the margins of the world of Casterbridge. Those who appear at a given signal, a whistle, to place bridges across the brook are described thus: 'A shape thereupon made its appearance on the other side bearing the bridge on end against the sky' (*MC* 255). This uncanny area beyond the knowable limits of Casterbridge itself can cause the uncanny sensation, merely through atmospheric conditions: 'Beyond the stream was the open moor, from which a clammy breeze smote upon their faces as they advanced' (*MC* 258). In each case, the familiarity of the world, signalled by its boundaries, is transformed, made strange in the act of representing the world, so that something almost ineffable emerges through the representation itself as a counter-signature to the natural in that representation.

There is one final figure of the uncanny yet to be mentioned. This involves neither a character nor a scene but, instead, a proper name: Farfrae. Of the man, we have already commented. To recap: he appears twice, seemingly as an apparition to Elizabeth-Jane and Lucetta. His face doubles the features of Henchard's dead brother, uncannily enough. Furthermore, he brings with him the strange ability to bring wheat back to life, acknowledged only in the vaguest terms as 'science', and all the more strange for being left undefined. Farfrae is, we might say, to use an idiomatic cliché, a 'canny Scot', a figure of the foreign who arrives with knowledge, which, kept to himself, interrupts Casterbridge and figures the introduction of the strange into the self-same. However, it is Donald Farfrae's surname which is of particular interest.[35] More than just a family name or surname, more than merely a proper name or signature – though it is, admittedly, all these things – *Farfrae* signs uncannily, and as a form of excessive, ghostly counter-signature within and yet supplementing the family name. English and yet not English, a compound name composed of two words (*far-frae*), the name speaks, as soon as it is named, as soon as it arrives, of spacing, of travel, of arrival from some other place. Partly the spelling out of dialect, while naming also dislocation and relocation, strangeness itself (he is defined as a 'stranger' [*MC* 52]), the proper name improperly signs its foreignness and unfamiliarity in the familiar space of Casterbridge as that which signals the stranger as being not only not at home, but also *far frae (from) home* or, to use his own dialect, which appears in his sentimental ballad, 'hame' (*MC* 52). Indeed, we might suggest, albeit tentatively, that *farfrae* inscribes a possible translation of *unheimlich*, even as it retains its own uncanny quality within English.

We might note more about this moment, in relation to Farfrae's name and its resonance. It is ironic, to say the least, that this strange figure first makes an impression on the town's inhabitants by singing a song about home. Indeed, so affecting, not to say unsettling, is his song that he is requested to repeat it at the moment its effect is partially erased by the snapping of a pipe stem (*MC* 52), thereby indicating the possibility of reiteration which haunts the text in so many other places. However, we must simply acknowledge that it is Farfrae's proper name, his surname or family name, which comes to be reiterated throughout the text. Signed, re-signed, and con-signed to the novel, *Farfrae* inscribes the uncanny, the unhomely, within the familiar, where the spectral unfamiliarity is that which haunts the family name. Oscillating as more than that name, while taking place within the name, the surname of *Farfrae* names that which leaves its traces everywhere in *The Mayor of Casterbridge*, and yet which is never recognized as such – the uncanny trace of the spectral.

## CONCLUSION

If by now, the reader has developed a sense of *déjà vu*, in either dictionary sense of 'an illusory feeling of having previously experienced a present situation' or 'tedious familiarity', this is deliberate (I assure you) ('*DV*' 4). The constant recourse to structural reiteration which haunts this essay is determined by *The Mayor of Casterbridge* where, as this reading has sought to demonstrate, the 'illusory feeling', similar in nature perhaps to that of the 'uncanny', occupies the same space (even as it spaces the same places in the novel) as the sense of 'tedious familiarity'. We read so many instances in *The Mayor* which remind us of so many others, and our having experienced them before – even as they appear in the guise of the present situation – that we may well read the text with a growing sense of that tedious familiarity. However, perhaps this is the point, structurally at least. For, if in the act of reading we become familiar, does something not always arrive – return – within the familiar as the unfamiliar, precisely in order that the sensation of *déjà vu* arises as a symptom of reading concomitant with those discernible instances of the uncanny? If the reiterative rhythms are imposed upon us without our awareness, so that we are at home with repetition, so that the nature of our familiarity blinds us to the constant chains of non-synonymous displacements and replacements, do not the spectral elements efface themselves in those moments when they are most insistent, becoming all the more spectral in the process?

There is still the question of structure haunting us here. The name of Farfrae is merely one structure which displays its own internal fracturing in a fairly straightforward manner. It is not unique, however, the question being one of degree rather than kind. For to come back to earlier comments, to return to the question of return: what cannot be stressed too often is the proposition that, whether we are speaking of the proper name, the matter of architecture or archaeology, the question of textual traces or cultural events, the office of the mayor in relation to the social order, or a communal identity based on the supposed stasis of civic office,[36] each figure repeats every other.

Think for one moment of the resounding bells heard by Susan and Elizabeth-Jane on entering the town as one exemplary moment in the novel:

> They came to a grizzled church, whose massive square tower rose unbroken into the darkening sky ... From this tower the clock struck eight, and thereupon a bell began to toll with a peremptory clang. The curfew was still rung in Casterbridge, ...
>
> Other clocks struck eight from time to time – one gloomily from the gaol, another from the gable of an alms-house ... a row of tall varnished case-clocks ... joined in one after another ... then chimes were heard stammering out ... so that chronologists of the advanced school were appreciably on their way to the next hour before the whole business of the old one was satisfactorily wound up. (*MC* 31)

Each sound reiterates every other in this, even though time is 'out of joint', so to speak. The passage in its movement from clock to clock, from chime to chime, performs the gradual and erratic sounding of the hour as the narrative moves. The hour is displaced from and within itself, even as each clock re-sounds the temporal punctuation of every other, and spaces the very idea of time. This one scene uncannily suggests the structure of the novel itself, where every form of return or reduplication signifies nothing so much as every other similar form. The clocks set the tone, if you will. Moreover, in this temporal disjointing the performance of which hints that there is no time like the present, there is no single present moment not always already divided, the spectral structure making itself felt in that residual trace of another time sounding within the present, that of the medieval curfew bell. Furthermore, the chimes in this scene anticipate and return in the moment, just prior to the election of Farfrae as Mayor, when the clocks strike half-past eight, and the streets are 'curiously silent' (*MC* 151).

The resounding of the time out of time with itself figures aurally both spacing and strata. The clocks trace the spatial and temporal movements which haunt the town of Casterbridge. The resonance is common and worked out in a particularly rich way in the opening of Chapter Eleven, when Hardy describes Casterbridge:

> Casterbridge announced old Rome in every street, alley and precinct . . . It was impossible to dig more than a foot or two deep about the town fields and gardens without coming upon some tall soldier or other . . .
>
> Imaginative inhabitants who would have felt an unpleasantness at the discovery of a comparatively modern skeleton in their gardens, were quite unmoved by these hoary shapes . . . (*MC* 70)

In the same chapter, the Roman amphitheatre, the Ring, is discussed. In particular, the commentary centres on the history of recurrence associated with the ruin:

> Apart from the sanguinary nature of the games originally played therein, such incidents attached to its past as these; that for scores of years the town gallows had stood at one corner; that in 1705 a woman who had murdered her husband was half strangled and then burnt there . . . In addition to these old tragedies pugilistic encounters almost to the death had come off down to recent dates in that secluded arena . . . though close to the turnpike-road crimes might be perpetrated there unseen at mid-day. (*MC* 71)

What is merely suggested in the first passage by the mention of architectural and archaeological detail is made clearer in the second. The past persists, though never as the past or as a presence, setting the tone through its ghostly persistence in and disturbance of the present. The remains of architectural detail are articulated – 'announced' – through the present structure of the town, so that the present is represented as disturbed by such traces; the land itself is built upon the remains and return of the past. In the case of the Ring, it is not a question of architectural structure or archaeological remainder. Rather, the persistence is of a particularly spectral kind. Events of a similar nature recur within the same space so that, as Hardy gradually dematerializes the return of the past – moving from overt structure, to what is hidden or sedimented, and then to forms of recurrence which are altogether more haunting – he traces a phantomatic temporal structure of revenance and insistence, of iteration, which is all the more disturbing and uncanny for the return of violence to the same location as an effective figure of spectral dislocation.

What haunts here, whether one is speaking of the sound of the bells, the description of the town, or the history of the Ring, is the ineluctable recurrence of what Derrida has termed a 'spectral motif' (*AF* 84). The spectral motif is spectral precisely because it disturbs any sense of presence or the present, any sense of undifferentiated moment or identity. It announces difference and iteration. It is therefore structural, a question of the structure, to repeat myself once more. In this, the novel resembles Derrida's description of the archive, the structure of which he suggests is spectral: 'It is spectral *a priori*; neither present nor absent, "in the flesh," neither visible nor invisible, a trace always referring to another . . .' (*AF* 84). Furthermore, there can be no archive, Derrida insists, '*without a technique of repetition*' (*AF* 11). Hardy capitalizes on repetition, on the return which he accumulates as a form of storage, where the numerous traces, citations, references, allusions are gathered. In being so formed, it traces a desire to remember perhaps, to maintain an archival memory in the face of effacement, of obliteration. It is perhaps this paradox which so haunts the novel, and which in turn haunts the reader, in the will of Michael Henchard, and on every page.

That the novel may be read as having the power to create uncanny feelings in its readers is one sign of its being haunted. That every subsequent generation of readers is enjoined to forget Michael Henchard by his will and yet receive his communication so unforgettably is another sign. The haunting condition is that effect by which language effaces itself even as what Maurice Merleau-Ponty calls its 'expression' remains.[37] If we do not read these remains in their disseminating signification of one another, we run the risk of misunderstanding to what extent this is a phantom-text, a haunted and haunting space. If we see each figure or character as essentially separate or separable from the circuitry of the text, we misrecognize the novel's attempt at opening itself to ghostly communication.

The constant pulsation of doubling, reiteration and return, of fleeting moments of citation, of ontological confusion through the interanimation of heterogeneous discourses, all serve to phantomize the text. Beginning to read such effects of ghostly troping, we may perhaps read the text of Hardy not simply as a text haunted by the residual traces of the past, but as one caught between the nineteenth and twentieth centuries, perhaps between realism and modernism, if this formulation can be read as suggesting an identity which acknowledges difference rather than seeking unity. We may even read *The Mayor of Casterbridge* as a text composed of the traces of spectres-to-come, a text haunted by the future. The phantomatic trace, sign of a sign without prior origin and without presence as such, takes place in Hardy's text. In doing so it undertakes the displacement of the familiar home of the novel in the nineteenth century, even as it makes possible a recognition of haunting as a condition of all narrative.

# Afterword: Prosopopoeia or, Witnessing

Perhaps, in conclusion, it is necessary to shift our ground, as does Hamlet when faced with the invisible ubiquity of the ghost. Nowhere as such, and yet everywhere; and yet everywhere different. Attuning ourselves to the possibility of spectral analysis, forcing ourselves to confront the *nothing-and-yet-not-nothing* and the *neither-nowhere-nor-not-nowhere* that nonetheless leaves a trace in passing and which has such a material effect – and what, after all, is ideology for example except the experience of this invisible nothing that we call beliefs, values, ideas? – we may perhaps discern a trembling of sorts. Whether we speak of 'the gothic', citation, ideology, or modalities of allusion and representation, if we seek to address ghosts, haunting, spectrality and the textual apparitions to which this book has sought to draw its readers' attention, then we need to acknowledge that we are responding to what has already come and gone – and which has returned again. As we intimated at the conclusion of the Introduction, it is thus a matter of reading as response, response as responsibility, and responsibility as witnessing. The experience of the spectral is, in being both responsive and responsible, the experience of being touched through reading by that which is other, that which is prosopopoeic: 'a voice or a face of the absent', as J. Hillis Miller has it, 'the inanimate, or the dead'.[1] Seeking to read the spectral is thus an effort to bear witness to this voice or face, and this witnessing is, moreover, not the presentation of proof on the part of the witness. As Derrida has commented recently, '[w]hoever bears witness does not bring a proof; he is someone whose experience, in principle singular and irreplaceable . . . comes to attest, precisely, that some "thing" has been present to him'. Expounding implicitly on the virtual, spectral condition of witnessing, Derrida continues: '[t]his "thing" is no longer present to him, of course, in the mode of perception at the moment when the attestation happens; but it is present to him, if he alleges this presence, as *re-presented* in the present in memory'.[2]

Derrida's remark, ever attentive to the virtual trace of the spectral by marking off with great caution the question of the non-present 'presence' of that which returns 'in memory' through the quotation marks which surround the 'thing', complicates our comprehension of witnessing, of reception and response. The experience of witnessing assumes an uncanny dimension through its temporal disruption and the revenance which is here invoked. In the present context, we can expand on this definition of witnessing to remark that what is being described is the condition of reading and of the text: That which we witness in any text, through any act of reading, is no longer present except as it is *re-presented*. Yet this 'representation' cannot be named this, properly speaking, for there is an indirection in the very idea of revenance which forestalls the desire for mimetic, anthropomorphic or logocentric relapse.

As the question of witnessing implies, there is an ethical dimension to the matter of reading the spectral, to responding to the revenance of the absent, the other. To paraphrase Hillis Miller, the dead continue to live on, to survive beyond life, in the afterlife that we call reading. And reading, as Miller informs us, 'is one major form of the responsibility the living have to the dead' (74–5). We see this in *Hamlet*, of course, in Hamlet's so-called vacillation in his efforts to read his father's ghost and the ethical dimensions of that ghostly return. In these last pages let us turn, undoubtedly too hastily, to three writers who address in different ways the matter of return and witnessing: Virginia Woolf, W. B. Yeats and Paul Celan.

Virginia Woolf's 'A Haunted House' is a brief tale, less than two pages in length.[3] An unnamed, unidentified, and, arguably, invisible narrator speaks to an equally unidentified, and unidentifiable, companion. The figure being addressed is indicated, disconcertingly, only through the use of the second-person pronoun, so that the number or location indicated by 'you' is undecidable. Thus, even the act of address is haunting; it disturbs comfortable, domesticated assumptions about identity and the conventions of narrators. The story concerns a 'ghostly couple', referred to thus twice, or, separately, as 'he' and 'she'. Once more, however, there are no names. The narrator speaks of the constant movement of this invisible couple throughout a non-specific house, sketched in only punctuated details such as doors, both open and in the process of 'shutting', window-panes, a drawing-room. The house is thus figured in part as so many thresholds. There is a certain, vague contextualization for the house. We are informed of the sound of 'the threshing machine . . . from the farm', the song of a wood pigeon, grass, stars in 'the Southern sky', trees, wind, moonbeams, the reflection of apples and roses, the 'shadow of a thrush'.

What is especially interesting about Woolf's representation of the house and its environs, composed equally of sound and images, is that it is a representation in fragments, of which there is more to be said. The conventions of narrative realism and its reliance on mimetic representation are seen to be involved in a process of decomposition, so that the very 'presence of form', if we can put it like this, appears to be shimmering, losing solidity, perhaps even disappearing. Reflections and projections, that is to say immaterial, yet manifest traces – a shadow, a sound, a reflection – trace a reality without either pretending to enact a totalizable construction or to suggest an architectural presence. Thus the house never quite coheres, its structure as an object capable of representation or as a 'system' or 'mechanism of representation' (*AD* 163) itself called into question through the narrative process itself. There is not simply an absence of coherence in 'A Haunted House'. Rather, the rhythms of the narrative, of its syntax and rhetoric, disable the structure of coherence and completion from within the structure itself. What we read through the haunting motion is a spacing process which spaces architecture within itself, displacing its unity and solidity, and yet, paradoxically, being intrinsic to the very idea of architecture, as that which makes available the domestic space as the illusion of coherent form. How does Woolf achieve this?

The story, moving between past and present tense, and between the unlocatable voices of, for want of better words, narrator and characters, oscillates with the ghostly motion of, and within, the narrative. If we speculate on the ghostly couple as the traces of the house's previous inhabitants, as the conventions of ghost stories dictate,[4] it is possible to imagine the disembodied voices through which the story is transmitted as yet more haunting figures of the house. They are the ghosts, if you will, of the house's future. Indeed, in that we read these traces, the voices are already those of phantoms returning from some indefinable anterior future moment at which the story has not yet arrived, and yet by which it is already marked. To an extent, then, the voices who narrate, who we imagine we hear, are always already spectral in that, while they are there, there is no presence behind the voice; indeed, the voice is not even a voice, strictly speaking, but the trace of a voice. It does not belong to someone. It is, instead, a fragment of the text, by which the text is formed, by which the narrative comes to be articulated, out of the reading of which house, narrative and character come to be formed, and through which invisible, yet material medium, they return and are doubled. The doubling is, according to Elizabeth Bronfen

in her reading of Freud, 'by definition also a figure for a split or gap . . .
The double, simultaneously den[ies] and affirm[s] mortality'.[5] Such
simultaneity is worked out between the invisible couples, between the
ghostly couple and the couple who figurally and yet invisibly trace the
text as narrator and listener, into which latter place we, as readers,
become uncannily translated. Thus in effect, the story implies our own
deaths and the fact that the memory of each and every reader will
come to be doubled in haunting fashion.

Such disruptive, iterable and doubling echolalia is signalled in the
narrative shift from past to present tense, a present tense without presence which, in its motion into a disembodied and incorporeal present
tense without the promise of closure conventionally produced by voices
within narrative, suggests uncannily and subversively a continuing temporal disturbance. This is a 'voice' which has always already returned,
and has done so, will have done so, from countless futures (this is the
spectral promise of reading), as a haunting figure which is disruptive
of the frames and stable concepts by which narrative operates. Ghosts
return, the narrative is told. But when and where? There is no 'once
upon a time' for Woolf's tale, for all time, and any normative conceptualization of temporality is disrupted in the telling of the tale and in
its play with the temporal. Straightforward narrative temporality is haunted
from within itself by anachronic displacement, opening narrative stability to its own undecidability. There is in operation a constant drift,
a ghosting caught in Woolf's phrase: '"Safe, safe, safe", the pulse of
the house beat softly' and '"Safe, safe, safe", the pulse of the house
beat gladly'. This pulse, doubled, splitting and simultaneously recon-
stituting, is itself split and doubled between the first and second phrases.
We read a structural interruption, refigured not only between phrases
but between the iteration of every safe, as the figure, in its articulation, is displaced from itself and in itself in its echoes. There is, we
read, no originary figure, only the haunting seriality of disinterred echoes.
And when this phrase is translated from itself into its third incarnation
– '"Safe, safe, safe", the heart of the house beats proudly' – we come
to recognize the displacement within place, haunting as the structural
constituent of architectural form and also, in uncanny doubling fashion,
as the spiritual 'heart' and its rhythm. Though not a heart at all but
rather this pulse, a somewhat uncanny metaphor, spacing itself from
within itself and denying the absolute stasis or identity of the architectural site. The mark of reiteration announces the ghostly 'because
iterability makes of the thing or text a ghost, something that begins by

returning'.[6] And because it can only begin by returning, the effect of haunting in its revenance is revealed as a 'remainder without origin' (Kronick 171).

The narrative moves, then, only through a spacing of figures: figures of speech, figures of the imagination, phantasmatic figures. These are the uncanny pulses if you will, the rhythms and cadences which discompose the reader as they compose both the story and the house identified by the story's title, 'A Haunted House'. What we read, to insist on this point, is that there is no house without haunting. The house does not come to be haunted. Instead, haunting is the condition out of which the sense of the house manifests itself: 'Whatever hour you woke there was a door shutting. From room to room they went, hand in hand, lifting here, opening there, making sure – a ghostly couple.' Figurally, there is constant discontinuous and fragmentary motion here, indicated through the relation of gerund to clause. Each gerund – *shutting, lifting, moving, making* – signals process rather than stasis, the lines composing themselves through a formal reiteration performative of the story's overall material effect; each gerund, arguably, signifies implicitly in an always present tense at odds with the past tense by which the sentences appear to operate normatively. The ghostly couple can be read, therefore, as installing into the text a doubling – of which they themselves are already a double figure – which is itself redoubled in the formal and temporal aspects of the narrative.

Furthermore, this apparitional drift is placed in tension against the shutting of the door. Beginning the story with a tension traced between the shift into consciousness and that closing door, closure and openness, framing and undecidability, architecture and spacing are announced as processes subject to an unresolvable spectral effect. And what the opening line of the story makes clear is that being (consciousness), haunting (invisible on-going motion) and the home (figured metonymically by the door) are intimately implicated into one another. The conditions by which the haunting makes itself felt are through a simultaneity of the establishment of the normative or domestic and the destabilization and estrangement of those same conditions. The classical ideas of the house as structure of representation or 'as an embodiment and abstract representation of the human body' (*AU* 69) are called into question by Woolf from the outset of the narrative through the persistence of the spectral.

There is thus at work, to cite Elisabeth Bronfen (on Freud's notion of the uncanny), a 'lack of clear definition' as a 'rhetorical strategy', producing 'a situation of undecidability, where fixed frames or margins [whether those of the house and surroundings, or notions of narrative's past, present and future] are set in motion . . . the question whether something is animate (alive) or inanimate (dead), whether something is real or imagined, unique, original or a repetition, a copy, cannot be decided' (113). 'A Haunted House' effects its uncanny disturbance as a condition of its narration because, like the Freudian concept of the uncanny, Woolf's story and the way in which it is structured 'in some sense always involves the question of visibility/invisibility, presence to/absence from sight' (Bronfen 113), and the rhythm of reiteration which this entails.

The story makes this clear in that the ghostly couple are comprehended repeatedly even though they are not seen ('Not that one could ever see them'). Each instance of comprehension signals return while also marking the return as the play of difference. The couple make their motions felt, while exceeding and escaping conventional representation: 'we hear no steps beside us; we see no ghostly lady spread her ghostly cloak'. We can neither allay the uncanny sensation within the house nor calm this spectral iterability by alluding to gothic convention. In this negation and denial, Woolf amplifies the haunting effect by dismissing the conventions of ghost narrative by which this 'haunted house' could be measured.

As with the very idea of the uncanny, the story implicitly 'entails anxieties about fragmentation' (Bronfen 113). Although Woolf's narrator appears lacking in all anxiety (again implicitly subverting the conventions of representation; characters are usually anxious about the possibility of spectral apparitions), there is nonetheless an imminent anxiety for the reader in the narrative's resistance to the conventions with which it toys. Woolf's short tale not only produces an uncanny sense, it also acts out the idea of the uncanny in the phantom form of a ghost story, contrived from simulacra of the uncanny experience. The ghosts, the images, the sounds and voices are not ghosts as such, so much as they are all interchangeable phantasms articulating repetition, doubling and processes of supplementation. There is thus what Bronfen describes as a blurring 'between the real and fantasy' (113). And this 'blurring' process is precisely that which, in its passage, reveals indirectly the apparitional instance of spectrality. For in this blurring is the movement, to recall the preface, between the living and the dead, between that which is neither alive nor dead.

Woolf's act of responsible witnessing resonates in W. B. Yeats' 1939 *Purgatory*, his penultimate drama.[7] An old, unnamed man stands with his son in the ruins of a house, the old man's parents' house, and the place of his conception. Though never presented as characters in the play, the man's parents return to him (the boy never sees them) as ghosts, coming back as they were on the night of the old man's conception. He witnesses as 'present in memory' the 'invisible' events leading up to his conception: his father's drinking, the sound of his father's horse's hooves as it approaches the house, and his mother's anticipation (*P* 433). What also returns through the haunting return of the parents is the revelation of the father's murder by his son, the old man. The old man subsequently kills his own son (*P* 435), only to hear the endless reiteration of the hoof-beats, which in its ghostly iteration (as with the ghosts of the parents, we neither see nor hear the horse or the sound it makes) evokes the endless revenance of the mother: 'And she must animate that dead night / Not once but many times' (*P* 436).

What is most startling about the play's revelation of witnessing and revenance is not that the phantoms of the past will return and that, inescapably, it is our responsibility to encounter them. Instead, the most haunting aspect, if you will, appears in Yeats' understanding of the ineluctable endlessness of the spectral, the phantomatic, the revenant. Furthermore, *Purgatory*'s structure, like the ruined house in which it takes place, is of the order of the phantasm – we are compelled to witness the spectralization of space as part of the encounter with the haunting that takes place. It is not simply, as with gothic conventionally understood, that the house or the old man are haunted; rather, the play takes place as the possibility of haunting, and as the various manifestations of reiteration make plain, haunting is not located as originating in any one place, person, or act. For what we witness, in seeing the old man's response to the dead and his misreading of the situation, is his own bearing witness to the hauntedness of memory in the figure of the mother's phantom. Even as her ghost 'must animate the dead night . . . many times', so there is nothing other than 'the impression upon my mother's mind' (*P* 435). A phantom herself, her mind is always already haunted, her 'soul' unable to be released from its 'dream' (*P* 436). It is the memory of her memory of the invisible, the absent, the other, which is *re-presented*, the implication being that the old man is merely the latest, and not the last, in this ghostly series. And that the old man is, himself, *re-presented* as being the momentary locus of memorial apparition and projection, intimates that it is to the memory of memory that we must be responsible. The old man is not the origin of events, as both the mother's dream and her spectral 'animation' make apparent, even though she is never witnessed as such but is only relayed, projected through her son's mind onto our imagination. She is in effect a figure for the trace of the spectral, her son the screen on which haunting comes to be projected momentarily. There is thus played out by *Purgatory* the poetics of an experience of 'self-referential self-presentation' (S-U 200) as being inescapably haunted, as marked immanently by the spectral to come, a marking of one's self always already displaced, haunted by one's other, as we have already considered. Coming face to face with this phantom other is refigured in another manner which is equally haunting by Paul Celan. Much if not all of Celan's poetry takes on the form of encrypted testimony, memory, of bearing witness, and addresses in complex, often labyrinthine fashion, the responsibility the living have to the dead, particularly in relation to the Holocaust. This is not the place, nor is there the space, to develop an analysis of Celan, much less a reading.[8] However, I do wish to consider, briefly and in conclusion, one poem, 'Ich kann dich noch sehn':[9]

> I can see you yet: an echo,
> palpable with feel-
> words, at the farewell-
> ridge.

> Your face shies faintly
> when all at once
> becoming lamplike bright
> in me, at the passage
> where one says the most painful never

'Ich kann dich noch sehn' appears to address a figure which, already having departed, nonetheless projects traces of itself, certain ghostly resonances to which the speaker is obligated to respond, and to which the poem, as reading of these apparitional marks, provides testimony. That 'yet' (translation of *noch*, which is also translatable as 'still' or, in some contexts 'only just' or 'one day') speaks of that which is barely visible, which is retained, and which remains on the edge, the limit of memory. 'Seeing' thus sees nothing as such, the verb being the displacement in language for memory, which further becomes 'translated' from itself in the invisible, yet resonant figure of the echo. The line seeks to reiterate that to which it responds, that which is invisible and which leaves its mark. This projection of the ghostly other emerges like a light 'in me', an illumination of the phantom as phantom, as nothing other than the phantasm to which the opening of the poem addresses itself, to which it responds and which returns even as the poem seeks to turn towards the figure of the other with its 'feel-words' (*Fühl* is also translatable as 'antenna', the translation used by Michael Hamburger, thereby translating the poem into an insect responding to various otherwise imperceptible, invisible stimuli). That point of lamplike brightness, that illumination as enlightenment whereby the speaker of the poem recognizes the spectral nature of the other, comes at the point, place or passage (*Stelle*) where the phantom, having returned, retreats. This passage is also a passing, a passing away, and Celan's poem records this motion in its own rhythmic fluctuations. The passage of the other takes place, coming and going, continuously in the text, and as the motion of the text, the two stanzas figuring this pulse, this breath. And what we come to read, between the lines as it were, from the first line to the last, is that the figure of the revenant haunts all the more powerfully for having always already passed beyond that farewell- or parting-ridge, which is, itself, nothing other than the very limit of *re-presentation*, the limit to which Celan's language goes.

However, this sketch of the poem's work is only provisional, in the face of the *way* it addresses us, moving as it does beyond its textual place or passage. In its performative operation, the ways in which the text enacts the condition of passage and limit, the illusion of a voice is merely that: one more phantom or phantasm returning to illuminate our comprehension and to enlighten us – as does the old man of Yeats' play in his own fashion – as to the responsibility which haunting imposes, that responsibility which the living have to the dead. As experience of witnessing, the poem testifies not only to that ghostly face or echo which has already returned and retreated; it also testifies before us, before each of its readers (as Derrida describes in speaking of the disjointing and haunting structure of testimony [S-U 200]). In operating in this manner, Celan's poem is spectralized, responding in its ethical obligation to the other, by returning as the apparitional address, testifying, as Derrida puts it, 'for someone who becomes the addressee of the testimony' (S-U 200).[10] We are translated, in effect, becoming the 'you' to whom the poem is addressed, haunted by its spectral, testimonial structure.

As Derrida says of another poem by Celan, what the poem means or says is ultimately of less importance than our experience of it, this experience of haunting, its uncanny power, and the experience also of the 'strange limit between what can and cannot be determined' about the experience of witnessing (S-U 184). The poem bears witness to an act of impossible witnessing and to witnessing as the marking of a limit between the possible and impossible, the visible and invisible. This question of witnessing, of the response and the responsibility that reading imposes on the living, is thus intimately implicated in every aspect of the poem before and beyond any consideration of content. This is what we name spectral persistence, and which comes to be figured through our acts of reading.

# Notes

PREFACE

1. Jacques Derrida, 'Marx c'est quelqu'un', in Jacques Derrida, Marc Guillaume, and Jean-Pierre Vincent, *Marx en jeu* (Paris: Descartes & Cie, 1997), 9–28. Hereafter Mcq.
2. Jacques Derrida, *Limited Inc.* Trans. Samuel Weber et al. (Evanston, IL: Northwestern University Press, 1988), 118. Hereafter *LI*.
3. John Updike, 'Books Unbound, Life Unraveled', *New York Times*, 18 June 2000.
4. Nicholas Royle, '*Déjà Vu*' in Martin McQuillan et al. (eds), *Post-Theory: New Directions in Criticism* (Edinburgh: Edinburgh University Press, 1999), 3–20; 11. Hereafter '*DV*'.
5. Jean-Michel Rabaté, *The Ghosts of Modernity* (Gainesville: University Press of Florida, 1996), xvi. Hereafter *GM*.


INTRODUCTION

1. Jacques Derrida, 'The Ghost Dance: An Interview with Jacques Derrida', trans. Jean-Luc Svoboda, *Public*, 2 (1989), 60–73; 61. Hereafter GD.
2. Derrida has taken up the connections between matters of technology and haunting more recently, with Bernard Steigler, in *Échographies: de la télévision: Entretiens filmés* (Paris: Galilée-INA, 1996). Hereafter *É*.
3. Samuel Weber, *Mass Mediauras: Form, Technics, Media* (Stanford, CA: Stanford University Press, 1996), 164; 162–3. Hereafter *MM*.
4. Avital Ronell, *Finitude's Score: Essays for the End of the Millennium* (Lincoln: University of Nebraska Press, 1994), 312–13. Hereafter *FS*. On television and tele-technology, see Richard Dienst, *Still Life in Real Time: Theory After Television* (Durham, NC: Duke University Press, 1994).
5. Walter Benjamin, 'The Work of Art in the Age of Mechanical Reproduction', in *Illuminations*, trans. Harry Zohn, ed. and int. Hannah Arendt (New York: Schocken Books, 1969), 217–52. Hereafter WA.

Seemingly anticipating Derrida's critique of the metaphysics of presence, Benjamin points out that the process of reproduction dissolves an object's 'presence in time and space, its unique existence' (WA 220). Furthermore, while never speaking in the essay directly of haunting or the spectral, Benjamin does turn approvingly to a remark by Paul Valéry, which remark comes close to tracing Derrida's own understanding of the spectral in relation to technologies of reproduction: 'Just as water, gas, and electricity are brought into our houses from afar off . . .', writes Valéry, 'so we shall be supplied with visual or auditory images, which will appear and disappear at a simple movement of the hand, hardly more than a sign' (Valéry cit. Benjamin, WA 219). Particularly interesting in Benjamin's reading of still and cinematic photography is the comprehension of technology's ability to make appear in its reproduction of human experience that which is invisible, that which haunts our actions and gestures and which, without the artifice of the medium, goes, as it were, unseen.

6. David Punter, 'Introduction: of Apparitions', in Glennis Byron and David Punter (eds), *Spectral Readings: Towards a Gothic Geography* (Basingstoke: Macmillan Press – now Palgrave, 1999), 1–8; 3.

7. Peggy Kamuf, *The Division of Literature or the University in Deconstruction* (Chicago: University of Chicago Press, 1997), 171. Hereafter *DL*.

8. Defoe's 'A True Relation' is reprinted in Stuart Sherman (ed.), *The Longman Anthology of British Literature: Vol. 1c, The Restoration and the Eighteenth Century* (New York: Longman, 1999), 2291–97, along with the two letters, by L. Lukyn and Stephen Gray, and the 'Interview' mentioned in the following paragraph (2298–2303). I have drawn on Stuart Sherman's notes throughout for contextual and historical detail.

9. On Defoe's interest in the spectral and apparitional phenomena, and, more generally, on the category of the uncanny, see Terry Castle's *The Female Thermometer* (FT 44–55, 175–6).

10. T. J. Lustig offers a telling commentary on the destabilizing effects of the figurative in Freud's essay 'The "Uncanny"', in *Henry James and the Ghostly* (Cambridge: Cambridge University Press, 1994), 24–7.

11. Jacques Derrida, *Archive Fever: A Freudian Impression*, trans. Eric Prenowitz (Chicago: University of Chicago Press, 1995), 86. Hereafter *AF*.

12. The term 'phantasm' is not synonymous with 'phantom', even though, as we will see in the chapter on Tennyson, both share a common etymology which haunts them (that which, we would say, haunts both figures, blurring absolute distinction between them). 'Phantasm' or 'fantasm', while having specifically psychoanalytic connotations, broadly conceived refers to forms of projection, figuration, fantasies and imaginary constructions which, though clearly having no 'reality' as such, nonetheless are comprehensible, visible we might suggest in their very invisibility. Being of this order, the phantasm crosses any distinct boundary between the visible and invisible, the so-called real and the imaginary (as does the phantom). As Peter Schwenger points out, the fantasm, in English, 'is both a ghost and an image in the mind'; Schwenger, *Fantasm and Fiction: On Textual Envisioning* (Stanford, CA: Stanford University Press, 1999), 5. Hereafter *FF*. Yet what the fantasm is, is not itself nor a representation of itself, but rather a figure, one amongst many, which spaces and haunts any identity. See Rodolphe Gasché's comment on the phantasmatic, below. On the persistence of the phantasm from Aristotle to Freud, see Giorgio Agamben, *Stanzas: Word and Phantasm in Western Culture*, trans. Ronald L. Martinez (Minneapolis: University of Minnesota Press, 1993). Hereafter *SWP*. On the figure and figurality of the phantasm, see Louis Althusser's commentary, cited below in the chapter on George Eliot's *The Lifted Veil*.

13. Abraham remarks that 'what haunts are not the dead, but the gaps left within us by the secrets of others'; Nicholas Abraham and Maria Torok, *The Shell and the Kernel*. Vol. 1, ed., trans., and int. Nicholas T. Rand (Chicago: University of Chicago Press, 1994), 171. Hereafter *SK*.

14. Rodolphe Gasché, 'The Witch Metapsychology', trans. Julian Patrick, in Todd Dufresne (ed.), *Returns of the 'French Freud': Freud, Lacan, and Beyond* (New York: Routledge, 1997), 169–208; 172.

15. Mark Wigley, *The Architecture of Deconstruction: Derrida's Haunt* (Cambridge, MA: MIT Press, 1993), 162. Hereafter *AD*.

16. Margaret Russett, *De Quincey's Romanticism: Canonical Minority and the Forms of Transmission* (Cambridge: Cambridge University Press, 1997).

17. Fred Botting, *Gothic* (London: Routledge, 1996), 14.

18. James R. Kincaid, 'Designing Gourmet Children or, KIDS FOR DINNER', in Ruth Robbins and Julian Wolfreys (eds), *Victorian Gothic: Literary and Cultural Manifestations in the Nineteenth Century* (Basingstoke: Macmillan Press – now Palgrave, 2000), 3–11; 8.

19. See, for example, Vijay Mishra, *The Gothic Sublime* (Albany: State University of New York Press, 1994).

20. Eve Kosofsky Sedgwick, *The Coherence of Gothic Conventions* (New York: Methuen, 1986), 3.

21. Robert Miles, *Gothic Writing 1750–1820: A Genealogy* (London: Routledge, 1993), 1.

22. Kelly Hurley, *The Gothic Body: Sexuality, Materialism, and Degeneration at the Fin de Siècle* (Cambridge: Cambridge University Press, 1996), 3. On the gothic body and the spectacle of the body in pain, see Steven Bruhm, *Gothic Bodies: The Politics of Pain in Romantic Fiction* (Philadelphia: University of Pennsylvania Press, 1994).

23. And, by implication, photography also. Inspired most directly by the work of Walter Benjamin and Roland Barthes on the technology of photography as one of shadows and spectres, critics have recently addressed the spectral nature of photographs. Particularly interesting amongst recent studies are Eduardo Cadava, *Words of Light: Theses on the Photography of History* (Princeton, NJ: Princeton University Press, 1997; hereafter *WL*), and Marianne Hirsch, *Family Frames: Photography, Narrative, and Postmemory* (Cambridge, MA: Harvard University Press, 1997).
    Both address the relation of photography to the death of the subject. Any photograph, in its reproducibility and its ability to bring back its subject, addresses that subject's mortality. When I look at a photograph of myself, I know that this image can be reproduced at any time, that it can be presented for another's view, not only during my lifetime but also after my death. In Hirsch's words (discussing Barthes' *Camera Lucida*), '[t]he referent is both present (implied in the photograph) and absent (it has been there but is not here now). The referent haunts the picture like a ghost: it is a revenant, a return of the lost and dead other' (5). The referent, the image of myself for example, confronts me with this duplicity, this act of paradoxical doubling, whereby I am here, as the observer, and both there and not there. What is returned through the photograph is only the spectre of an irrecoverable and, therefore, haunting past which

can never be present, and which moreover disorganizes temporality in its ability to return repeatedly in the future. Photography, remarks Hirsch, 'bring[s] the past back in the form of a ghostly revenant, emphasizing, at the same time, its immutable and irreversible pastness and irretrievability' (20). As the trace of phantoms and ghosts, photographs are readable, remarks Hirsch, as 'fragments of a history we cannot assimilate' (40). In this, they bear a passing resemblance to the fragmented text in the gothic (of which more in the section of the chapter on the gothic) and, more generally, to the irretrievable fragment as the sign of spectrality. Fragments are themselves akin to snapshots, phatic images resistant to incorporation.

While Hirsch comments on the personal in photography, Cadava's interest is directed to the phantoms of history which return. As he puts it:

> [l]ike an angel of history whose wings register the traces of this disappearance, the image bears witness to an experience that cannot come to light. This experience is the experience of the shock of experience, of experience as bereavement. This bereavement acknowledges what takes place in any photograph – the return of the departed . . . the return of what was once there takes the form of a haunting . . . The possibility of the photographic image requires that there be such things as ghosts and phantoms . . . the lesson of the photograph for history – what it says about the spectralization of light, about the electrical flashes of remote spirits – is that every attempt to bring the other to the light of day, to keep the other alive, silently presumes that it is mortal, that it is always already touched (or retouched) by death . . . In photographing someone, we know that the photograph will survive him – it begins, even during his life, to circulate without him, figuring and anticipating his death each time it is looked at. (11, 13)

Thus whether it is a matter of the most personal and private snapshot, or the documentary record of historical events, photography is a spectral medium and the ghost, suggests Cadava, after Benjamin, 'is the residue of technological reproduction' (137 n.14). On Barthes, photography and ghosts, see Rabaté (*GM* 67–83).

24. Jacqueline Howard, *Reading Gothic Fiction: A Bakhtinian Approach* (Oxford: Oxford University Press, 1994), 13, 12.

25. Sigmund Freud, 'The "Uncanny"', in *Writings on Art and Literature*, Foreword Neil Hertz (Stanford, CA: Stanford University Press, 1997), 193–233. Hereafter *U*.

26. For a discussion of the literary texts of which Freud makes mention, see Phillip McCaffrey, 'Freud's Uncanny Woman', in Sander L. Gilman, Jutta Birmele, Jay Geller, and Valerie D. Greenberg (eds), *Reading Freud's Reading* (New York: New York University Press, 1994), 91–108.

27. Terry Castle, *The Female Thermometer: Eighteenth-Century Culture and the Invention of the Uncanny* (Oxford: Oxford University Press, 1995), 7. Hereafter *FT*.

28. Royle addresses theories of the ghost and the double in terms of *déjà vu*, which, he argues, is all the more powerfully at work in Freud's essay on the uncanny for being nowhere mentioned. Though – or, perhaps, *precisely because* – Freud does not discuss the sensation of *déjà vu*, it 'appears' invisibly to propel, in an uncanny fashion, the various turns of that text. Apropos of *déjà vu* as one possible name for haunting or doubling, Royle remarks that 'it is difficult to imagine a theory of the ghost or double without a theory of *déjà vu* . . . The double is always ghostly and cannot be dissociated from a sense of *déjà vu* . . . *Déjà vu* is the experience of the double *par excellence*; it is the experience of experience *as* double. There can be no uncanny perhaps, without some experience of this duplicity' (*'DV'* 15).

   Royle also touches on an area of interest shared by Terry Castle, though in a different manner: sight. While Castle addresses that aspect of Freud's essay which concerns the apparition as that which, in becoming visible, comes to light and thus brings enlightenment as an effect of this figural visibility (*FT* 7), Royle speaks of the gaze implicit in the sense of *déjà vu*: 'it is to be oneself *already seen*, watched (over)' (*'DV'* 16). The concerns of light, enlightenment, sight, insight, second sight, projection, and illumination in relation to the issue of spectrality are of concern throughout these essays.

29. Hélène Cixous, 'Fiction and its Phantoms: A Reading of Freud's *Das Unheimlich* (The "Uncanny")', trans. Robert Dennomé, *New Literary History* 7:3 (1976): 525–48; 525. Hereafter FP.

30. Neil Hertz, *The End of the Line: Essays on Psychoanalysis and the Sublime* (New York: Columbia University Press, 1985), 101–2.

31. Martin Heidegger, *History of the Concept of Time: Prolegomena*, trans. Theodore Kisiel (Bloomington: Indiana University Press, 1985), 283–92. Hereafter *HCT*.

   Heidegger's 1925 lecture course provides an early version of Heidegger's *Being and Time* (1927), trans. Joan Stambaugh (Albany: New York University Press, 1996), in which the question of uncanniness is discussed in a number of places. See, in particular, §188–90, §276–8, §286–7, §295–6, §342–4. Hereafter *BT*.

32. Hent de Vries, *Philosophy and the Turn to Religion* (Baltimore: The Johns Hopkins University Press, 1999), 271. Hereafter *PTR*.

33. Jacques Derrida, *Dissemination*, trans. Barbara Johnson (Chicago: University of Chicago Press, 1981), 220 n.32. Hereafter *D*.

34. Paul de Man, *The Rhetoric of Romanticism* (New York: Columbia University Press, 1984), 243. Hereafter *RR*.

35. Ernesto Laclau, *Emancipation(s)* (London: Verso, 1996), 67, 69.

36. Slavoj Žižek *The Plague of Fantasies* (London: Verso, 1997), 95. On Žižek's discussion of the de Manian comprehension of reading, see my *Readings: Acts of Close Reading in Literary Theory* (Edinburgh: Edinburgh University Press, 2000), 138–40.

37. Jacques Derrida, *Specters of Marx: The State of the Debt, the Work of Mourning, and the New International*, trans. Peggy Kamuf, int. Bernd

Magnus and Stephen Cullenberg (New York: Routledge, 1994), 11. Hereafter *SM*.

38. Slavoj Žižek, 'The Spectre of Ideology', in Žižek (ed.), *Mapping Ideology* (London: Verso, 1994), 1–33; 20–21. Hereafter SI.

39. Which returns in relation to the question of haunting-as-political in Žižek's most recent publication, *The Fragile Absolute – or, why is the Christian Legacy Worth Fighting For?* (London: Verso, 2000).

## CHAPTER 1

1. James B. Twitchell, *The Living Dead: A Study of the Vampire in Romantic Literature* (Durham, NC: Duke University Press, 1981), 33.

2. Antony Easthope, *Englishness and National Culture* (London: Routledge, 1999), 161.

3. On doubling, repetition and the uncanny, see the Introduction.

4. H. L. Malchow, *Gothic Images of Race in Nineteenth-Century Britain* (Stanford, CA: Stanford University Press, 1996), 110f.

   See also Chris Baldick, *In Frankenstein's Shadow: Myth, Monstrosity, and Nineteenth-Century Writing* (Oxford: Oxford University Press, 1987), 106–20, on the monstrous and Dickens' gallows humour. Baldick discusses the comic references to galvanism, from Sawyer and Allen forward, and also to the 'animation of the apparently inanimate' (107). He also considers how the comedic effect is achieved through a dark exuberance on the author's part, discussing as well the question of dismemberment and dissection. Baldick argues that there is 'more to all this ghoulishness than a gratuitous *frisson*; it is of a piece with Dickens' synecdochal, Carlylean representation of character and of the fragmented body' (110). Furthermore, for Baldick Dickens maps monstrosity onto the body as a product of 'crushing social pressures' (112). This may be true in part, but there is a certain distortion in Baldick's argument inasmuch as he takes the issue of fragmentation as directly Carlylean – Dickens' productions being a manifestation akin to the anxiety of influence perhaps – rather than seeing Carlyle's writing as similarly produced, and not the original source as Baldick seems to assume implicitly. Arguably, the 'contamination' of fictive discourse with traces of scientific, anatomical and gothic textuality speaks of the general historicity and materiality of Dickens' text, in which materiality Carlyle is also enfolded. The gothic as genre provides Dickens with a recognizable form of bourgeois entertainment which misshapes and in turn is distorted by contemporaneous discourses of the period.

5. Harry Stone, *The Night Side of Dickens: Cannibalism, Passion, Necessity* (Columbus: Ohio State University Press, 1994), 77–9.

6. On flesh, fatness, and their carnivalesque relation to the erotic in *Pickwick*, with particular attention to the Fat Boy, see James R. Kincaid's essay 'Fattening up on Pickwick' in *Annoying the Victorians* (New York: Routledge, 1995), 21–35. Elsewhere, in *Erotic Innocence: The Culture*

*of Child Molesting* (Durham, NC: Duke University Press, 1998), 10–13, Kincaid argues that the stories we tell today concerning child abuse are, in their structures and circuitry, essentially gothic narratives, filled with so much terror that we become paralysed by them, unable to act. From this perspective, what is perhaps particularly terrifying in Dickens' gothic reinventions is that he is able to invest the gothic with humour. The spectralized gothic mode can be read as being put to use as a revenge, rather than a return of, the repressed.

7. José Gil, *Metamorphoses of the Body*, trans. Stephen Muecke (Minneapolis: University of Minnesota Press, 1998), 99.

8. James R. Kincaid, *Child-Loving: The Erotic Child and Victorian Culture* (New York: Routledge, 1992), 95.

9. For a full-length study of mesmerism and its popularity as a form of entertainment, see Alison Winter's *Mesmerized: Powers of Mind in Victorian Britain* (Chicago: University of Chicago Press, 1998).

10. Bailey is not the sole proponent of the comic-gothic in *Martin Chuzzlewit*, though he is its most knowing practitioner. As an instance of the way in which the comic-gothic overflows the limits of the individual to make itself manifest in the discourse of others, in a particular setting or in the atmosphere of a scene, we might recall the moment when Merry, in conversation with old Martin Chuzzlewit in the churchyard, sees Jonas Chuzzlewit, crying out, 'What a perfectly *hideous monster* to be wandering about church-yards in the broad daylight, *frightening people* out of their wits! Don't come here, Griffin, or I'll go away directly' (*MC* 466; emphases added). Arguably, Merry is not conscious of her comic abilities as is Bailey (or, at least, she is not as conscious). However, her comment partakes of the gothic mode even while it is comic. It nicely conflates the conventions of gothic narrative – while chastising Jonas for appearing in daylight; Merry appears to be aware that in gothic tales monsters in graveyards only appear at night – with a particular feature of gothic architecture, the griffin. If Merry were more conscious, and less indebted to the gothic for the expression of her repulsion, she might recognize Jonas for the monster that he is, rather than the one she imagines him to be. Dickens appears to be offering us a warning, not so much against the gothic as against the gullibility of the gothic novel reader.

11. As I have argued elsewhere, Todgers' boarding house serves as a synecdochic figure for the condition of London; Wolfreys, *Writing London: The Trace of the Urban Text from Blake to Dickens* (Basingstoke: Macmillan Press – now Palgrave, 1998), 167–9.

    This symbolic and structural relationship, in its play between domestic architecture and urban topography, provides a suitably gothic space. This is intimated in the passage above with regard to Todgers, while Kelly Hurley has argued that Dickensian narrative 'figures the urban space . . . as a gothic one' (Hurley, *Gothic Body*, 165). Certainly this is true in Dickens' city narratives, where boys can be kidnapped, women frightened, and men stalked.

12. On the body in pain as gothic trope, see Bruhm, *Gothic Bodies*, on which I have drawn in this section of the essay.

13. John David Moore, 'Coleridge and the "Modern Jacobinical Drama": *Osorio, Remorse,* and the Development of Coleridge's Critique of the Stage, 1797–1816', *Bulletin of Research in the Humanities,* 85:4 (1982), 443–64; 444.

14. Clery writes: 'In Gothic Fictions, smugglers and bandits opportunistically inhabit spaces . . . [such as] the deserted wing of the castle, the ancestral crypt. Like spectres they are of necessity creatures of the night and they exploit this kinship by using popular superstition as a cover for their illegitimate activities'; E. J. Clery, *The Rise of Supernatural Fiction, 1762–1800* (Cambridge: Cambridge University Press, 1995), 133–4.

   I am not suggesting that Bailey is either supernatural or criminal, merely that Dickens brings together in the boy's performance, in his names and acts, the discursive kinship discussed by Clery and frequently exploited in Gothic narrative.

15. Mark Edmundson, *Nightmare on Main Street: Angels, Sadomasochism, and the Culture of Gothic* (Cambridge, MA: Harvard University Press, 1997), 32.

16. If the difference between the child who causes laughter and who is laughed at in Dickens can be described briefly, perhaps the question is one of class, and of the child's class position. Both Bailey and the Fat Boy are working class, their 'low' position indicated through their speech, through non-standard spelling and the emphasis by Dickens on idiomatic expression. Neither boy speaks the standard English of the middle classes or of the narrator. Oliver Twist and Pip, on the other hand, always speak standard English, without the trace of idiom or accent peculiar to the working class. They are thus implicitly given 'universal' voices. Within the narrative logic of *Great Expectations* Pip's 'voice' may of course be explained away: he is the adult narrator, recalling his own boyhood, and he has undergone education which has erased any signs of local accent which he may have had as a child. Oliver, on the other hand, always speaks English 'correctly', thereby signalling that, even as a child, in the workhouse or Fagin's hideout, he has always already transcended both class and locale. It would seem then, as a provisional thesis by which to explain the difference between those who generate humour and those who are its objects, that the comic-gothic is, for Dickens, a working-class mode of articulation, which shares certain proletarian affinities with the grotesque, the carnivalesque, the melodramatic, and the music hall; in short, with all forms of popular entertainment.

17. The words are of course those of Ebenezer Scrooge in response to Marley's ghost (*CC* 19). Although not a child, Dickens has Scrooge respond in a manner which is instructive with regard to the comic-gothic. Following the well-known retort, Dickens remarks, 'Scrooge was not much in the habit of cracking jokes, nor did he feel, in his heart, by any means waggish then. The truth is, that he tried to be smart, as a means of distracting his own attention, and keeping down his terror; for the spectre's voice disturbed the very marrow in his bones' (*CC* 19). Despite Dickens' protestations, the line is, of course, funny, whether it was intended or not. However, the inadvertent recourse to humour in opposition to terror provides the reader with one more comic-gothic moment, which

is, again, connected to consumption, to what is inside us. This is expressed both in Scrooge's remark, and in those preceding the gravy pun, but also, importantly in Dickens' own expression of spectral disturbance in 'the very marrow in [Scrooge's] bones'. The ghost makes Scrooge's flesh creep, while the text moves spectrally across the boundary of the character's remarks to those of the narrator.

18. Adrian Poole, 'Introduction', in Charles Dickens, *Our Mutual Friend* (London, 1997), ix.

19. De Man's comment comes from an essay on aesthetic formalization in Kleist's *Über das Marionettentheater* (*RR* 263–90). There is a possible reading of the marionette-like aspects of Jenny to be developed from both Kleist's essay and de Man's commentary.

20. Joseph Andriano, *Our Ladies of Darkness: Feminine Daemonology in Male Gothic Fiction* (University Park: Pennsylvania State University Press, 1993), 139.

21. Andriano cites both Jackson and Warren on this point. Jackson suggests that 'the history of the survival of Gothic horror is one of progressive internalization and recognition of fears generated by the self', while Warren states that 'the phantom lady is essentially the man's most vital spirit' (Jackson and Warren cit. Andriano 2 n.3). The works to which Andriano refers are Rosemary Jackson, *Fantasy: The Literature of Subversion* (London: Methuen, 1988), and Barbara Warren, *The Feminine Image in Literature* (Rochelle Park: Humanities Press, 1973).

22. Malcolm Andrews, *Dickens and the Grown-Up Child* (Basingstoke: Macmillan Press – now Palgrave, 1994), 89.

23. Mary Russo, *The Female Grotesque: Risk, Excess, and Modernity* (London: Routledge, 1994), 5.

24. Fiona Robertson, *Legitimate Histories: Scott, Gothic, and the Authorities of Fiction* (Oxford: Oxford University Press, 1994), 74. In establishing the conventions of the gothic for a reading of Walter Scott, Robertson highlights the ways in which there is narrative and architectural correspondence in gothic novels, where passages, in both senses of the word, lead nowhere. Jenny's fantastic transport also promises to lead nowhere, strictly speaking.

25. J. Hillis Miller, *The Disappearance of God: Five Nineteenth Century Writers* (New York: Schocken Books, 1965), 65.

26. See, for example, the well-known cartoon by John Tenniel, 'The Irish Frankenstein', published in *Punch* (20 May 1882), where in a typical conflation between the name of the creator and his creature, the Irish are represented as monstrous, bloodthirsty, masked creatures. H. L. Malchow's *Gothic Images* provides what is to date the most sustained consideration of the relation between the aesthetics and politics of representation, from *Frankenstein* to the *fin-de-siècle*. On related matters of race and the connections made between 'foreigners' and women see Susan Meyer, *Imperialism at Home: Race and Victorian Women's Fiction* (Ithaca, NY: Cornell University Press, 1996); also on the issue of race and degeneration, see William Greenslade, *Degeneration, Culture and the Novel, 1880–1940* (Cambridge: Cambridge University Press, 1994).

27. Jean-François Lyotard, *The Postmodern Explained*, trans. Don Barry et al., Afterword Wlad Godzich (Minnesota: University of Minnesota Press, 1992), 93.

## CHAPTER 2

1. Immanuel Kant, *Religion within the boundaries of mere reason*, trans. George di Giovanni, *Religion and Rational Theology*, trans. Allen W. Wood and George di Giovanni (Cambridge: Cambridge University Press, 1996), 39–216; 167.
2. Isobel Armstrong, *Victorian Poetry: Poetry, Poetics and Politics* (London: Routledge, 1993), 261.
3. Michael Wheeler, *Death and the Future Life in Victorian Language and Theology* (Cambridge: Cambridge University Press, 1990), 264.
4. Graham Ward, *Barth, Derrida and the Language of Theology* (Cambridge: Cambridge University Press, 1995), 151. The phrase cited is coined by Edmund Husserl in his *Cartesian Meditations* 'in an attempt', as Ward puts it, 'to answer the question of how, given his own commitment to a transcendental subjectivity, there can be an experience of and an acknowledgement of someone else'. It is precisely this Husserlian or phenomenological problematic of mediation which we encounter in Tennyson's recourse to analogy throughout *In Memoriam*.

    On the subject of analogy in the poem, see Christopher Craft, *Another Kind of Love: Male Homosexual Desire in English Discourse* (Berkeley: University of California Press, 1994), 53; Donald S. Hair, *Tennyson's Language* (Toronto: University of Toronto Press, 1991); Wheeler, *Death and the Future Life*, 230; Elaine Jordan, *Alfred Tennyson* (Cambridge: Cambridge University Press, 1988), 123.
5. On the poem as a series of fragments resistant to unification, see Hair (89–95); Timothy Peltason, *Reading In Memoriam* (Princeton, NJ: Princeton University Press, 1985), 5, 14. Isobel Armstrong reads the 'fragmented syntax' of particular lyrics (264). Elaine Jordan regards the question of unity as a problem (109). Alan Sinfield and Richard Dellamora both address the rhetoric of fragmentation and discontinuity in the poem's representation of male subjectivity (Sinfield, *Alfred Tennyson* [Oxford: Oxford University Press, 1986], 124; Dellamora, *Masculine Desire: The Sexual Politics of Victorian Aestheticism* [Chapel Hill: North Carolina University Press, 1990], 23). I would like to thank Pamela Gilbert for bringing Dellamora's essay to my attention.
6. We can legitimately define the text as a machine, given its proto-modernity and its anticipation of modernist poetics observed by critics of the poem. George Landow suggests that, in its fragmentary expression of subjective states at particular moments, the poem 'fulfills Paul Valéry's definition of poetry as a machine that reproduces an emotion' (http://landow.stg.brown.edu/victorian/tennyson/im/intro.html).

    Donald Hair points to expressionist connections between the formal fragmentation of the text and the theologically oriented consideration of expressionism set out by Keble in his Oxford lectures on poetry (90). Timothy Peltason remarks that, '[a]s a long poem made up of fragments, *In Memoriam* stands significantly between the long poems of the early nineteenth century and the self-conscious patchwork of such modern poems as *The Waste Land* and Pound's *Cantos*' (14). More explicit than either Peltason or Hair, Alan Sinfield draws our attention 'to . . . the persistent stylization of language . . . [which] makes us always aware of the artificiality of *In Memoriam*' (197), while also commenting at length on Tennyson's cultivation of a modern sensibility marked by negation, 'small or personal affirmation' and 'a tentative irony which eschews large statements', which gestures have subsequently become typical of 'Twentieth-century English poetry' (201). Sinfield also likens Tennyson's endeavours to 'seize the essence of a mood . . . in evoking the quality of an immediate experience' (202) to the effects of Symbolist poetry, while the 'dependence on mystical experience' is common to both (203).

Michael Wheeler has commented on questions of polyvocality and intertextuality, addressing the 'many voiced quality [as] . . . a series of acts of memory in which disparate reminiscences, both personal and literary . . . drawn together and made present in the imagination. The poem memorializes Hallam, for example, by echoing his words and thoughts; and close editorial work has only recently revealed the great range of literary and biblical allusion and parallelism in the work (222).

7.  While I cannot pursue such a reading here, arguably Tennyson's poem is notable for its being informed by various signs of gothic discourse and with uncanny echoes, not least in the image of the yew, the roots of which are 'wrapt about the bones' of the dead (*IM* 1–4; XXXIX). Dark and troubled houses are frequently the sites of the poet's disturbing memories, and return to particular locations serves to return strange or apprehensive sensations (*IM* VII); there are towers, crypts, vaults, graves, and catacombs (*IM* LVI; LXXVI; LXXXI; XCVIII), while the story of Lazarus is refigured as a ghost story (*IM* XXXI 1–2: 'When Lazarus left his charnel-cave, / And home to Mary's house return'd'). The sky is rewritten as the location of a ghostly architecture, where 'Cloud-towers' are built by 'ghostly masons' (*IM* LXX 5). The lost one has become uncanny, having been transformed 'to something strange' (*IM* XLI 5). This uncanny resonance later informs the days themselves (*IM* LXXI 11: 'The days that grow to something strange'), and typical of the uncanny is the tracing of process and the ineffable in both remarks. That which troubles the narrator is a 'spectral doubt' (echoed later as 'spectres of the mind'; *IM* XCVI 15), the apparition of which occurs 'when sundown skirts the moor', a temporally liminal moment wholly consonant with gothic narrative (*IM*, XLI 17–19). There are phantoms (*IM* III 9; XX 1.16; XCII 4; CVIII 10), the last a projection of the poet's other. Bats 'haunt the dusk' (*IM* XCV 11), while, in several stanzas, the Shadow of death returns (*IM* XXII 12, 20; XXIII 4; XXVI 15; XXX 8).

8.  T. S. Eliot, 'In Memoriam', *Essays Ancient and Modern* (London: Faber and Faber, 1936), 200–1.

9.  Samuel Taylor Coleridge, 'On the Constitution of the Church and State,

According to the Idea of Each' (1829) in John Morrow (ed.), *Coleridge's Writings on Politics and Society*. Volume 1 (Princeton, NJ: Princeton University Press, 1991), 152–220. The passage cited is from 173–4.

10. Immanuel Kant, 'Preface to the Second Edition', *Critique of Pure Reason*, trans. and ed. Paul Guyer and Allen W. Wood (Cambridge: Cambridge University Press, 1997), Bxxx, 117.
11. Kevin Hart, *The Trespass of the Sign: Deconstruction, Theology and Philosophy* (Cambridge: Cambridge University Press, 1989), 130–1. Hart provides a useful overview and critique of onto-theology, from Kant, through Heidegger and Derrida (75–96).
12. Werner Hamacher, *Pleroma: Reading in Hegel*, trans. Nicholas Walker and Simon Jarvis (Stanford, CA: Stanford University Press, 1998), 3. Hereafter *PRH*.
13. For the consideration of a materiality of inscription, and for the specific thinking of a materiality that forestalls anthropomorphism and the normalization of analogy, I am indebted to Paul de Man's consideration of materiality in Kant's third *Critique*, in *Aesthetic Ideology*, ed. and int. Andrzej Warminski (Minneapolis: University of Minnesota Press, 1996), 70–90. Hereafter *AI*.

    I am also indebted to the various considerations of de Man's late work, particularly on the matter of materiality, in Tom Cohen, Barbara Cohen, J. Hillis Miller, and Andrzej Warminski (eds), *Material Events: Paul de Man and the Afterlife of Theory* (Minneapolis: University of Minnesota Press, 2000). The phrase, materiality without matter, is used by the editors as the subtitle for their introduction, and is taken from Derrida's contribution to the collection.
14. Jacques Derrida, 'How to Avoid Speaking: Denials', trans. Ken Friedan, in Sanford Budick and Wolfgang Iser (eds), *Languages of the Unsayable: The Play of Negativity in Literature and Literary Theory* (New York: Columbia University Press, 1989), 3–70; 4. Hereafter HAS.
15. Immanuel Kant, *Lectures on the philosophical doctrine of religion*, trans. Allen W. Wood, *Religion and Rational Theology*, trans. Allen W. Wood and George di Giovanni (Cambridge: Cambridge University Press, 1996), 335–452; 385.
16. Eleanor Bustin Mattes, *In Memoriam: The Way of the Soul: A Study of Some Influences that Shaped Tennyson's Poem* (New York: Exposition Press, 1951), 114. Michael Wheeler, discussing the theological thought of Maurice, Coleridge, and Jowett, refers to the latter's arguments as 'Kantian' in tone (228). Wheeler also points to the ways in which Tennyson's argument in the poem for the 'immortality of the soul' is 'derived from Kant (partly from reading Goethe and listening to Hallam)' (240).
17. James R. Kincaid, *Tennyson's Major Poems: The Comic and Ironic Patterns* (New Haven, CT: Yale University Press, 1975), 81, 99.
18. Jacques Derrida, 'Faith and Knowledge: The Two Sources of "Religion" at the Limits of Reason Alone', trans. Samuel Weber, in Jacques Derrida and Gianni Vattimo (eds), *Religion* (Stanford, CA: Stanford University Press, 1998), 1–78; 6. Hereafter FK. One might also usefully connect

Derrida's assertion to another, that one ought to be able to begin with haunting (*SM* 175).

19. This phrase, 'haunting to-come', should be read as internally doubling *and* displacing: it suggests the experience of a haunting yet to arrive, while also implying that the 'to-come' – and the thought of a to-come which, though imagined, is not a moment which will arrive as a present – is, in this condition, haunting.

20. Referring to the Epilogue, Eleanor Bustin Mattes comments on the 'progress of the universe toward some remote goal' has nothing 'specifically Christian' in it (91). In reading this, she is correct in observing the idiomatic aspect of Tennyson's expression of faith, already commented on above.

21. Elsewhere, in a reading of Lyric XXX Wheeler comments in the following fashion on Tennyson's notion of the 'future state': '. . . the future state, which from a limited this-worldly perspective is fundamentally paradoxical, must be progressive, opening up worlds of experience which are beyond the grasp of our mortal imaginations, yet remaining somehow in "sympathy" (an important concept for Hallam) with mortal experience' (241); there is, moreover, a 'provisionality' about Tennyson's comprehension 'which suggest[s] that those who seek for final answers concerning the future life are asking the wrong kind of question' (243).

22. As Isobel Armstrong points out, Tennyson plays on the double and paradoxical meaning of 'incorporation' in the poem, whereby the term means both embodiment and the experience of being disembodied (257). There is a simultaneity of movement (which I discuss in the body of the essay) in Tennyson's play, which he employs elsewhere in the text, in figures such as Type, for example, which plays between notions of biological species and biblical exegesis, discussed, again by Armstrong (257), and by George Landow.

On Christian Typology, see Craft, Wheeler, and Sue Zemka, *Victorian Testaments: The Bible, Christology, and Literary Authority in Early-Nineteenth-Century British Culture* (Stanford, CA: Stanford University Press, 1997).

Though having no sustained discussion of Tennyson, Zemka's study, in its reading of Ruskin, points usefully to 'the social and psychological patterns of Victorian worship [which] were structured by . . . the perception of a God at once internal and external' (115). Clearly, this perception informs Tennyson's comprehension, though his understanding is more radically articulated because it exceeds the conventional reliance on direct forms of representation which inform early Victorian Christology.

Armstrong is not alone in noticing Tennyson's word-play and the instability it produces (264). There are, furthermore, other aspects of instability in the text, as critics have noted. Dellamora has noted a doubleness of address in the poem directed simultaneously towards 'normal domestic relations' (36) and 'expressions of male homosocial desire' (38). On the formal nature of *In Memoriam* and the ordering of its lyrics, Timothy Peltason has argued that the poet's organization allows for no claim to 'final authority', while, frequently, the 'relationship of the part to the whole is antagonistic as well as constructive' (6). Alan Sinfield argues that reading the poem for its 'discontinuities' (117) and the lack of a 'unifying principle' (124) in relation to the fragmentary formation of the human subject is the 'more interesting and necessary project' (117).

23. On Hallam's androgyny and the Victorian perception of an androgynous Christ, see Richard Dellamora, who describes Hallam as a 'male Beatrice' (10). See also Craft, and Diane Long Hoeveler, *'Manly-Women and Womanly-Men': Tennyson's Androgynous Ideal in 'The Princess' and 'In Memoriam'*, Michigan Occasional Papers XIX (Spring 1981).

24. Jacques Derrida, *Adieu: To Emmanuel Levinas*, trans. Pascale-Anne Brault and Michael Naas (Stanford, CA: Stanford University Press, 1999), 13. Hereafter *AEL*.

## CHAPTER 3

1. Fredric Jameson, 'Marx's Purloined Letter', in Michael Sprinker (ed.), *Ghostly Demarcations: A Symposium on Jacques Derrida's Specters of Marx* (London: Verso, 1999), 26–67; 38.

2. Jacques Derrida, *Memoirs of the Blind: The Self-Portrait and Other Ruins*, trans. Pascale-Anne Brault and Michael Naas (Chicago: University of Chicago Press, 1993), 213. Hereafter *MB*. Derrida works through these ideas, in part as a critical response to and extension of the work of Maurice Merleau-Ponty, *The Visible and the Invisible*, ed. Claude Lefort, trans. Alphonso Lingis (Evanston, IL: Northwestern University Press, 1968).

Merleau-Ponty's phenomenological study of visibility and invisibility has proved invaluable in recent studies of Victorian photography, particularly those by Lindsay Smith, *Victorian Photography, Painting and Poetry: The Enigma of Visibility in Ruskin, Morris and the Pre-Raphaelites* (Cambridge: Cambridge University Press, 1995) and Carol Mavor, *Pleasures Taken: Performances of Sexuality and Loss in Victorian Photographs* (Durham, NC: Duke University Press, 1995). Mavor's discussion of the concept of invisibility also incorporates Lacan's response to Merleau-Ponty (80–4), and is particularly useful in thinking through the possible relationship between invisibility and spectrality.

Also of particular interest is Luce Irigaray's critical reworking of the question of the invisible, in 'The Invisible of the Flesh: A Reading of Merleau-Ponty, *The Visible and the Invisible*, "The Intertwining – The Chiasm"', in *An Ethics of Sexual Difference*, trans. Caroline Burke and Gillian C. Gill (Ithaca, NY: Cornell University Press, 1993), 151–84.

3. Athena Vrettos, *Somatic Fictions: Imagining Illness in Victorian Culture* (Stanford, CA: Stanford University Press, 1995), 110.

4. Charles Swann, 'Déjà Vu: Déjà Lu: "The Lifted Veil" as an Experiment in Art', in *Literature and History*, 5:1 (1979), 40–57; 43, 40. Elsewhere, Swann suggests that 'Eliot uses "The Lifted Veil" to dramatize an enquiry into the nature of artistic production and narrative method' (46).

5. Sally Shuttleworth, *George Eliot and Nineteenth-Century Science: The*

*Make-Believe of a Beginning* (Cambridge: Cambridge University Press, 1984), 78.

6. Nicholas Royle, *Telepathy and Literature: Essays on the Reading Mind* (Oxford: Blackwell, 1991), 110. Hereafter *TL*.

7. Terry Eagleton, 'Power and Knowledge in "The Lifted Veil"', in *Literature and History*, 9:1 (1983), 52–61; 58.

The question of science and pseudo-science occupies several of the commentators on Eliot's novella. Judith Siford comments on the story's emphasis 'on the supernatural, on bizarre pseudo-scientific experiments, attempted murder and gothic horror' as those elements which most persistently 'interrupt and fragment' the narrative and its realist conventions; Judith Siford, '"Dismal Loneliness": George Eliot, Auguste Comte and "The Lifted Veil"' in *The George Eliot Review*, 26 (1995), 46–52; 46. B. M. Gray's 'Pseudoscience and George Eliot's "The Lifted Veil"', *Nineteenth-Century Fiction*, 36:4 (1981), 407–23, places Eliot's novella in 'the social milieu to which she immediately belonged' before living with George Henry Lewes, which 'embraced the now debunked, intrinsically Victorian phenomena of phrenology, mesmerism and clairvoyance' (409).

There is of course, in the story's interest in phrenology, telepathy, clairvoyance and mesmerism a somewhat supernaturalized manifestation of other nineteenth-century interests in contemporary psychological debates which traverse the boundaries between science and pseudo-science, particularly as these pertain to matters of the individual's heightened sensibility and nervous disorders, as these are given expression through Latimer's narration of his own pathological condition and the symptoms thereof. For a study of the Victorian fascination with mesmerism, see Winter, *Mesmerized*.

8. Kate Flint, 'Blood, Bodies, and *The Lifted Veil*', in *Nineteenth-Century Literature*, 51:4 (1997), 455–73; 456.

9. George Eliot, 'The Natural History of German Life', in Thomas Pinney (ed.), *Essays of George Eliot* (London: Routledge and Kegan Paul, 1963), 433.

10. George Eliot, *Janet's Repentance* (245–412) in *Scenes of Clerical Life*, ed. David Lodge (Harmondsworth: Penguin, 1985), 364.

11. Of the phantasm in the text of Freud, Althusser remarks that it '... designates something other than objective reality, an other – no less objective – reality, although it does not appear to the senses ... The phantasm is thus a reality sui generis. The phantasm is linked to desire. The phantasm is unconscious. The phantasm is a kind of "fantasy", of "scenario", of "*mise en scène*", in which something serious happens and in which nothing happens, for all transpires in an extreme affective tension (the affect) that literally congeals the characters (the "imagos"), which are also phantasms, in their reciprocal positions of desire or interdiction. One thus sees that the phantasm is *contradictory*, since something occurs in it, but nothing happens; that everything is immobile, but in an intense form of tension that is the very opposite of immobility, in which everything is desire and all is interdiction; and finally, one sees that the

phantasm is a totality composed of phantasms, that is, of itself, of its own null repetition . . . *The concept of the phantasm is nothing other, in Freud, than the concept of the unconscious in all its extension and all its comprehension.* . . . in the phantasm Freud designates something extremely precise, an existent – though nonmaterial – reality . . . that is the very existence of its object: the unconscious. But we are also obliged to observe that the name Freud gives to that reality, in other words, the name Freud gives to the unconscious when he attains the zenith of his theory in order to think it is the name of a *metaphor*: phantasm.' Louis Althusser, *Writings on Psychoanalysis: Freud and Lacan*, trans. Jeffrey Melhman, ed. Olivier Corpet and François Matheron (New York: Columbia University Press, 1996), 103–4.

12. On the movement of doubling, division and interchangeability of identities as constituent processes in the production of the uncanny feeling, see Freud (*U* 210–12).

   Hélène Cixous comments on the 'network of the manifestations of the double' in her reading of Freud's essay, in which, in elaborating on the aspects of the double, she notes the 'identification made from one to the other' (which occurs in the phrase of Eliot's with which we are concerned) and the 'recurrent return of what is similar' (FP 539).

13. Jacques Derrida, 'Sending: On Representation', trans. Peter and Mary Ann Caws, *Social Research* (Summer 1982), 294–326; 314.

14. The Latin epitaph, from Swift's tomb as Eliot informs us, translates as 'where savage indignation can no longer lacerate the heart'.

15. Jacques Lacan, *The Four Fundamental Concepts of Psycho-analysis*, ed. Jacques-Alain Miller, trans. Alan Sheridan, int. David Macey (London: Penguin, 1994), 72.

16. Charles Darwin, *On the Origin of Species*, cit. Gillian Beer, *Darwin's Plots: Evolutionary Narrative in Darwin, George Eliot and Nineteenth-Century Fiction* (London: Ark Press, 1983), 167.

   Beer comments that 'web imagery is found everywhere in Victorian writing', citing not only Darwin but also Hardy, Lewes and Tyndall (168). The metaphor is picked up by Elizabeth Deeds Ermath, for whom George Eliot's fictional world is structured as 'a web of relationships, a network of crossing and recrossing pathways that has immense mutual resonance across space and centuries . . . Her historical narrative is a perspective system made up of perspective systems . . . Every narrative moment in George Eliot belongs to an entire . . . system of awareness'; Ermath, *The English Novel in History* (London: Routledge, 1997), 159–60. Royle cautions against getting caught in the skein of 'intratextuality and all the metaphors, motifs, concepts, representations of webs and weaving in Eliot' (*TL* 87).

## CHAPTER 4

1. Peter Nicholls, 'The Belated Postmodern: History, Phantoms, and Toni Morrison', in Sue Vice (ed.), *Psychoanalytic Criticism: A Reader* (London: Polity Press, 1996), 50–67; 52.

2. Charles Dickens, *Little Dorrit* (1857), ed. and intro. Stephen Wall and Helen Small (London: Penguin, 1998). Hereafter *LD*.

3. See, for example, Peter Claus, 'Languages of Citizenship in the City of London 1847–1867', *London Journal*, 24:1 (1999), 23–37. Hereafter LCC.

4. Richard Price, *British Society 1680–1880* (Cambridge: Cambridge University Press, 1999), 182. Apropos urban politics, it is important to recognize, as does Price, that from the 1780s through the 1830s and 40s interests are not necessarily always addressed along party lines, so much as they are according to divisions of interest between the urban and rural, and between London-urban and other urban centres of manufacture, such as Birmingham, Leeds, or Manchester, for example. Thus Whig interests in the City of London may well find opposition or, at least, dissent, in the opinions of rural politicians of the same party.

5. Manning has commented of *Little Dorrit* that it is 'a text paradoxically enmeshed in the system it is trying to criticise'; Sylvia Manning, 'Social Criticism and Textual Subversion in *Little Dorrit*', *Dickens Studies Annual*, 20 (1991), 127–46; 131.

6. Andrew Sanders, *Dickens and the Spirit of the Age* (Oxford: Clarendon Press, 1999), 142. Hereafter *DSA*.

7. William J. Palmer, *Dickens and New Historicism* (New York: St. Martin's Press – now Palgrave, 1997), 2.

8. Anny Sadrin, *Parentage and Inheritance in the Novels of Charles Dickens* (Cambridge: Cambridge University Press, 1994), 77. Hereafter *PINCD*.

9. Hilary M. Schor, *Dickens and the Daughter of the House* (Cambridge: Cambridge University Press, 1999), 129.

10. John Glavin, *After Dickens: Reading, Adaptation and Performance* (Cambridge: Cambridge University Press, 1999), 149.

11. Soultana Maglavera, *Time Patterns in Later Dickens: A Study of the Thematic Implications of Temporal Organization of* Bleak House, Hard Times, Little Dorrit, A Tale of Two Cities, Great Expectations, *and* Our Mutual Friend (Amsterdam: Rodopi, 1994), 93.

12. Hans-Jost Frey, *Interruptions* (1989), trans. Georgia Albert (Albany, NY: State University Press, 1996), 48.

13. Ibid., 49.

14. Pierre Nora, 'Between Memory and History: *Les lieux de mémoire*', *Representations*, 26 (1989), 12.

15. 'The Power of Nobody is becoming so enormous in England, and he alone is responsible for so many proceedings ... The hand [of Nobody] ... in the late war [Crimean] is amazing to consider ... it was Nobody who made the hospitals more horrible than language can describe, it was Nobody who occasioned all the dire confusion of Balaklava Harbour, it was even Nobody who ordered the fatal Balaklava cavalry charge ... In civil matters we have Nobody equally advise ... The government ... is invariably outstripped by private enterprise; which we all know to be Nobody's fault': Dickens, *Household Words*, 336 (30 August 1856), 145–7.

16. Anny Sadrin also points to the fact that 'the name of the father is ... the name of the son' (*PINCD*, 76).

17. The phrase is taken from Martin Heidegger, 'Building, Dwelling, Think-

ing', in *Poetry, Language, Thought*, trans. and int. Albert Hofstadter (New York: Harper and Row, 1971), 157. Heidegger's phrase, expressing the idea of being as a form of dwelling, resonates strongly here for the reading of Clennam's memory as not originary, suggesting as it does the thinking of being and location beyond the individual.

18. Peter Ackroyd, *London: The Biography* (London: Chatto and Windus, 2000), hereafter *L:TB*; Bruce R. Smith, *The Acoustic World of Early Modern London: Attending to the O-Factor* (Chicago: University of Chicago Press, 1999); John Stow, *The Survey of London*, (1598), ed. H. B. Wheatley, int. Valerie Pearl (London: Everyman, 1987).

19. Ulrich Baer, *Remnants of Song: Trauma and the Experience of Modernity in Charles Baudelaire and Paul Celan* (Stanford, CA: Stanford University Press, 2000), 253.

20. See Introduction.

21. Jacques Derrida, '"Eating Well", or the Calculation of the Subject: An Interview with Jacques Derrida', trans. Peter Connor and Avital Ronell, in Eduardo Cadava, Peter Connor, and Jean-Luc Nancy (eds), *Who Comes After the Subject* (London: Routledge, 1991), 96–119; 117. Hereafter EW.

22. Thomas Keenan, *Fables of Responsibility: Aberrations and Predicaments in Ethics and Politics* (Stanford, CA: Stanford University Press, 1997). Hereafter *FR*.

## CHAPTER 5

1. Keith Wilson, 'Introduction', in Thomas Hardy, *The Mayor of Casterbridge*, ed. Keith Wilson (London: Penguin, 1997; xxi–xli), xxxi.

2. Avery F. Gordon, *Ghostly Matters: Haunting and the Sociological Imagination* (Minneapolis: University of Minnesota Press, 1997), 8.

3. Wigley offers a highly useful summary and discussion of the Freudian concept of the uncanny and its structural condition, specifically the relationship between haunting and habitation, the ghost and the structural space of the house (*AD* 109–12, 161–71).

4. Ned Lukacher, *Time-Fetishes: The Secret History of Eternal Recurrence* (Durham, NC: Duke University Press, 1998), 156–7.

5. See, for example, John R. Cooley, 'The Importance of Things Past: An Archetypal Reading of *The Mayor of Casterbridge*', *Massachusetts Studies in English*, 1 (1967), 17–21; W. Eugene Davis, 'Comparatively Modern Skeletons in the Garden: A Reconsideration of *The Mayor of Casterbridge*', *English Literature in Transition (1880–1920)*, 3 (1985), 108–20; Rod Edmond, '"The Past-Marked Prospect": Reading *The Mayor of Casterbridge*', *Reading the Victorian Novel: Detail into Form*, ed. Ian Gregor (London: Routledge, 1993), 111–27.

6. J. Hillis Miller, *Thomas Hardy: Distance and Desire* (Cambridge, MA: Harvard University Press, 1970); Bruce Johnson, '*The Mayor of Casterbridge* and *The Woodlanders*', in *True Correspondence: A Phenomenology of Thomas Hardy's Novels* (Gainesville: University Press of Florida, 1983), 76–83; Tess O'Toole, 'Fictitious Families', in *Genealogy*

*and Fiction in Hardy: Family Lineage and Narrative Lines* (Basingstoke: Macmillan Press – now Palgrave, 1997), 17–23.

7. Suzanne Keen, *Victorian Renovations of the Novel: Narrative Annexes and the Boundaries of Representation* (Cambridge: Cambridge University Press, 1998), 127, 132, 134, 140.

8. Raymond O'Dea, 'The "Haunting Shade" That Accompanies the Virtuous Elizabeth-Jane in *The Mayor of Casterbridge*', *The Victorian Newsletter*, 31 (Spring 1967), 33–6.

9. Robert Langbaum, *Thomas Hardy in Our Time* (Basingstoke: Macmillan Press – now Palgrave, 1995), 128.

10. Jacques Derrida, *Mémoires: for Paul de Man*, rev. edn, trans. Cecile Lindsay et al. (New York: Columbia University Press, 1989), 64. Hereafter *MPdM*.

11. Jim Reilly, *Shadowtime: History and Representation in Hardy, Conrad and George Eliot* (London: Routledge, 1993), 65.

12. J. Hillis Miller, *Fiction and Repetition: Seven English Novels* (Oxford: Blackwell, 1982), 6.

13. Florence Emily Hardy, *The Life and Work of Thomas Hardy*, ed. Michael Milgate (London: Macmillan Press – now Palgrave, 1985), 183.

14. Nicholas Royle, *After Derrida* (Manchester: Manchester University Press, 1995), 61. Hereafter *AfD*.

15. Dale Kramer, 'Introduction' in *The Mayor* (*MC* xi–xxix), xxiii, xxii. As Kramer also puts it, 'scene after scene in this novel of specific locale takes place within the context of a past custom' (xxiii).

16. Keith Wilson is surely correct in describing the effect of doubling as having an 'uncanny appeal' for Henchard (xxv).

17. Scott Durham, *Phantom Communities: The Simulacrum and the Limits of Postmodernism* (Stanford, CA: Stanford University Press, 1998), 3.

18. Marjorie Garson, '*The Mayor of Casterbridge*: The Bounds of Propriety' in *Hardy's Fables of Integrity: Woman, Body, Text* (Oxford: Oxford University Press, 1991), 94–129.

19. On Hardy's use of the archaism 'seed-lip', see Earl G. Ingersoll on the significance of technology and the 'conflict between the new and the old' in the novel, in his *Representations of Science and Technology in British Literature Since 1880* (New York: Peter Lang, 1992), 33.

20. See also Keen's discussion of Mixen Lane (131).

21. Derrida suggests that a condition of the spectral is that it observes us before we see it, if we see it at all (*SM* 101), on which see the commentary by Lacan in Chapter 3 above. Seeing yet being unseen, the spectral returns to inhabit the event, in this case the narrative, to effect and disturb the way in which the narrative unfolds. Although there is not the space here to follow this through, I would like to suggest, albeit provisionally, that Hardy plays on the question of what Derrida terms the 'visibility of the invisible' (*SM* 100). Henchard and other characters have brief moments of uncanny apperception, as if they dimly realize, intuitively as it were yet not completely consciously, that they are haunted. However, Hardy, through the constant recourse to the sight of the narra-

tor (as in the opening, highly visualized scene), implies a sense of spectral surveillance over everyone and everything.

22. Another tragic/gothic context for Henchard is noted by Earl Ingersoll, who describes the wife-sale in terms of a 'Faustian bargain' (Ingersoll, *Representations*, 24). In the same passage, Ingersoll notes the assumption of a '"lurid" glow' in the furmity woman's tent as a sign of the Faustian compact. I would however suggest that this 'lurid colour' (*MC* 14) belongs to a more general gothic aspect of the scene, especially as the furmity woman is described as a 'haggish creature of about fifty' (*MC* 8).

23. The architectural features appeal to the details of both gothic narrative and a Victorian interest in the reinvention of gothic architecture; they are thus doubled – internally haunted – in their function. The Tudor arch of the King's Arms (*MC* 42) belongs to the Perpendicular gothic style, while the gothic age is mentioned with particular reference to architecture (*MC* 141). There are numerous brief mentions by Hardy of architectural detail throughout the novel, whether these are the remnants of past styles persisting in present buildings as decaying features or pieces in good repair, or whether they are pastiche details. While this part of the essay concentrates on the literary gothic, it is important to note that Hardy's references to various architectural details, alongside those discussions of stones, architectural history, grave-sites, and so on, are forms of citation and reference. They cite the past within the site of Casterbridge's present, constant textual rem(a)inders returning in the text as untimely traces displacing both the spatial and temporal frames of Casterbridge and the novel. Dale Kramer's notes in the edition of *The Mayor* to which I refer are particularly helpful on the various architectural styles and their histories (*MC* 337–403).

Interesting, and perhaps teasing for this reading of the novel, is Kramer's comment on the gothic. He points out that, while gothic architecture had 'identifiable features', it nonetheless 'evaded fixed canons', evolving and transforming even in the building of a single structure (*MC* 369–70). We may provisionally apply this to the writing of the novel, which is structured by the identifiable features of other genres and yet which adheres to no one form in particular. Furthermore, in mixing genres, Hardy effectively translates them even while the ghosts of genres remain discernible. This is not only a formal or experimental concern however, for it alludes in turn to the historical and archaeological intimations of transformation and return which are to be read throughout the text. Moreover, and to reiterate again an earlier point, such use of architectural 'fragments' in the composition of the text (discursive delineations of architectural fragments intrude into and disturb the movement of the narrative) and their more general function as traces or ruins refer us not to an architectural past, but to those other textual traces, of myths, folklore, tragedy, and so on. All operate as articulations of the spectral truth of return.

24. See also Anthony Vidler, *The Architectural Uncanny: Essays in the Modern Unhomely* (Cambridge, MA: MIT Press, 1992), 17–44. Hereafter *AU*.

25. As Wigley goes on to point out in this passage, the words 'haunting' and 'house' are etymologically related. Closer still is the family relationship between 'haunt' and 'home', where the shared sense is that of frequenting places or finding a home. The ghost thus always belongs to the home, and there is no home that is not haunted. As we have suggested above, haunting is a not merely a temporal condition, that of a return, but is also a spatial or structural condition also, hence the argument of this essay, that the space, the structure and time of *The Mayor of Casterbridge* are haunted. Hardy seems aware of the doubleness within the term 'haunt', for he uses it to describe those who frequent both the near and the far bridges (*MC* 223). In that the term is used concerning those architectural structures which effectively cross the boundary of the river, its use appears uncannily apposite.

26. J. Hillis Miller, *Topographies* (Stanford, CA: Stanford University Press, 1995), 20–1.

27. The history of research and composition in relation to Hardy's return to Dorchester and the building of Max Gate is discussed by Keith Wilson and Dale Kramer in their introductions to *The Mayor of Casterbridge*, referred to in the notes above, and also by Norman Page in his introduction to the novel (Page, 'Introduction', *The Mayor of Casterbridge* [Peterborough, Ontario: Broadview Press, 1997], 7–23).

28. See note 3.

29. The question of writing and the importance of letters and other scraps of written communication going astray are important in the novel. On the ambivalence of writing and technology in the novel, see Earl Ingersoll (*Representations*, 29–30), which draws on Derrida's consideration of writing as *pharmakon*, poison *and* cure (*D* 95–116). Ingersoll develops his reading of writing and memory in the novel, in relation to the Biblical story of Saul and David, from a Derridean perspective in his 'Writing and Memory in *The Mayor of Casterbridge*' in *English Literature in Transition 1880–1920*, 33:3 (1990), 299–309.

30. J. Hillis Miller, *Reading Narrative* (Norman: University of Oklahoma Press, 1998), 110. On the effects of the will, see also Ingersoll ('Writing and Memory', 307–8). Also on the will, see Joe Fisher, *The Hidden Hardy* (Basingstoke: Macmillan Press – now Palgrave, 1992), 134–5.

31. On questions of destination and receipt, and the transformation of addressees, see J. Hillis Miller, 'Thomas Hardy, Jacques Derrida, and the "Dislocation of Souls"' in *Tropes, Parables, Performatives* (Durham, NC: Duke University Press, 1991), 171–80.

32. Jacques Derrida, 'Desistance', trans. Christopher Fynsk, in Philippe Lacoue-Labarthe, *Typography: Mimesis, Philosophy, Politics*, ed. Christopher Fynsk (Cambridge, MA: Harvard University Press, 1989), 1–42; 27. Hereafter D. On this passage, and Derrida's reading of rhythm as the haunting of the space of tradition, see Wigley (*AD* 162).

33. Jacques Derrida, 'Living On • Border Lines', trans. James Hulbert, in Harold Bloom et al., *Deconstruction and Criticism* (New York: Continuum, 1979), 75–176; 76. Hereafter LO.

34. Martin Heidegger, *An Introduction to Metaphysics*, trans. Ralph Manheim

(New Haven, CT: Yale University Press, 1959), 150. Wigley draws on Heidegger's discussions of dwelling and of the uncanny in relation to Being throughout his study.

35. Neither Kramer, Wilson, nor Page offer explanations for Farfrae's name in their editions of the novel, although Wilson does point out (330, n.3) that the character's name was to have been Alan Stansbie. There is also little rational explanation for Farfrae's circuitous journey, from Scotland, via Casterbridge, to Bristol. Kramer suggests that perhaps Farfrae is merely curious to see England (*MC* 348), otherwise he might have travelled to America from either Glasgow or Liverpool.

36. Arguably, this is the project of that area of Hardy criticism, prominent in the 1960s, 1970s and 1980s, which sought to read Hardy as a social historian or 'sociologist of Wessex'. At the risk of being reductive, such criticism tends towards reading Hardy's novels as documents of rural life, and the losses to a way of life attendant on changing technologies of farming. See, for example, Douglas Brown, *Thomas Hardy: The Mayor of Casterbridge* (London: Edward Arnold, 1962); Noorul Hasan, *Thomas Hardy: The Sociological Imagination* (London: Macmillan Press – now Palgrave, 1982); Peter Widdowson, *Hardy in History: A Study in Literary Sociology* (London: Routledge, 1989); Merryn Williams, *Thomas Hardy and Rural England* (London: Macmillan Press – now Palgrave, 1972).

37. Maurice Merleau-Ponty, *The Prose of the World*, trans. John O'Neill (Evanston, IL: Northwestern University Press, 1973), 9.
    Merleau-Ponty's consideration of the signifying functions of language is highly suggestive for readings of the various spectral effects in *The Mayor of Casterbridge* which would intersect with a number of the readings put forward here. At a number of points, and in particular in suggesting that 'I *become* the one to whom I am listening' (118), Merleau-Ponty anticipates the discussions of Hillis Miller and Derrida on the effects of communication on the addressee in the former's essay on Hardy, already mentioned, and Derrida's essay 'Telepathy', on which Miller draws: 'Telepathy', trans. Nicholas Royle, *Oxford Literary Review*, 10 (1988), 3–41.

## AFTERWORD

1. J. Hillis Miller, *Topographies* (Stanford, CA: Stanford University Press, 1995), 57.

2. Jacques Derrida, '"A Self-Unsealing Poetic Text": Poetics and Politics of Witnessing', trans. Rachel Bowlby, in Michael P. Clark (ed.), *Revenge of the Aesthetic: The Place of Literature in Theory Today* (Berkeley and Los Angeles: University of California Press, 2000), 180–207; 190. Hereafter S-U.

3. Virginia Woolf, 'A Haunted House', *The Complete Shorter Fiction*, ed. Susan Dick (London: Grafton, 1991), 122–3.

4. George M. Johnson, in his consideration of the ghostly in Woolf's essays and early fiction, remarks on 'A Haunted House', and on its subversions of the 'conventions of the traditional haunted house story'

as a response in part to the work of Henry James: George M. Johnson, 'A Haunted House: Ghostly Presences in Woolf's Essays and Early Fiction', in Beth Carol Rosenberg and Jeanne Dubino, *Virginia Woolf and the Essay* (New York: St. Martin's Press – now Palgrave, 1997), 235–56; 245.

As Johnson goes on to suggest, 'the traditional effects of horror and terror are conspicuously absent'. In his discussion of the ghostly in the text of Woolf, Johnson draws on Nicholas Royle's essay on 'Kew Gardens', written by Woolf two years before 'A Haunted House', and which, in Royle's words, appears to 'satirize telepathy and spiritualism' (*TL* 111). Despite the initial air of satire, this earlier essay turns out to be a ghost story, according to Royle: 'Without destination, "Kew Gardens" seems to gather the ghosts of ancestral voices, including the voices of children, bringing war into the phantom nosegay of a moment's rhetoric' (*TL* 120).

5.  Elisabeth Bronfen, *Over Her Dead Body: Death, Femininity, and the Aesthetic* (Manchester: Manchester University Press, 1992), 114.
6.  Joseph G. Kronick, *Derrida and the Future of Literature* (Albany: State University of New York Press, 1999), 67.
7.  W. B. Yeats, *Purgatory* in *Collected Plays* (New York: Macmillan, 1953).
8.  John Felstiner's critical biography, *Paul Celan: Poet, Survivor, Jew* (New Haven, CT: Yale University Press, 1995), provides a comprehensive introduction to Celan's writing. Clarisse Samuels examines Celan's response to the Holocaust through the aesthetic and philosophical influences of surrealism and existentialism on the poet's work in *Holocaust Visions: Surrealism and Existentialism in the Poetry of Paul Celan* (Columbia, SC: Camden House, 1993). Shira Wolosky's *Language Mysticism: The Negative Way of Language in Eliot, Beckett, and Celan* (Stanford, CA: Stanford University Press, 1995) relates experimentation with language in relation to questions of Christian and Judaic mysticism. She provides a reading of 'Ich kann dich noch sehn' (232–4), drawing on Kabbalistic tradition and Emmanuel Levinas's consideration of one's relation to the Other, in particular the impossible encounter with the face of God; see Levinas, *Totality and Infinity: An Essay on Exteriority* (1961), trans. Alphonso Lingis (Pittsburgh, PA: Duquesne University Press, 1969), 187–220. *Word Traces: Readings of Paul Celan*, ed. Aris Fioretos (Baltimore, MD: The Johns Hopkins University Press, 1994) brings together a number of essays on different aspects of Celan's poetry, including Derrida's 'Shibboleth: For Paul Celan', 3–74.

    The translation of 'Ich kann dich noch sehn' is my own. For copyright reasons, I cannot reproduce the original in German. A translation of this poem, with the original, is to be found in Celan's *Selected Poems*, trans. and int. Michael Hamburger (Harmondsworth: Penguin, 1990), 298–9.
9.  Celan's careful choice of words makes translation difficult, if not impossible. There is a 'multiplicity of layering', a 'multilayered, precise concreteness', to quote Anders Olsson, 'Spectral Analysis: A Commentary on "Solve" and "Coagula"', trans. Hanna Kalter Weiss in collaboration with the author, in Fioretos (ed.), *Word Traces*, 267–79; 274. Such encryption, where even the most seemingly commonplace words – such

as *noch* – push the readability of language to its limits, also offers the reader a sense of the haunting resonance at which the material trace hints, and which, responsibly, reading should not attempt to control. One particular translation above might be seen as contentious, where I have translated *Stelle* as passage, rather than 'point' or 'place'. This translation immediately refers to a location in a text, but, given the poem's address, its passage if you will between addresser and addressee, and the poem's turning upon a movement, I have risked the more unlikely translation.

10. On this transformation of address, see J. Hillis Miller, 'Thomas Hardy, Jacques Derrida and the "Dislocation of Souls"', 171–80. In a remark which is uncannily pertinent to Celan's poem, Miller says that '[r]eading the poem, I, you, or anyone becomes its addressee, since it has no name or specified destination' (180).

# Index